THIS I KNOW

THIS I

KN●W

MARKETING LESSONS FROM
UNDER THE INFLUENCE

TERRY O'REILLY

CHICAGO
REVIEW
PRESS

Copyright © 2017 by Terry O'Reilly
Published by arrangement with the author

All rights reserved
Published in the USA in 2018 by Chicago Review Press Incorporated
814 North Franklin Street
Chicago, Illinois 60610
ISBN 978-1-64160-014-9

Library of Congress Cataloging-in-Publication Data
Is available from the Library of Congress.

Cover and interior design: Andrew Roberts
Cover image: Copyright © H. Armstrong Roberts / Classic stock / Getty Images

Printed in the United States of America
5 4 3 2 1

For Pete Watts,
who took a chance on me in my first copywriting job

For Trevor Goodgoll,
who took a chance on me in the big leagues

And for Debbie,
who took the biggest chance of all

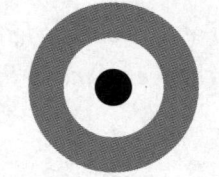

Contents

Foreword

I've spent most of my work time the last five years trying to help entrepreneurs grow their businesses.

Some of the businesses are start-ups. Others have been around for decades.

Some of the businesses offer products. Others offer services.

Some of the businesses use complex algorithms to offer digital solutions to enterprises. Others have invented new bathroom mats or shovelling aids.

Some of the businesses are run by individuals out of their homes. Others employ dozens and own their own production facilities.

But they all have one thing in common: They need customers to survive. They have to convince people or other companies to give up hard-earned money in return for their offerings.

That is not easy to do.

They are competing with other businesses. They are competing with inertia. They are competing with society's ADD. Heck, whether they realize it or not, they are competing with Netflix.

They need to get their potential customers' attention and they need to convince them that their business's solution is the right one.

They need to accomplish those two very difficult tasks cost-efficiently.

They need to read this book.

Terry O'Reilly is a marketing genius. I call him the Prince of Persuasion. A few months ago I begged him (literally) to come out of retirement to orchestrate a campaign for a company I'm involved with. He declined because he was too busy writing this book. At the time I was disappointed, but after reading the manuscript I am so glad he decided to focus on this project.

You will be, too.

Dave Chilton,

a.k.a. The Wealthy Barber

Introduction

By the time the Sex Pistols came to America in 1978, they were already a profane sensation in the UK. But their savvy manager, Malcolm McLaren, knew breaking into the States would be a different matter. The US market was hard to impress, and it had seen it all before. So McLaren devised a strategy.

He limited the Sex Pistols to performing in small towns in southern states. He knew the largely fundamentalist Christians would be absolutely appalled at the antics of Johnny Rotten & co. He counted on the press in those cities to generate a lot of scandalous publicity; the more notorious the Sex Pistols became, the more intrigued New York and LA would be.

It was a brilliant plan. Most bands set their sights on New York and LA immediately, but can't get noticed in these two competitive markets. McLaren knew the power in holding back, and having created pandemonium in conservative towns like Tulsa and Baton Rouge, he was able to use that outrage as a calling card in the Big Apple and Los Angeles.

While the Sex Pistols were offending audiences from coast to coast, I was a young man just starting my career in advertising. Originally, I sent sixty resumés to sixty advertising agencies across

Canada hoping to land a junior copywriter job, writing ads. I got back sixty-one rejection letters. Yes, one company rejected me twice. So I set my sights a little lower and dropped off a more creative resumé at a small radio station called FM 108 in Burlington, Ontario. The sales manager, Pete Watts (a man named for his career destiny), liked my resumé and hired me. It wasn't where I really wanted to be—my dream was to work at a major advertising agency—and radio wasn't my passion, but it was a copywriting job.

Pete brought in a handful of advertising contracts every day, and I was the only copywriter for the station's hundred or so retail clients. The days were twelve hours long, but I got to experiment with creative ideas because I had a lot of freedom; I answered only to the station's clients. Some of those commercials worked and some fell flat on their face. It was baptism by hellfire. And wouldn't you know it, I fell in love with radio.

My next stop was a small advertising agency in the same town. The client list there was a jump up from my last job, and along with radio I got to write print ads, billboards and the odd television commercial. As it turned out, the owner of that agency didn't really like my work and rarely approved anything creative. I think he booed my car in the parking lot. After two years of creative rebuffs, the final straw came while writing a campaign for a new concrete roofing tile. The product's main benefit was that the tiles lasted fifty years. I came up with the headline "No more fiddling on the roof."

I loved it. He didn't.

So I resigned.

I still clung to my dream of working as a copywriter in a big national advertising agency in Toronto, which was mission control for the advertising industry in Canada. At my kitchen table I worked on a portfolio of made-up ads to show creative directors the kind of ideas I was capable of generating if given the chance.

When ready, I got on the phone and called a long list of big-time Toronto creative directors. Four of them agreed to see me.

My very first meeting was at an agency called Campbell Ewald. Its impressive client list included GMAC Financing, Fiberglas Canada, Eastern Air Lines, Gilbey Distilleries, DuPont, Burroughs Computers and investment firm Nesbitt Thomson.

The creative director was a flamboyant South African named Trevor Goodgoll, who blew into the office the morning of my interview sporting a floor-length fur coat. He whisked through my portfolio at a speed that blew my hair back and then offered me two weeks' employment. I thanked him and asked, "If you like my work, you'll keep me on?"

He said, "We'll see."

Nevertheless, I was to start the following Monday and I was thrilled. Then I did a crazy thing; I cancelled the other three interviews. If I had no plan B, plan A had to work. My wife thought I was crazy.

That Monday, Trevor gave me my first assignment. It was a print ad for pipe insulation. Riveting stuff, but I didn't care. I was in the big leagues, or at least sitting at a desk in the big leagues. But it was the second assignment that made my eyes widen. Trevor asked me to come up with a print ad for a Fiberglas roofing product. The tiles lasted forty years. So I scribbled up an ad with the headline "No more fiddling on the roof."

When I brought it to Trevor's office about ten minutes later, he looked up at me and said, with raised eyebrows, "You have an idea already?" I shrugged yes, and laid the ad down on his desk. He took one look at the headline, and yelled, "I love it!"

A few days later, he hired me full-time.

Trevor loved creativity. He taught me that the world was my oyster, and that that oyster was *big*. About three weeks into my time with Trevor, I presented him with a radio campaign for Eastern

Air Lines and he asked me what kind of actor I had in mind. It was a musical idea, so I mentioned I had seen a comedian named Pete Barbutti on the Johnny Carson show recently who played the piano while telling jokes. If I could find someone like him, I said, that would be perfect.

"Get him!" Trevor said, and walked away. One week later, I was in a studio with that very comedian I had seen on *The Tonight Show*.

Welcome to the big leagues.

Trevor paired me up with a very talented art director named Steve Chase, and in that first year alone we won over sixty national and international awards. But my time with Trevor was marked by another experience: his intense desire to explore and explain the motivations, psychology and marketing strategies behind every product we advertised.

Once he and the account service department had worked out the larger strategy for any big new campaign, Trevor gathered his creative staff in the boardroom. There, he unravelled a long roll of brown paper and pinned it to the wall from one end of the room to the other. Then he grabbed a handful of coloured markers and the tutorial began. (See Fig. 1.)

He started with the product, explaining its history, its features, its hidden qualities and where it fit into someone's life. He distilled the product's benefit to consumers down to its very essence, then refined it even further until he arrived at a perfectly articulated summation of what made this product unique and why it was worth owning. He wrote it all on that brown paper, slowly moving across the room, circling words and drawing arrows to link ideas. Then he talked about the potential customer for this product. If it were women, aged twenty-five to thirty-four, for example, Trevor would talk about the life of such a woman. What her day consisted of, her family, her responsibilities, her job, her purchasing habits, the TV shows she watched, the psychology behind her choices, her peer pressure and how our product fit into her life. Then he moved along the wall and began sketching out the state of the marketplace, circling a list of competitors, drawing arrows to the advertising they were doing and linking that back to the greatest area of opportunity for our product.

Then he got to the best part. Trevor funnelled all this thinking down to what our creative opportunity would be. He suggested clever ways we could outmanoeuvre our competitors, and he served us the insights and nuggets that would inform our creative thought process. Trevor wanted award-winning creativity, but he wanted it grounded in a solid understanding of who our market was and how we could best reach them.

At the end of those strategy sessions, the length of the boardroom wall was covered in writing, in different-coloured markers, with circles and arrows and exclamation marks, culminating in a penetrating insight into the task at hand.

I loved those sessions, and we all left the boardroom pumped up and guided by a clear sense of the marketing mission.

It wasn't lost on me that my two employers in Burlington had provided their clients with no such clarity. The radio station offered them no advertising insights, and the small agency I had worked at offered only marginally better marketing counsel. That meant those retailers and merchants were spending hard-earned dollars on advertising that wasn't grounded in fundamental selling principles or sharpened with seasoned marketing insights.

I later worked for two other highly creative advertising agencies—Doyle Dane Bernbach and Chiat/Day. The level of marketing savvy at both was excellent, although neither matched Trevor's depth and exhaustive exploration. So in 1989, I decided to become my own boss and to recapture some of that energy in a company of my own.

I left agency life to launch O'Reilly Radio Inc., to direct and produce radio commercials for advertising agencies. A year later, I joined forces with another director and co-founded Pirate Radio. It was an audio production company with a difference: we had a creative department. All of our competitors in Toronto executed agency-written work, they didn't create it. They were artisans, not artists. But in me Pirate had an ex-agency creative man as a principal, and that set us apart. We could produce entertaining agency-generated radio scripts while protecting the selling strategy. More importantly, we could also create commercials for clients who couldn't afford a high-priced ad agency, and offer them strategic advertising combined with bold creativity.

During my many years at Pirate, I staged an annual creative radio seminar in Toronto. Over two hundred young copywriters from agencies all over the country would attend. For six hours, I would stand onstage teaching them how to produce effective radio commercials. Topics included scriptwriting and script structure, the intricacies of humour versus drama, sound effects, casting, music, how to present radio scripts, studio protocol and the implications of creating a thirty-second commercial versus a sixty-second one (thirty seconds is much more difficult).

One day over lunch with a few radio buddies, Larry MacInnis, the creative director of CHUM Radio, suggested my seminar would make a great radio show. I asked, "What station would possibly air that?" He thought for a second, and said, "The CBC." To which I replied, "You mean the advertising-free CBC would air a show on advertising?"

He said, "They would air that one."

We laughed, had a few more beers, and enjoyed the rest of our lunch. But when I went home that day, I couldn't get the idea out of my head. Freelance radio writer Mike Tennant was also at that lunch, and he called me up later that week saying he thought Larry's idea was worth pursuing. So we wrote up a simple presentation.

Mike had some connections at CBC and arranged a meeting. In a CBC boardroom, we explained that advertising was like architecture: it was everywhere in people's lives. Most hate it, most find it annoying, but in reality, advertising is a fascinating business. Fascinating, because it is the study of human nature. It offers a granular look at what makes us tick. We told the CBC we weren't journalists, we weren't academics and we weren't pundits. We were working admen in the trenches—with access. We wanted to give Canadians a backstage pass to the closed world of advertising.

To our amazement, CBC bought *O'Reilly on Advertising* as a ten-episode summer replacement series. The response from listeners was so enthusiastic, CBC asked us to stay on for the entire season. When they invited us back for a second season, we retooled the show and renamed it *The Age of Persuasion*. That was 2006. Many years later, that show has transitioned to become *Under the Influence* and I've expanded its focus to examine not just advertising but the ever-expanding and much broader world of marketing in all its forms.

Over the past decade, the show has collected a lot of marketing wisdom. From the marketing strategies of the world's biggest brands to the smart selling tactics of small businesses, the program has become a sort of library of great moments, trends and ideas for the practice of selling.

After a few wonderful decades at Pirate I sold my share of the company I co-founded, but held on to my marketing habit. Along with doing the radio show, I still consult for companies and associations, and give dozens of speeches a year at marketing conferences. My talks focus on the fundamentals of advertising (the building blocks of actual campaigns) and marketing (the bigger, overall business strategy), because in my experience that's where most campaigns go tragically wrong.

Right out of the starting blocks.

When I finish those talks there is usually a Q&A period. And what becomes quickly apparent is that many business owners and their staff feel lost when it comes to marketing. They have limited budgets and get no guidance on their advertising. They are usually wearing several hats in their companies, don't have dedicated marketing departments, aren't sure how to craft a real marketing strategy and feel they aren't getting a return on their advertising dollar.

This is a book for all those people.

It is for the entrepreneurs who can't afford a big downtown advertising agency to guide them. It is a collection of the insights and marketing lessons from the many years of my radio show, gathered in one volume. It also draws on the experience I've gained over my advertising career. It's a book that will challenge you, ask you interesting questions and help you formulate your own marketing.

When you've been in the high-stakes game of advertising for over thirty-five years and have produced over ten thousand advertisements, the lessons are many. I'm a pack rat when it comes to epic blunders, sly observations and unintended tutorials. And when you've worked with that many clients, wrestled that many briefing documents to the ground, wrangled that many creative people, laughed with that many actors, dealt with that many celebrity egos, recorded in that many studios and won and lost that many battles, you learn a thing or two.

Because this I know: If it weren't for great marketing, you would never have heard of the Sex Pistols.

Chapter One

SLUDGE OR GRAVY
What Business Are You Really In?

What business are you really in? Don't answer that question too quickly. Most people get it wrong. Yet it's the most important marketing question you can ask yourself. Until you can answer it correctly, your marketing will always lack focus. A truism of business is that what you sell and what people buy are almost always two different things. Companies look to sell products, and customers look to buy solutions. While seemingly related, the definitions of each can be miles apart.

For example, Molson isn't in the beer business. Even though Molson's plants are designed to manufacture beer and every Molson delivery truck you see is full of beer cases, Molson isn't in the beer business. It's in the party business.

Look at almost any Molson beer commercial. It's all about having fun, being in groups, flirting, laughing and socializing. That is what the majority of Molson beer fans are really buying into when they put their money down. Molson is a savvy marketer and it knows the solution it offers is social lubrication. That presents a delicate communication task, because alcohol marketing is heavily regulated in this country. So the partying scenes are tightly controlled. The number of beers in a scene must equal no more than the number of people in said scene. Five people in a shot, five beers max. No one holding a beer can be involved in an activity requiring skill—like waterskiing or chainsaw carving. No one can appear to be underage. The activity of the participants can't be "over exuberant." I once had a beer commercial turned down by regulators because one of the actors toasted above shoulder level. The charge: too exuberant. The advertising can't suggest beer promotes sex. (I know, I know. It's the most elastic rule of the bunch). But say what you will, Molson knows what business it's in.

Michelin is not in the tire business. It's in the safety business. Its purpose is to offer the utmost tire safety for automobiles. Michelin once had the best tire tagline of all time. The company's TV ads showed a baby strapped into a radial, with the line "Because so much is riding on your tires." That's the business Michelin is in. Not vulcanized rubber. Safety. So if it just sold tires, it was in trouble. But if it sold safety, it was golden. (Why Michelin abandoned that line, I will never know.)

Häagen-Dazs isn't in the ice cream business, it's in the sensual pleasure business. Whitewater rafting companies aren't in the personal transportation business. They are in the personal transformation business. Starbucks isn't in the coffee business. It's in the coffee *theatre* business, with baristas, elaborate java machinery and five-word mocha-choco-lotta coffee names.

Apple isn't in the computer business. It's in the personal empowerment business. If you want to understand Apple's massive success, just draw a straight line back to late 1983. To Super Bowl XVIII. To late in the third quarter. To a TV commercial called *1984*. (See Fig. 2.)

Within the advertising business, it is arguably the most famous TV commercial in history (google it). This single advertisement positioned Apple for all time in the minds of the buying public. It showed a bleak image of George Orwell's *1984* future, where people shuffle in drab uniforms and listen to the hypnotic ranting of

Big Brother on a gigantic screen. But meanwhile, we see dramatic cuts of a female athlete, dressed in white and red, holding an Olympic-sized hammer, being pursued by a squad of futuristic police. She runs down a long tunnel into the gathering, stops, swings the hammer and lets it go with a scream—smashing the gigantic screen, to the amazement of the catatonic crowd. The message from Apple: "On January 24th, Apple Computer will introduce Macintosh. And you'll see why 1984 won't be like *1984*." Translation: We're going to take the computing power that IBM has hoarded all these years and give it to you.

That single message—or contemporized variations of it, echoed ever since by everything Apple does and everything Steve Jobs has said—is why so many people buy so many Apple products. To put a finer point on it, you can google a photograph of Steve Jobs at IBM's head office, standing under its massive logo, flipping the bird. People loved that rebel stance. When Apple announces a new product, people line up overnight to be the first to get their hands on it. No one does that for Dell. People are drawn to Apple's promise of personal empowerment on a very deep level, topped with a little seasoning of "us versus them." That is what Apple sells. There are more powerful computers out there, and certainly cheaper ones, yet Apple has become the most valuable company in the world after Exxon. It accomplished this by completely understanding what business it is in.

Nike isn't in the shoe business. It is in the motivation business. The mantra "Just Do It" has been called the last great slogan of our time. While it may have motivated millions of people to step up and enjoy life, it was actually inspired by someone's death. Dan Wieden, co-founder of advertising agency Wieden + Kennedy, located in Portland, Oregon, coined the slogan. He remembered watching a news report on the execution of spree-killer Gary Gilmore in 1977. Gilmore, who had grown up in Portland, was being executed in

Utah by firing squad. His official last words to the warden were "Let's do it." Wieden was struck by the impact of that line. He thought it remarkable that Gilmore could face that much uncertainty and just push through it. It stayed with Wieden, and when he needed to come up with a tagline to tie eight different TV commercials together for his agency's first presentation to Nike, he remembered Gilmore's words. He simply changed one word and "Just Do It" was born. The rest is marketing history.

The power of that line cannot be understated. At first glance, it says, If you have a body, you're an athlete. But a quick frisk reveals something more profound. That phrase is the answer to so many of life's bigger questions. Should I tell the boss my idea? Should I quit this horrible job? Should I start my own business? Should I pop the big question?

The majority of the people who wear Nike sneakers don't work out. That should tell you everything. "Just Do It" is a line that ignites millions of dreams, only a small percentage of which are exercise-related. Nike knows what people are buying. It's not shoes. It's motivation.

Conjure up all the commercials you can for Molson, Apple and Nike. Nearly all Molson ads show people happy and partying. After the *1984* TV commercial, virtually all Apple commercials show an individual achieving something on a computer. Every single Nike ad you've ever seen shows pros and amateurs reaching for a dream. Good Molson ads don't tell you how the beer is made. Apple doesn't analyze gigabits. Nike rarely discusses sneakers.

You have to know what business you're in.

I once interviewed Playboy founder Hugh Hefner. I asked him this: If you were to stop wearing pyjamas to work and ceased dating twins, would it affect your business? He didn't hesitate. His immediate answer was yes. You've got to hand it to old Hef; he knew what business he was in. In order to keep the entire grotto-filled enterprise afloat, he had to sell the lifestyle. Men weren't buying a magazine; they were buying the fantasy of living the *Playboy* life.

If you are a company big enough to hire an advertising agency, then a smart one will help you uncover what business you are really in. But if you can't afford an agency, you have to do the homework on your own. Believe it or not, answering this question is not as easy as it appears. It requires sober objectivity, one of the most important things an ad agency can offer a client.

Agencies need to strive for objectivity because in order to appeal to a customer, you have to think like a customer. Not like a company. Most companies fall in love with their product. The passion you feel for your company is good, but that passion can be fuelled by your immersion in how your product is created—which, if you are marketing that product, is bad. You are lost in the weeds. Have you ever asked an Internet installer a question and had to stand through a thesis on routers and megabit-per-second download rates when all you really wanted to know was whether you could download an HD movie?

That's what I mean.

Smart marketers know when their nose is too close to the glass and their breath is fogging up the view. You have to develop the ability to leave your office and look back in through the windows. Ruthless objectivity is the key. Customers are drawn to a brand— be it a product or a service—for many reasons. But the most important, overriding reason is how it makes them *feel*. Price, location, colour and so on all rank well below this single criterion.

Remember the cola wars in the eighties? Remember the Pepsi Challenge commercials? We all sat at home and watched real people take the challenge of sipping two hidden colas, and choosing one, which, when revealed, was Pepsi. Coke's management all sat at home, too, watching the same commercials every night, and it made them nuts. Here's the important thing to know: Coke had an ocean of market share over Pepsi. It couldn't even see Pepsi in its rear-view mirror. But the sight of those commercials playing out every single night made Coke executives crazy. So what did they do? Coke actually changed its formula. If you remember, the reaction to that was so negative, so swift and so overwhelming, Coke brought back its original formula only seventy-seven days later. Can you imagine what that cost Coca-Cola? Untold millions. The company not only changed its packaging, and spent millions with Bill Cosby (!) marketing New Coke, it changed its entire manufacturing process.

But I maintain Coke should have been really happy about that. It proved how much people loved the brand. If they didn't, that change would have passed like a ship in the night. As one journalist noted, it just happened to be the most expensive focus group in history. Follow this math with me: In hidden taste tests, Pepsi beats Coke slightly. In taste tests where respondents can see both brands, Coke beats Pepsi decisively. Interesting, isn't it? Nothing has fundamentally changed in that scenario. But get this: in another taste test, where Coke was pitted against a hidden cola, in other words, where people could see Coke but not the other brand, Coke beat that other brand 99 to 1. Guess what that other brand was?

Coke.

Coke clobbered Coke.

Let's analyze what happened there. When people saw the branding information—the familiar Coke bottle and logo—they made an automatic assumption. Coke was vastly superior to whatever that other cola was. That's how powerful branding is. It can make a product taste better than itself in your mind. So how does Coke do this? With a century of smart marketing. Coke knows what business it is in.

Look at the one thing Coke sells in all its advertising: happiness. It's only sugared water in a bottle. Yet Coke is one of the most valuable corporations in the world. It has attached *happiness* to its product. Think all the way back to the famous *I'd Like to Buy the World a Coke* commercial in 1971.

Happiness.

That commercial was inspired by an interesting moment. When adman Bill Backer was flying over to London, England, to record a new jingle for Coke, his plane had to land in Ireland since Heathrow was fogged in. Pan Am didn't want to bus the passengers to a major hotel in a large city forty minutes away, because the airline wanted everyone nearby and ready to board on short notice in case the fog lifted. Instead, it sent them to a small, local motel. But it didn't have enough vacancies to accommodate two hundred passengers, so everyone was asked to double up. Having to share a room with a stranger put the passengers in an even worse mood. Some refused and curled up to sleep in the corner of the lobby. Others grouped themselves by nationality or sex.

The next day the passengers weren't allowed to leave the airport. They could only shop in the duty-free store, eat, snack and feel sorry for themselves. As Backer says, they had been placed on permanent standby. By midmorning, all the duty-free shopping that could be done was done. The second hand on the airport clock seemed to move once a minute. Passengers began collecting in small groups in the coffee shop. Slowly, the mood started to lift as people began having conversations. The common icebreaker was a bottle of Coke. That scenario was being repeated all over the restaurant—people who spoke different languages, from different countries, forced together by circumstance were enjoying each other's company over a Coke. As Backer watched this unfold, he realized that Coke wasn't just a liquid refreshment, it was a tiny bit of commonality. He scribbled, "I'd like to buy the world a Coke, and keep it company" onto a napkin, and stuffed it into his pocket.

When he eventually got to the recording session in London, Backer pulled the napkin out of his pocket, and that line he'd scribbled down became the heart not only of the jingle but also of one of the most famous TV commercials of all time. The original tune was sung by the Hillside Singers, an ad hoc group put together by jingle producer Al Ham. When the jingle became a sensation, Ham issued it as a single (with a slight tweak from "I'd like to buy the world a Coke" to "I'd like to teach the world to sing"). The New Seekers, who had originally been approached, didn't think much of the jingle when they first heard it, considering it too syrupy and simple (". . . apple trees and honey bees and snow white turtle doves"). But when the Hillside Singers had a hit with it, the group decided to release its own version. The melody was sticky, and the song contained a profound message of peace and harmony at a time when America was still wading through the swamps of Vietnam. Never underestimate the power of the right message at the right time. It sold twelve million records.

Don't you think, in this day and age, that a competitive company could analyze a bottle of Coke and figure out its secret formula? Then manufacture a product that tasted just like Coke? The answer is yes. It's been done many times, but those companies don't succeed. Why is that? Because people aren't buying sugared water. They're buying Coke's powerful branding and its consistent promise of happiness. Let's follow that through to its logical conclusion. Why does Coke succeed around the world, across borders, with many different cultures, in spite of hundreds of competitors? Answer: because happiness is a universal emotional desire, and Coke has been masterful at linking its product to that emotion. Coke knows what business it's in.

Molson makes people feel like partying. Apple makes people feel they can compete with corporations. Nike makes people feel they can achieve any goal. Hugh Hefner makes men feel they, too, could date twins, if only they had more time on their hands.

So when you look at your business, you have to divorce yourself from your product, from the manufacturing process, from the sugared water, the hops and the air soles. You have to think like a customer. To do that, you have to quietly observe what customers are really buying from you. They will tell you, but you have to listen carefully. I have always believed the best marketers are the best listeners. I once had a business partner who would ask a client a question about their company, then proceed to answer it himself. He would then look to the client for a nod in agreement. But two monologues don't make a dialogue.

When I ask a client a question, sometimes I already know the answer, sometimes I don't. But I always want to hear the exact words the client chooses in their response. That answer is like a suitcase; it's packed with insights and clues and tiny epiphanies. Many clients can't articulate what they want to say about themselves or their product in a short, concise way. So you have to read between the lines. It's the same with the buying public. Ad legend David Ogilvy once said that consumers don't know what they feel, don't say what they know, and don't do what they say. But with Presbyterian patience, you will see and hear the information you need. You have to ask the right questions that prompt the revealing answers. The clues to their true desires—what they really want to buy from you—are in their adjectives and their adverbs.

Customers are most forthcoming during two occasions: when they are knocking on your door, and after the task is completed or the product is purchased. For example, at Pirate, we produced the audio for radio and television commercials. Our biggest customers were the creative departments in advertising agencies. Copywriters and art directors would bring their radio scripts or film to us, and we would add the sound effects—every footstep, every bird chirp—compose the music and direct the voiceovers. We offered audio directors, music composers, sound engineers and line producers. In marketing Pirate to advertising agencies, we could have focused on any number of those things, as well as our beautiful studios, our state-of-the-art equipment, our exhaustive casting, our competitive rates, and so on.

But that's not what creative teams were buying.

When they came to Pirate, they wanted to leave with award-winning commercials. Period. Pirate had a long track record for winning awards, so that's how we marketed the company. We held annual daylong seminars to teach young agency copywriters how to create award-winning radio. We staged Lunch & Learns where we would bring a catered lunch into ad agency creative departments and play them award-winning radio commercials we had discovered from around the world, break them down and show creative teams the hidden building blocks of outstanding radio. We sponsored advertising award shows. We contributed scholarships for college marketing awards. When our work won awards around the world, we invested in public relations.

While Pirate was a honeycomb of features we were proud of, creative teams were really buying commercials that attracted trophies. Selling anything else was just talking to ourselves. Sure, there's a time and a place to break your company's features down and discuss them one by one. It just can't be the core of your marketing. People make decisions based on emotion, then rationalize that decision with details. Our advertising agency clients were after the emotional reward of commercials that won awards.

If you are an owner or founder of your business, you have an intimate relationship with the minutiae of your company's mechanics.

You built it from nothing. You may have struggled to build a unique internal blueprint. You may have pioneered a technique. You may have battled untold forces to streamline your systems. All of it is a badge of honour to you. But to your customers, it's a megabit-per-second lecture.

So, what business are you in?

A few paragraphs back, I mentioned that your customers will be most vocal about what they want from you when they first come knocking and when the job is done. Let me give you another example.

In my company, the first conversations with the ad agency creative team about a radio campaign revealed a lot. They were excited to show me the scripts. They would make references to other award-winning commercials: "We'd love to find an actor like the funny guy in the Volkswagen ad that ranked number one in the Super Bowl ratings" or "We loved the music in that CLIO award–winning radio commercial for BMW."

Now, those suggestions are not just about finding the right actor or sourcing a specific piece of music. Sandwiched between the lines is the creative team's desire to create an award-winning ad, because winning awards is how creative teams are judged. Yes, selling products for their clients is extremely important, but doing that with a high degree of creativity is the currency within the industry. Awards can be tallied. Product sales are fuzzy and result from many forces, only one of which is advertising. Knowing this, I listen carefully to the words the team uses to decipher their desires. I have to balance their personal goals with their client's objectives. That's why the words your customers choose are so revealing. The reason they are bringing their business to you is on display. They are telling you why they came to you. They are telling you the business you are in.

The next most important message from your customers comes when the job is done, the product is purchased or the service is rendered. Your customer will tell you how close you came to fulfilling their initial expectation. The middle bit—the process of fulfilling a customer request—is too fraught with the fog of screaming deadlines, problems, details, budgets and heavy lifting. The before and after is the richer soil. The general public only retains an impression of a brand. There is just too much information zooming along our cranial highways. Too much advertising congestion, too much data smog. So a mere impression is the thin document the public files in their mental cabinets. That impression is the business your customer believes you to be in. It is what they are buying and it is the reason they come back to you again.

True, if you are a new company, you have a wonderful window in time where you can actually plant that impression. In those early, important days, your image is net zero. But if your company has been around for years, that original core reason your business was founded may have faded in the sun or it may have hopped sideways. Or you may have lost sight of it internally because you are too laser-beamed into internal issues or running red-cheeked to keep up with a competitor. Either way, you have lost sight of your original purpose.

I don't think anyone has summed up this dilemma better than Simon Sinek in his book *Start with Why*. Sinek (don't read anything into that name) proposes that customers are attracted to companies who are fully aware of *why* they went into business in the first place. He maintains that the *why* is the most important asset of a company. It contains the company's original spark. Its driving force. Its unique mission. The trap most companies fall into over time is that they become fixated on the *how* and the *what*, how they create their products and what goes into them. Companies become more and more self-absorbed as time moves on. Especially if they are successful, because success can be a trap. Success can tempt a company to stand still and become resistant to change.

That inward focus then starts to manifest itself in the marketing. But people are only moderately interested in *how* and *what* goes into a product; they are much more drawn to *why* you are making it in the first place.

Apple is the classic example. Yes, the design of Apple products is sexy and what they enable you to do is limitless. But many tech companies can make that claim. What separates Apple from everyone else is *why* Steve Jobs created his company. He wanted to throw a grappling hook over IBM's walls, swing over the moat Big Blue had dug around its power, scale the wall and storm the castle. Then, when he caught IBM asleep in its jammies—and this is the important part—he wanted to lower the drawbridge and let everyone in. He wanted to give you the same computing power IBM had only previously shared with rich corporations. That was Steve Jobs's *why*. That *why* is the pivot point for Apple. Every ad Apple has created, from *1984* to the Apple ad you saw last night, shows a single individual creating things that only corporations could do back in 1983.

Not long ago, the president of a non-profit foundation was struggling to define its *why*. He asked me for help. I suggested he go back in time to the day the foundation began. I asked, "What did your founder say that day he banged his fist on the table and said, 'There has got to be a better way!'" In that moment is the best distillation of your *why*.

There are many reasons why corporations cut ties with their founders. Sometimes it's age; there comes a time when founders must retire or expire. Sometimes it's a business decision, when a founder must step aside to allow for a fresh point of view in a rapidly changing marketplace. But when corporations turn their backs on founders completely, I think a great disservice is done. By doing so, they are severing the connection to their original spark. That spark is a glowing ember inside most founders, and while it may dim, it's rarely extinguished. Almost categorically, companies lose the connection to their *why* when the founder retires or dies or is pushed aside.

Years ago, I was doing work for a string of KFC franchises in Hamilton. The Colonel had sold KFC back in 1964 but was retained as spokesperson and quality controller. The owners told me stories of how much they dreaded visits from Colonel Sanders. (The Colonel was actually living in Mississauga at the time, so it was easy to make surprise visits.) He would always be grouchy and complain about the way the franchisees were preparing the food. They rolled their eyes when talking about the Colonel. But in hindsight, I see what was happening. The Colonel started Kentucky Fried Chicken because he was passionate about his recipe and loved the idea of feeding people a Sunday dinner any day of the week. When he saw his dream distorted over time and miles and profit efficiencies, it just steamed his grits. He was testy because he was trying to preserve the initial spark.

In the mid-seventies, KFC did the unheard of and sued the Colonel. The corporation actually took its spokesperson to court for libel after he publicly described KFC's gravy as "wallpaper paste to which sludge was added." You gotta love that description—it was a right cross followed by an uppercut. In making that charge, Sanders wasn't driven by ego, he was driven by the pain of watching his *why* being corrupted. He had started Kentucky Fried Chicken for the love of good food. Now KFC was a massive corporation more interested in the *what* and the *how* of the fast-food industry. KFC lost the case, by the way.

Before I co-founded my company, I was a frustrated ad agency copywriter. Whenever I had to hire a director to produce my radio or television commercials, most of them would run roughshod over my scripts, sacrificing the marketing strategy in favour of the humour. The majority of the directors didn't have marketing backgrounds, they were talent directors. The resulting commercials might be amusing, but they sold little product. It was a recurring issue, from Toronto to New York to Los Angeles. Instead of having directors save my scripts, I ended up having to save the scripts *from* the directors. So we created the company I could not find. Pirate was to be a production company that created award-winning commercials while protecting the marketing strategy.

You just heard the sound of my fist hitting a table as I yelled out, "There has got to be a better way."

That was Pirate's mission. When we opened our doors, we were inundated with work. Clearly, I wasn't the only copywriter starved for respect.

Whenever we veered from that stated purpose, Pirate's business suffered. Whenever we got sucked into the internal workings of our business and confused it for marketing, we suffered. Like when we expanded to New York City. We spent a lot of money and time marketing that fact in Canada. No one cared. It was just Pirate expanding its business to the States. Whenever we got sucked into price wars with competitors, we suffered. Whenever we went against our instincts to please overly aggressive agency producers (who cared about budgets, not creativity) we suffered. And when we sold a piece of our company to an outside investment firm that specialized in the advertising space—hoping its Rolodex would help us expand our business—we suffered. That firm was bottom-line driven and had little sensitivity to our *why*. Ironically, our *why* was what attracted it to us in the first place, because at the time, Pirate was producing the majority of radio commercials in Canada. Then its corporate rigidity slowly seeped into our engine and put sand in the gears. Our original spark slowly started to suffocate.

All of which is to say, when I ask what business you are really in, it's the most important question in this book. Because if you don't know the answer, how can your marketing ever be relevant?

If you can't articulate why you're in business, how can you protect that delicate spark? And if you don't have a firm grasp on your why, how can you articulate it to your staff? A company needs one shared purpose, not a bunch of individual ones.

Recently, I found an old book titled *The Lasker Story: As He Told It*. Albert D. Lasker was probably the most fascinating adman in history. He built the Lord & Thomas advertising agency into the biggest agency in North America in the 1920s, and he did it by pioneering what was then called "reason-why" copy. Prior to that insight (giving people reasons to buy a brand), advertising was just news. Put another way, Lasker turned advertising into persuasion. This book is the verbatim speech Lasker gave to his staff over two days back in the twenties. He was giving the speech because he wanted his agency, which had grown substantially over the years, to connect back to its original spark. Over those two days, Lasker articulated the philosophy of Lord & Thomas, its principles, what he expected of his agency and his staff, and why he loved the advertising business so much. It wasn't about profit and loss, it wasn't about systems and it wasn't about accounting. Lasker wanted the agency to be of one mind, to move as one machine. It was about understanding what made Lord & Thomas unique. It was about his pioneering love of persuasion. It was about embracing the agency's *why*.

Fifty years later, ad icon David Ogilvy realized he couldn't be a constant presence at his sixty Ogilvy & Mather offices around the world. So he would issue letters and memos and print his speeches for staff, so they would stay connected to the *why* of the shop. Ogilvy instinctively knew a leader's job is to continually fan the vital flame. When he retired, his executives bound all his memos and speeches into a book titled *The Unpublished David Ogilvy* and presented it to him. It has since been published. I highly recommend it.

The key to articulating what business you're in is a purely emotional exercise. It was an emotional moment for the founder on day one and it's emotion that pulls in customers. When Michelin abandoned its powerful tagline "Because so much is riding on your tires" and adopted "A better way forward," the decision was completely lost on me. There is not a scintilla of emotion in the new line. It sounds like a slogan coined by Walter in accounting. Again, Apple is about thumbing its nose at IBM and tearing down the barriers between people and technology. Molson is about letting off steam with your friends. Nike is about getting off the couch and accomplishing something.

Not an accountant in the bunch.

Look at those previous sentences. They have power, they have thrust. "A better way forward" is stuck in neutral. Now, to make this exercise even harder, you should be able to sum up the driving principle of your company in one compelling sentence. It's an elevator pitch of sorts (more on that next chapter). Your core driving purpose cannot be a paragraph. No successful business ever points to the company paragraph. Sure, you can argue that many causes have been won after someone gave a rousing speech. But no one remembers the details of a speech, they only remember how that speech made them *feel*. That feeling is captured by the elevator pitch. That feeling is the business you are really in, and that sensation is what creates a repeat customer.

Remember, customers never want the product. They want the benefit of the product, and to purchase that benefit from a company whose purpose feels like a cavalry coming over the hill. Apple's cavalry hoists a pirate flag and attacks corporations from ingenious angles. Molson's troops say nine to five may belong to your boss, but 5:01 to midnight is yours. Nike's militia says go for it.

People don't buy ¾-inch drill bits. They buy ¾-inch holes.

I have used that line for over thirty years and took full credit for it until I reread a book written by Theodore Levitt and realized I had unconsciously stolen it from him. But it's a beautiful articulation of what marketing is all about. People buy benefits. Not products. Not features. And they buy those solutions from companies they can relate to.

That's why knowing what business you are really in is so imperative. The worst possible marketing scenario is when you keep selling tires but your customers are buying safety. With that kind of disconnect, the future of the company will get very difficult.

Smart companies sweat over this. But once you look back through your own windows, once you pull out a stethoscope to listen to the beating heart of your company, everything will change. Your marketing will be clear. Concise. Relevant. Not only that, but it will lend itself to more creativity. Think of the endless ideas "Just Do It" has inspired. Think of all the iconic marketing Apple has done for thirty years off the launch pad of its *1984* commercial. Coke's consistent "happiness" marketing has made it number four on the *Forbes* list of the World's Most Valuable Brands, a list that includes Apple, Microsoft and Google. Very telling—a brand invented in the late nineteenth century, still relevant and valuable near the top of that tech-heavy list.

More than anything, if you truly know what business you're in, you will be selling the right thing and solving the right problems. Your burning ember will be alive and well. Customers will ignore closer competitors with lower prices, drive across town and do business with you. Your staff will have a fixed North Star to follow.

All you have to know is what business you're really in and articulate it in one clear, compelling sentence. Which is fiendishly hard to do. But don't panic. Step into my elevator.

Chapter Two

PRAYING TO THE GOD OF OTIS
Perfecting Your Elevator Pitch

Back in 1974, *Time* magazine had a People column. This feature told short stories about people who had done something outstanding. Over time, the People column became so popular the magazine's editors wondered if they could spin it out into a standalone publication. To succeed, it would need a unique editorial point of view. So managing editor Richard Stolley and his team started to refine the idea. Stolley knew about hot properties. He was the man who had acquired the Zapruder JFK assassination film for *Time* in 1963.

A magazine about ordinary people probably wouldn't survive, but a magazine that was weighted 50:50 between celebrities and regular people just might. When that idea was presented to parent magazine *Time*, the pitch was distilled down to one line: *A magazine that would feature celebrities and ordinary people doing extraordinary things.*

That angle was irresistible. *Time* backed *People* magazine and today it has the largest audience of any American magazine. Even in the battered print industry, *People* recently attracted over a billion dollars in advertising, while most other publications were struggling. And it all started with a pitch.

Pitches are an exercise in clarity.

The task of marketing is a never-ending exercise in reduction. For a business, it's about summing up the company's purpose in one crisp statement. For that company's advertising, it's about stripping a selling message or idea down to its essence. It's about honing a briefing document repeatedly until there is only one powerful selling point left. Every effective advertisement or commercial should sell one thing well. This may seem like Advertising 101, but it is the rule most often broken in the world of marketing. "Nine-tenths of wasted copywriting work comes from having to write copy before we determine what we are trying to sell." Adman James Webb Young wrote that. In 1942.

What has changed since then? Nothing.

In my opinion, the fault lies mostly with advertisers, not advertising agencies. Agencies are always pushing clients to focus and be single-minded in their communications. Clients, generally speaking, love to shoehorn as many selling points as they can into every ad, or are famously hazy when it comes to articulating what makes their company unique. Here's the problem with that. The amount of selling points in an advertisement is inversely proportionate to how much it will be noticed. The more stuffed into it, the less will be absorbed. The world of marketing is a world of clutter.

One rule of thumb states that people are subjected to over three thousand advertising messages a day, which is, I think, laughably low. As an experiment one morning, I counted the number of messages I was exposed to from the time I got up at 6:45 a.m. until the moment I stepped into my office at nine. I did all my usual rituals. My clock radio woke me up. I showered, and listened to the radio while I shaved. I perused the newspaper as I ate my cereal, with a morning TV show humming in the background. I jumped into my car and drove the thirty-five minutes to work, listened to more radio and passed dozens of billboards and posters. Then I pulled into my parking space.

Total number of commercial messages: ninety-nine. And it was only 9 a.m., when the real advertising onslaught begins.

Conventional ad wisdom also states that of those three thousand messages, people notice six and retain two. So how do you get into that exclusive country club of two ads? The answer, my friend, is simplicity. A single-minded advertisement, founded on a compelling strategy and expressed creatively has the greatest chance of penetrating and persuading. It's like this: If I have five apples in my hands and I throw them at you, chances are you'll drop them all. But if I lob one, chances are good you'll catch it. Welcome to communication in the twenty-first century. The debate over single-mindedness in advertising has ignited more arguments between client and agency than fee structures and commissions.

But this I know: Simple, clear messages always win.

In order to be single-minded, you have to distill the advertisement into its most basic message. That's why an advertising brief is called an advertising brief. It's supposed to be short. In the thousands of briefs I was handed in my career, that was rarely the case. Most went on for pages. The ideal brief is one page long, with plenty of white space. That means the person in charge of drafting it has to do a lot of rewriting. As they say, hard writing makes for easy reading. It's about chiselling away at the stone to reveal a statue within. It's succinct, it's insightful and it's to the point. But before we expand on that, let's back up a few F-stops.

The classic definition of an elevator pitch is this: How would you describe an idea to someone in the brief time it takes for an elevator to go from the first floor to the second floor? It's also been called an escalator pitch. Even more punishing, in this definition you are going up the escalator on one side, your customer is going down the escalator on the other, and the time you have is the few seconds you are passing each other.

When I asked what business you are really in, the answer should be framed in one compelling sentence. If you need a paragraph to answer it, your mission is fuzzy. And if your mission is fuzzy, your marketing will be, too. An elevator pitch is about forced clarity. It insists you encapsulate the core of your offer or company. Without it, your story, your marketing or maybe even your entire company has no focus, no bubble at the centre of the level.

I read an article about Comedy Central not long ago. It was lauding the consistent success of the channel. At one point, the astute executive in charge of original programming wanted to build a show around a pair of very talented comedians. He said to the team, "We know you guys are great sketch performers, but what is the voice of the show?" The comedy team was stuck for an answer.

The executive was asking for the elevator pitch.

He was forcing the team to find their comedic axle, the thing that would allow the show to go round. You might be surprised to learn that many business owners and marketing directors have difficulty articulating what makes their business unique. I've been in many a meeting where a successful businessperson cannot succinctly express the purpose of their company or the objective of their advertising campaign. Often, they'll just give me the basic category benefit.

The problem with a commodity statement is the domino effect it has on marketing. Brands that haven't gone through the exercise of distilling their message end up with frustrated copywriters creating average advertising. Every company should have a hot, burning core. Everything a company embarks on should emanate from that fist-slamming-on-the-table moment. It is a platform. A foundation. A sharp articulation of what a company was born to change. All the marketing a company produces should be measured against that benchmark. By always referring back to it, a company will never stray from its purpose. That elevator pitch turns into a lighthouse whenever the horizon gets foggy.

But why is articulating an elevator pitch so fiendishly difficult?

Often, the enemy is the passage of time. Imagine drawing a dot in the centre of a page. Then draw a circle around that dot. Then another one. And another. Keep drawing concentric circles until you run out of space. That first tiny dot was the original spark for starting a company. The circles are time, growth, success, failures, market conditions, staff growth, management changes, competitive pressures and business cycles. With each circle, the company moves further away from its flashpoint. When enough circles are drawn, the difficulty of formulating an elevator pitch increases.

A brand-new company has the best window for articulating its mission. The fist-slam is fresh. I suggest that, while it's still fresh, a founder record that moment for posterity and hang it on the wall for all to see. This encapsulation of the company's founding spark will be especially critical for staff over time, as market forces start to smudge the sense of purpose. If the moment is stated and preserved, the company will always have a crisp vector to refer back to.

When you are going through the exercise of distilling your purpose into one compelling statement, you have to drill down and identify what is unique about your particular company. Most importantly, you have to resist offering up a promise all your competitors can match. "Cleaner clothes" describes the detergent category, not your detergent company. So begin with isolating the overall category promise. Write that down and put it up on the wall. Now you've identified the one promise your company should never claim. That benefit belongs to the category. It's a commodity stance.

Now, from that starting point, begin the exercise: What gap does your company fill in the market? What was the founding insight? *Why* does your company do what it does (remember Sinek)? What, aside from profit, is the single driving factor? What is your battle cry? What makes your company different from its biggest competitor? How does your founder differ from your rival's founder? If you stood in the middle of your biggest rival's office, how would it feel different from yours? What is your company's philosophy? What is your company's unique understanding of its customers? How does your company fit into people's lives—realistically? Why do people want to work at your company? If all other things were equal, why should someone choose your company over a competitor? How has your company taken the category benefit and turned it into something unique? What special magic is at work?

If you whittle all this down to a statement your competitor could still claim, you haven't nailed your elevator pitch. This is about capturing your distinctive purpose in a bottle. When Cheer carved out its place in the market, it said you could use the detergent in hot *or* cold water. Hence the line "All Tempa-Cheer!" No other brand had staked out that territory. The process of isolating your unique benefit is like looking through binoculars. You're asking questions to slowly make the creative opportunity come into focus. When you identify that opportunity, lock it in and start the creative process of generating an advertising campaign idea.

Once you come up with something interesting, test it with an elevator pitch. Can you describe your idea in an exciting sentence or two? If you can, it's probably a strong idea. If it takes a paragraph, it's not ready yet.

Let's look at some great elevator pitches to inspire you. My favourite of all time comes from *Wired*. Launched in 1993, *Wired* is a magazine that reports on how trends and innovations are changing the future of business, culture and science. According to its website, *Wired* and Wired.com reach over fourteen million readers every month. But back when it was just a start-up looking for funding, it existed only as a concept in the minds of the founders. And when a company is only an idea, the elevator pitch is all there is.

When the founders of *Wired* met with potential investors, they were funded immediately. The reason was their elevator pitch. It was absolutely captivating. They simply said: Wired *was going to feel like a magazine mailed back from the future.*

When financial backers heard that pitch, they could instantly imagine the magazine. They knew immediately what it stood for and gave the founders what they were looking for on the spot. Over twenty years later, that elevator pitch is still the plumb line for everything *Wired* does. Let's analyze that pitch for a moment. The founders could have just as easily said, "*Wired* is a magazine that will report on future tech trends." That pitch, I maintain, would have induced more narcolepsy than funding. But the phrase "like a magazine mailed back from the future" was such a powerful combination of words. The suggestion that the publication was sending knowledge back through some kind of time/space continuum was intoxicating. Combining the words "mailed back" with "the future" was a stroke of brilliance. So simple, so memorable, so full of potential. It's the nagging thought that won't let you rest, the match-strike to a fascinating fuse.

If a captivating elevator pitch is important when a company is a just a doodle on a notepad (like *Wired* in 1993), it's vital when a company is being established (Apple circa 1983), and it's crucial when a company matures (Nike today). It's the swim lane. When competitors are scrambling and getting lost in their concentric circles, your company is Michael Phelps slicing through the water like a torpedo. On target. On point. Unstoppable. Elevator pitches not only have locked-in coordinates; they contain an insight that is undeniable.

Movie studios, for example, know consumers make quick decisions about which film to see. They know there are infinite choices out there for your entertainment dollar. So they try to make that decision easier for you. The crux of all movie marketing answers one question: What is the movie about? That line underpins movie posters, movie ad campaigns and especially movie trailers. Clint Eastwood rocketed to superstardom when he did *Dirty Harry* in 1971. If you're old enough to remember that film, here's a test. What was it about *Dirty Harry* that was so utterly compelling? What was it about that character that evoked such a visceral reaction in audiences? What was that film really about? You may be thinking it's about a rogue cop. Or that Dirty Harry was a guy who broke all the rules. Wrong. Those two storylines had been done dozens of times before. The secret ingredient of *Dirty Harry* was this: he was more violent than the criminals he chases. That's exactly what was so mesmerizing about Inspector Harry Callahan. It's the reason the studio made the movie. It's what attracted millions of moviegoers, making it one of the top films of the seventies. It's what established Clint Eastwood as the classic tough guy for all time, much more so than the series of spaghetti westerns he had done previously.

When Hollywood executives decided to make a movie based on Robert Ludlum's *Bourne Identity*, they didn't really have to read the 523-page book. They just had to hear one line to green-light the movie: *What if a man with amnesia has forgotten he's the world's most dangerous assassin?*

Frank Oz, who voices Miss Piggy, says the core of the character is that Miss Piggy is a "trucker who wants to be a woman." When you think about it, that's exactly what is so funny about Miss P.

Then there's *Snakes on a Plane*. Actor Samuel L. Jackson signed to do the film based on the stipulation that the studio couldn't change the title. He knew a perfect trifecta when he saw one. "*Snakes on a Plane*" was an elevator pitch, a movie title and a marketing campaign all rolled into one.

It's remarkable what a finely honed elevator pitch can accomplish. One day in 1986, a pair of would-be screenwriters decided to spend their summer vacation going to Hollywood to pitch their movie idea. When they arrived, they looked up "Agents" in the phone book and went down the list until one agreed to a meeting. When they met with the agent, they handed him the screenplay and outlined the story. The agent said, "Listen, I have an appointment with a studio exec this afternoon to pitch an idea, but my writer just cancelled on me and I don't want to lose the meeting. Let's go pitch this." So the novice screenwriters said sure, and off they went. They had no idea how lucky they were to be with an agent on the way to a movie studio to pitch a screenplay during their first week in Hollywood.

When they got to the studio executive's office, they shook hands, sat down and pitched their movie idea. The studio exec listened then said, "I hate it. What else you got?" The writers only had *one* idea. So they excused themselves to run down to the car and get their *other* idea. Moments later, they ducked into a washroom and stared at each other in a mild panic. Then one guy turned to the other and said, "Remember that idea you had where twins are separated at birth and meet later in life?" His partner said yes, but that was all he had. No storyline.

"What if the twins are Schwarzenegger and DeVito?"

So they march back into the office and say to the studio executive, "Okay, twins separated at birth who meet later in life. One's Arnold Schwarzenegger and the other is Danny DeVito." There was a big pause in the room.

Then the exec said, "I'll take it."

Because in that instant, the movie executive could imagine not only the movie, but also the marketing, the poster and most of all the scene where Schwarzenegger tells DeVito he is his long-lost twin brother. To which DeVito says, "Obviously. The moment I sat down I thought I was looking into a mirror." That's the story of *Twins*. An entire movie sold with just an elevator pitch.

In his screenwriting book titled *Save the Cat*, screenwriter Blake Snyder says if a writer can't sum up their story in one intriguing line, they haven't thought the story through. Until you have your pitch, you don't have a story. Again, it's the discipline of clarity. The one-line pitch forces you to articulate the core idea.

Or forces you to admit there isn't one.

That's why an elevator pitch is so crucial. It's a metal detector that only beeps when it hits gold.

It's the same in marketing. First, the company has to have a burning quest. All marketing efforts should rise from that purpose. Within an advertising agency, pitching an advertising idea must pass through that same kind of gauntlet. If a creative team can't sum up their idea in a line or two, the creative director will say, "What else you got?" If it can be relayed in a few powerful words, it's probably a solid idea. If it can't be, chances are it is unfocused, rambling or can't exist fully within the harsh walls of a thirty-second commercial. In a cluttered world of distracted attention, complication is kryptonite.

Many years ago, El Al airlines refurbished its fleet with faster airplanes. Ad agency Doyle Dane Bernbach was charged with coming up with an ad to promote that fact. The creative team came back to creative director Bill Bernbach with a photo of the ocean with a portion of its breadth torn away. (See Fig. 3.)

Bam. Done. No further explanation necessary.

If you've ever wondered how a product can connect with huge swaths of people who seem to have nothing in common, drill down to the core message. That essence—the elevator pitch—will tap a universal desire. Apple products are used by teens *and* by my parents, who are in their eighties. How can one product appeal to such a wide demographic? Because Apple's core promise is to take technology from the hands of the few and put into the hands of the many. That allure knows no generational boundaries.

When Steve Jobs was trying to lure John Sculley to leave his top job at Pepsi to run Apple, he offered him a salary that looked like a long-distance phone number. Sculley demurred. Then Jobs offered him stock options that would vest at over fifty million dollars. Sculley still refused. Jobs peppered him with phone calls, hoping to sway him. Sculley politely declined. So Jobs flew up to New York to ask him to reconsider one last time. Sculley said thank you, but no thank you. He had invested too many years in Pepsi and he had a future there. That's when Jobs looked Sculley in the eye and said, "Do you want to spend the rest of your life selling sugared water, or do you want a chance to change the world?"

As Sculley later said in his book *Odyssey*, that challenge took the wind out of him. After all the meetings, all the phone calls, the huge salary offer and the millions in stock options, it was that one sentence that haunted him. It gnawed at his gut and wouldn't let him sleep. It was so seductive, it overpowered all his loyalty to Pepsi and convinced Sculley to join Apple. It's gone down in history as one of the most famous elevator pitches of all time.

When Ronald Reagan was running for president against incumbent Jimmy Carter, he posed one simple question to America: "Are you better off now than you were four years ago?" When voters were in the booth, that line hung in the air like cologne. The majority of Americans answered no, and put an *x* beside Reagan's name.

When the jury was deliberating O.J. Simpson's fate, defence attorney Johnnie Cochran's elevator pitch, "If it doesn't fit, you must acquit," rang in their ears.

A sharply worded idea whetted on the stone of brevity is capable of remarkable persuasion.

When Michael Jordan was asked what made the Chicago Bulls so dominating, he simply said: "One Team, One Dream." It was a phrase that perfectly captured the team's spirit, expressing their burning desire to win as one unified squad. Those four words became their mantra in practices, in the locker room and during games. The Bulls won six championships between 1991 and 1998, and are the only team in NBA history to win more than seventy games in a single season.

In his book *Tell to Win*, movie producer Peter Guber tells a fascinating story about legendary basketball coach Pat Riley. He had led the Los Angeles Lakers to four championship titles before moving on to coach the Miami Heat. In 2006, the Heat wasn't even supposed to get into the finals. Even though Miami had Shaquille O'Neal, they were still overshadowed by many more powerful, well-rounded teams. But under Riley's insightful coaching, they made it to the championship.

The Heat were playing the Dallas Mavericks and defied all odds to go ahead three games to two. They only had to win one more for the championship. But the last two games were to be played in Dallas, the Mavericks' home court. Statistically, the team with home-court advantage wins three out of every four series in the playoffs. The Heat's handicap would be most intense in the seventh game. If they lost the sixth, winning the seventh game in an enemy stadium would be almost impossible.

But Riley was certain his team could beat the Mavericks as long as he could find a way to convince *them* they could win. He had to make his players believe they could win the championship in game six. He didn't want them having to play that dangerous seventh game in the Maverick's house. So how did he motivate his players to win game six? He simply told the team the whole story of their upcoming victory in a single line: "Pack for just one night."

That line telegraphed Riley's intention not to allow Dallas a seventh game. His team wouldn't need a second change of clothes because they were coming home the night of the sixth game as NBA World Champions.

He said it. They got it.

And the Miami Heat won the NBA championship in their first-ever appearance in the finals.

An elevator pitch isn't just an exercise in clarity, it is also a detonator. It ignites excitement. Skeptics often say elevator pitches leave too much on the table. They leave no room for important nuance. But I think skeptics miss the big picture. An elevator pitch is a test of an idea. It is a ruthless strainer an idea must pass through in order to determine if there really is a workable concept there. An elevator pitch is like the checklist a pilot goes through before take-off. It is not meant to be the entire presentation. This is an important point. An elevator pitch is about testing the validity of an idea in the early stages. Then, in the boardroom, an elevator pitch is meant to excite. Once you unleash it, two things should happen immediately. First, everyone will lean in, and then the next thing you hear is "Tell us more." That's when you bring out the nuances, the colour, and put flesh on the bones.

Or in the case of the Miami Heat, eliminate the need for game seven.

Even if your company is doing well, constantly refining your elevator pitches will make it capable of even bigger leaps. Your marketing will be crisp, your staff will have GPS coordinates for success, new management hires will have a playbook, your customers will have a clear understanding of your offering, and you will even make better operational decisions.

An elevator pitch can articulate an idea, define a story, keep a marketing campaign on the rails and express the soul of your company. Any company that can't express its vision in a single, vivid sentence is a company that is underachieving.

And now that you've distilled your elevator pitch down to your company's very essence, you're ready to begin writing your marketing strategy.

Chapter Three

STRATEGY
It Tastes Awful. And It Works

During a kung fu class one evening, our instructor was teaching us how to calm down during a real-life confrontation. When violence triggers fear, fear triggers adrenaline. And adrenaline can either give you superhuman clarity or freeze you in place. Knowing tactics to calm your mind quickly is critically important because anger and fear make you inefficient. You begin to breathe shallowly, then tense up, then run out of energy quickly.

But in class that day, we pressed our kung fu master further, asking him what he would do if a fight was clearly inevitable. In other words, what would he do in the taut moments leading up to a confrontation? He said he would probably show fear and trepidation. He would cower and keep his hands up in a surrendering posture. He would plead with the aggressor not to hurt him. That answer shocked us. We expected him to say that he would sink into a fighting stance and begin closing the distance between his fists and the attacker's pressure points. When we asked why he would show alarm, he said it was a strategy. His projected weakness would fool his attacker into thinking he was an easy mark, making the attacker overconfident, and when our teacher finally did attack, it would be an utter surprise.

That was an astounding insight to us all. It meant submerging your ego to act like a scared lamb in front of an aggressive A-Type, to absorb their ridicule, to let their swagger grow—then attack when their overconfidence revealed a window of opportunity.

Whenever you have an opponent, or a competitor in the marketplace, you must employ strategy. Marketing should never be just a blunt instrument. If you are just creating ads to "get your name out there," you are selling yourself short. If your marketing is confined to month-end specials or Christmas gift ideas, you're underachieving. Most marketing lurches from one short-term need to the next crisis, and that's why a huge percentage of marketing money is wasted.

When you employ an advertising agency, the first thing it will do is analyze your business, your customers, your competitors and the marketplace, looking for strengths, weaknesses, threats and opportunities—then use that reconnaissance to formulate a marketing strategy. It's what Trevor Goodgoll was doing with his brown paper sessions. It sounds like warfare, and in a way, it is. The reason so much marketing language sounds militaristic is because the men who rebuilt Madison Avenue in the 1950s had just come back from World War II. Therefore, marketing involves strategies, campaigns, tactics, missions, territory, targets, blitzes and battles to capture ground.

The most important of those is strategy.

When you can't afford an advertising agency, you have to formulate a marketing strategy on your own. It's a daunting task, especially if you don't fully understand what a marketing strategy is. When I travel across the country talking to companies and associations, marketing strategy is the topic they struggle with most.

To begin, let's look at some familiar brands.

You probably know that Crest toothpaste "fights cavities." You probably know that Volvo automobiles are known for safety. That an M&M "melts in your mouth, not in your hand." Tim Hortons is "Always Fresh." "You're in good hands" with Allstate. That once upon a time, when you shopped at Eaton's, it promised, "Goods satisfactory or money refunded." Coffee Crisp makes "a nice light snack." You know Buckley's Cough Mixture "Tastes awful. And it works." No doubt, many of those advertisers created good commercials. But here's a question: How many specific commercials can you actually remember?

Next to none, I bet. What you are remembering is the strategy.

When Eaton's promised to refund your money, it was a strategy to instill confidence in your purchases. The plan was to use that confidence to pull you into Eaton's doors, bypassing the competition. Buckley's knew its taste repelled people, so it employed a strategy to assure people that it worked *because* it tasted bad. Crest could have talked about white teeth, but instead it chose to link itself with fighting cavities. Coffee Crisp wanted to position the candy bar as a snack, not a treat.

Every one of these thoughts is a selling strategy. Each brand looked at the marketplace, found an area not yet claimed by a competitor and created an all-encompassing plan to invade and own that space. Every advertisement or communication from that point on aimed at that target. If a new message didn't align with that strategy, it was discarded. The strategy became a benchmark, a route map and an end goal.

The simplest analogy is this: When you go vacation, first you decide on the kind of holiday you want. Then you identify the destination, plot the trip carefully, and budget your money accordingly. You wouldn't jump in your car or board an airplane without knowing where you are headed, what route to take or how much money to bring. Same with a marketing strategy.

You should never spend money on advertising without a master plan. Put another way, you want to formulate an overall direction for your business or product that clearly articulates which part of the available marketing real estate you want to own and how you're going to get there. To do that, you have to analyze the marketplace and determine what territory is already staked out by the competition. I suggest going competitor by competitor, and writing down what each stands for on separate cards. Put those cards up on a wall so you can stare at them all. Somewhere on that wall will be an opening, an opportunity to wedge your card in between the others. A way to catch the competition between bases.

When Crest looked at its marketplace, the cards on the wall said white teeth, fresh breath and social acceptance. The opportunity was to be the brand that prevented cavities. When Volvo surveyed the global automotive marketplace, the cards on their wall said luxury, high performance and practicality. The opportunity was safety. Buckley's Cough Mixture has been around since 1919. It's a heritage brand, so other cough medicines have to swirl around Buckley's orbit. Buckley's mixture had worked all these years because the lousy tasting ingredients it contained were effective. The slogan became: "It tastes awful. And it works." It's a brilliant strategy because it gives Buckley's a unique selling point in a crowded category. Other brands had to wedge their card in with artificially flavoured cough mixtures.

Coffee Crisp wanted to increase sales. The brand analyzed the competition in the candy bar category, and realized most were positioned as treats. But a treat only triggers an occasional purchase. So Coffee Crisp decided to occupy the "snack" real estate in your mind. Therefore, when Coffee Crisp said it was a "nice light snack," it was vying for frequent usage. Not monthly treats. That strategy had a big impact on Coffee Crisp sales. By remaining consistent with that message, it persuaded people to double or triple the frequency of their purchases.

When Malcolm McLaren surveyed the American music scene, he realized he had a short time to make a big impact with the Sex Pistols. So he crafted that strategy of offending small southern cities and let the resulting press become his advertising.

In each of these examples, the marketplace was analyzed, an opportunity was identified and all subsequent marketing was aimed at that gap.

When you analyze your marketplace, it shouldn't be difficult to get a pretty accurate reading of rival companies. The thing that bugs you most about them is probably their greatest strength. It's the pea under the mattress as you lie in bed thinking about your competition in the middle of the night. Now, compare that to what your company stands for in the marketplace. If you have a strong position, you'll want to vigorously defend it. If you suffer from a weak position, you need to find a smarter, more effective strategy. If your company is brand new, the sheet is clean. Look for a gap in the market, then determine if there is a market in the gap.

That, in a nutshell, is what a smart strategy does. It plants a flag in people's minds and plots a way to generate business. There is always a flag to be had. You just have to be willing to dig and analyze.

Ideally, your strategy should hinge on the thing that makes your company unique. Pirate Radio was the only Toronto production company with an ex-agency copywriter as a principal. That was an important distinction, because most other production companies were run by music composers who had never spent a day inside an advertising agency. Pirate understood not just sound, but also marketing. We could produce radio commercials that were award-winning *and* sold product. We enhanced the script's creativity while protecting the selling strategy. That became the unique selling proposition in our marketing. Our award-winning production attracted agency creative people as our clients, and our marketing chops attracted direct advertisers. That was Pirate's unique flag in the marketplace.

And that strategy generated business.

When radio station CHUM-FM asked me to analyze its marketing, I asked the station what made it unique in the marketplace, beyond good music. (That's a given in the radio category, and you should never advertise a given). One of the features their people told me about was the many contests and giveaways they organized throughout the year. When I asked for more detail—after all, many radio stations give away prizes—they told me about the annual trip to the Barbados, where they send a planeload of listeners to be part of CHUM's live annual broadcast from the tropical location. They told me about inviting listeners to sit in on the morning show in Toronto when celebrities were being interviewed. And about bringing listeners backstage to the green room to meet the bands before big concerts CHUM-FM sponsored.

The strategy was immediately apparent to me: CHUM-FM gave listeners experiences money can't buy.

Other stations gave away CDs, money, shopping sprees, and so on. But CHUM-FM gave listeners VIP experiences unavailable to the average person. From that point, CHUM-FM's marketing emphasized that it was the only station that gave away priceless experiences. It was a unique and powerful statement. That's the power of strategy. It framed a unique selling feature of CHUM-FM. It gave the station a marketing roadmap. It allowed the station to own a piece of mental real estate that wasn't bound by music. And at the same time, it diminished the offerings of other radio stations (more on this shortly).

On the other hand, if you discover that a rival has already staked out a powerful position in the marketplace, congratulations, you have formidable competition. But don't lose heart. Strong competitors only make you better. In the Ultimate Fighting Championship, for example, many elite fighters do poorly against weaker opponents. They manage to win, but they look lacklustre doing it. Yet when a top UFC fighter is matched against a highly ranked opponent, their best game emerges. Worthy competition only makes you better, forcing you to be absolutely sharp and present. In my own experience, whenever Pirate had a strong competitor, we always did better work and smarter marketing. We had a healthy respect for our top rivals, and their presence consistently kicked our performance up a few notches.

But one of the things that's rarely discussed when it comes to marketing is that if you want to grow your business, that business has to come from somewhere. Namely, from your competitors.

It's important to recognize this. Customers don't just materialize. Revenues don't just appear in a rainbow of pixie dust. Like the amount of water on the planet, customers are a finite resource. That means you have to carefully figure out where you're going to get those new customers, and how.

One of the most effective strategies is to reposition your competition. It's a strategy within a strategy: you position your brand in the public's mind while disabling the competition at the same time. A classic example of repositioning was Avis versus Hertz. Hertz was the number-one car rental company in the 1960s, and Avis wanted to steal some of its market share. So Avis said: "We're number two, but we try harder." That was a radical statement in the sixties. First, no one had ever boasted about being number two in a category before. But more importantly, it repositioned Hertz as a company that wasn't trying that hard anymore. Another Avis ad said: "Our lines are shorter." It was classic Achilles heel repositioning. It leveraged the weakness in Hertz's strength. Avis was saying you would get faster service at its counters because they weren't as busy, and because it was number two, it would try harder to keep your business.

By repositioning Hertz as too big and too busy, Avis increased its market share by 35 percent in just a few years.

When Tylenol entered a market dominated by Bayer Aspirin for over seventy years, Tylenol analyzed the opportunities and decided the way to gain dramatic market share was to reposition Aspirin. It achieved that by employing a strategy that said Tylenol was "easy on stomachs." Aspirin occasionally irritated the stomach lining in some patients and created a small amount of bleeding in some others. By saying Tylenol didn't irritate stomachs, it repositioned Aspirin as the pain reliever that did.

Tylenol effectively adjusted people's perceptions of Aspirin. In the ad copy, Tylenol acknowledged Aspirin's leading pain-relieving abilities but questioned the strong ingredients it used to relieve that pain. When people were exposed to that strategy, two things happened. First, people with stomach problems stopped using Aspirin. And second, people who didn't have stomach issues thought, why tempt it? As a result, Tylenol stole huge swaths of market share and eventually surpassed Aspirin to become the number-one brand in pain relief.

A repositioning strategy depends on a couple of rules. First, you have to find the weakness in your competitor's strength. Then you reposition your rival by adjusting the perception the public has about that brand and take advantage of that shift. In other words, their sword becomes your sword. It's a gutsy strategy, but it is a powerful way to steal customers.

Royal Doulton, the fine china company based in Stoke-on-Trent, England, found itself competing in the United States with a company called Lenox Fine China. Over 50 percent of Royal Doulton's products were exported, so the American market was important. Royal Doulton decided to defend its position in the US marketplace by repositioning Lenox. To do that, it ran ads that stated: "Royal

Doulton. The china of Stoke-on-Trent, England versus Lenox. The china of Pomona, New Jersey."

Lenox also made fine china, but it made that china in New Jersey. And say what you will, Jersey doesn't conjure up images of bucolic villages, rolling fields and mannered British aristocracy. As a result of that advertisement, Royal Doulton increased its revenues by 6 percent.

Listerine had dominated the mouthwash category since the early twentieth century. Then in 1966 along came Scope. It was a pleasant tasting, minty mouthwash. In order to take customers away from the mighty Listerine, Scope chose to reposition its larger rival. It simply asked: "Why settle for medicine breath?" As all effective repositioning strategies do, it attacked the leader's strength. Everyone knew Listerine tasted terrible. Everyone knew that terrible taste killed germs. Scope didn't challenge that belief. But what Scope did was alter a perception, suggesting that clean, *medicine* breath could be just as unpleasant as bad breath. As a result, Scope stole a healthy mouthful of market share away from Listerine.

When BMW first came to North America, it was ranked number eleven in the European car category. It had the weakest image of all imports and many thought BMW stood for British Motor Works. The leading brand, of course, was Mercedes. So in the 1980s, BMW set its sights on younger professionals with big paycheques. This upwardly mobile generation rejected the luxury symbols of their parents—a list that happened to include Mercedes.

Because BMW was an underdog, it hired an underdog ad agency called Ammirati & Puris, which coined the slogan "BMW. The Ultimate Driving Machine." The strategy was to emphasize performance rather than force BMW into the luxury category dominated by Mercedes. To do that, BMW chose to reposition Mercedes.

So the carmaker created ads that effectively said: BMW, the

ultimate driving machine versus Mercedes, the ultimate sitting machine. That repositioned Mercedes as a living room on wheels and BMW as a sleek, high-performance automobile. In essence, BMW attacked the weak spot in Mercedes's strength. No one doubted the luxury of Mercedes, they now just doubted the power and handling. With that, BMW sales soared.

Now that you understand repositioning, you'll realize you've seen it at work many times. Remember the famous "I'm a Mac and I'm a PC" television campaign? It was a humorous but vicious repositioning campaign, framing the perception of PCs as the computer of choice for nerds. Pepsi tried to reposition the mighty Coke by calling itself the "Choice of a New Generation," recasting Coke as the soft drink for older folks. Prego spaghetti sauce repositioned Ragú by saying it was the "thick sauce," leaving market leader Ragú to be perceived as thin. When Löwenbräu was the leading German import beer in North America, another German beer called Beck's wanted to steal its market share. So it took a leaf from Royal Doulton's playbook and said: "You've tasted the German beer that's the most popular in America. Now taste the German beer that's the most popular in Germany." A powerful repositioning. It acknowledged Löwenbräu's success, but zeroed in on its failure with the world's most discerning beer drinkers. It didn't take long for Beck's to overtake Löwenbräu.

In each of the above examples, one brand was repositioning another brand. But sometimes, a brand can try to reposition an entire category. In the late 1800s, Ivory soap began saying it was "99.44/100% pure" because it contained no perfumes, creams or dyes and only 0.56 percent of the ingredients were non-soap. That was its way of repositioning all other soaps as impure.

When I was writing ads for fashion retailer Bretton's, the retailer wanted to attract shoppers away from department stores. Because Bretton's specialized in fashion and department stores didn't, I saw an opportunity and wrote the line: "I won't buy my fashion where I buy my appliances." Putting the image of a stylish dress beside a washer in people's minds was all I needed to taint the perception of department stores as fashion destinations. When CHUM-FM said it gave listeners experiences money couldn't buy, it devalued the offerings of the other stations in the market, in essence, repositioning them all.

Then there are times when a company is facing a strategic hurdle within the company itself. Often, an established way of thinking internally is preventing an organization from adapting to new competitive pressures externally. "That's the way we do it around here" is the phrase of death in marketing. There comes a time when a strategy must be first aimed at the company itself. In Paris, the Metro subway system is the second-busiest in Europe. It carries over 1.5 billion passengers a year. But not long ago, it had a big problem. Ridership numbers were falling, surface traffic was increasing, revenue was in a death spiral. People were avoiding the subway. Cars, cabs and walking were all eating into the subway's business. The Metro had to change its strategy in order to become more appealing to the people of Paris. To achieve that, the Metro management made the most extraordinary decision. Instead of trying to change their user's minds about how they viewed the subway, they decided to change the way *they* viewed their users.

The first step was to change their terminology. So subway "users" became subway "customers." And when users became customers, it completely changed the Metro's thinking process. It meant the subway was no longer in the business of moving people from A to B, but rather a *provider of services for mobile people*. With that change of mindset, the Paris Metro's entire strategy was recalibrated.

First, the Metro installed Internet terminals in the subways. Then it added ATM machines, three hundred shops, fifteen hundred vending machines and a hundred newspaper distributors. All of which, by the way, happily paid royalties to the Metro. Works of art were put on display at many stations. New theatrical spaces were installed so performers could busk. A new customer website provided traffic information, customized itineraries and a guide to what was going on in the City of Light. Ridership and customer satisfaction soared.

But look at what happened.

By making that change internally, it changed the way customers thought about them externally. And it all started with a completely bold thought—let's stop thinking like a train. Not many marketers would have the guts to pursue that wholesale change. I believe 99.9 percent would have defaulted to convincing subway patrons to change *their* way of thinking. Most marketing is aimed at customers; it is rarely redirected at the mother ship. Don't forget that the Paris subway is 115 years old. Changing the ingrained behaviour of a twenty-year-old company is almost impossible; imagine rewiring a 115-year-old organization. It's like trying to turn the *Queen Mary* around in a bathtub.

But amazingly the Paris Metro did it, proving that a bold strategy has a combustive energy. Once you can accept the brazenness of the idea, once you can see the powerful logic it contains, a counterintuitive strategy can leapfrog an organization over obstacles, competitors and occasionally, even market forces.

So ask yourself: What is your business strategy? What makes your company utterly unique? How does your strategy position your company against the competition? Does it plot your company's direction? Is your strategy meaningful to your customers and potential customers? Is there an opportunity to reposition the competition? Where will your new customers come from? Where is the gap?

This is the thinking I find most lacking with smaller marketers. Most haven't formulated a marketing strategy, their advertising has a slightly willy-nilly feeling to it, the gains are incremental and frustrating and they find themselves running out of funds before an effective marketing position can be achieved.

I often see companies confuse strategy with tactics. Creating ads for the holiday shopping season is a tactic for moving product, not a marketing strategy. While a smart strategy should be able to embrace tactical requirements, they are only a subset of your overall strategy. So if you have to advertise gift ideas during the Christmas season, all your seasonal messages should still riff off your main strategy. For example, Volvo messages can transform into Christmas messages by saying Volvo is the vehicle of choice for bringing families together safely during the holiday travel season.

Tactic: advertising to Christmas shoppers. Strategy: safety.

Tactics are a necessary part of marketing. Opportunities will present themselves and you'll want to take short-term tactical advantage of them to help achieve your overall strategy. But a tactic is not a marketing strategy. That means when deciding on a tactic, it must first pass the benchmark test. If it can fit into the main strategy, it's right. If it needs to be shoehorned in, it's wrong. Never deviate from your brand's marketing. You will always pay dearly for detours.

For as long as I can remember, my father was an Oldsmobile man. He loved the luxury branding of Oldsmobiles. Then, somewhere along the way, Oldsmobile stopped talking to my father. The advertising theme actually became "Not your father's Oldsmobile." Little by little, its advertising became less aspirational and began focusing on more tactical marketing aimed at increasing short-term sales. That decision probably seemed like a good move in boardroom meetings, but over the long haul it had an impact on its customer base. General Motors eventually shut down its Oldsmobile division in 2012 after a run of over a hundred years. My father has driven imports for the last twenty years. Oldsmobile had lost its proud, long-term customers.

Always play the long game.

If you are Coffee Crisp, you can do tactical Christmas messages (need a snack while shopping?), you can sponsor marathons (need a quick fuel-up at the thirteen-kilometre mark?), you can stock vending machines in office buildings (quell the four o'clock munchies!). But everything Coffee Crisp does revolves around "a nice light snack."

Let's take an even deeper dive.

Good marketing makes a company look smart, but great marketing makes a customer look smart. The former is just a company talking to itself. The message has little relevance to its customers and results in annoying, cloying advertising. But the latter is about having a conversation with customers about something that is on their minds, making them look smart and enhancing their lives. It's a relevant message that makes a customer sit up and pay attention.

Tylenol won't irritate your stomach.

Really? Tell me more.

That is interesting marketing at work.

Remember that a great strategy is a competitive advantage. Most of your competitors probably don't have a business strategy in place. They are just reacting to the marketplace like a pinball machine. They are pouring marketing money into short-term tactics. The creativity of their advertisements is low, because nothing is more debilitating than an empty strategy. Their marketing isn't propelling the company toward a definable and defendable position.

Think of a football game. It's about advancing down the field. Every huddle is a short-term plan (tactic) to get closer to the goal line (strategy) in order to deliver a touchdown (goal). Think baseball: every pitch is customized to that batter's weakness (tactic); every out is part of a bigger plan to win the inning (strategy) in order to win the game (goal).

When Muhammad Ali fought George Foreman in the Rumble in the Jungle, and realized after round one that he couldn't out-punch the much more powerful Foreman, he quickly changed strategy. As he stood in his corner between round one and round two, Ali decided—then and there—to let Foreman punch himself out. From that point on, Ali just leaned back on the ropes, letting the big man punch himself into exhaustion, each round draining a little more fuel from Foreman's tank (strategy). Meanwhile, Ali covered up and absorbed Foreman's heavy fists, waiting patiently. When his left side started to go numb from Foreman's thunderous rights, Ali whispered in Foreman's ear that he obviously didn't have much of a left (tactic). So in round six, Foreman switched hands and started pummelling Ali with his left, which allowed the feeling to come back into Ali's side. Then in the eighth round, Ali saw fatigue spider across Foreman's face for a millisecond. He seized the moment and unleashed an explosive eight-punch combination to knock Foreman out. Watch the eighth round on YouTube, and see the crowd absolutely reel in shock at the sight of Foreman on the canvas. Note that the boxing commentator doesn't even twig to Ali's strategy until moments before the knockout. No one saw it coming.

Except Ali.

I was in my teens when that fight took place in 1974 and was a huge Ali fan, but Ali's "Rope-a-Dope" performance was a snooze-fest in my mind. Where was the dancing Ali we all knew and loved? I've completely revised my opinion since then. I now think the match was Ali's greatest, because he didn't beat Foreman with his fists, he beat him with his mind.

It was a glorious example of the power of strategy.

In the twenty-first century, UFC mixed martial arts has overtaken boxing as the top pugilistic sport. Many of its trainers and champions have made a prediction about the future of fighting.

They believe that as mixed martial arts progresses and becomes more intelligent, the fighters will become smaller. They will rely less on brute force and more on the "art" in martial arts. In other words, they will rely more on *strategy*.

For smaller marketers, this is a crucial insight. Think of your deeper-pocketed rivals as the George Foremans of your business. You can't beat them going mano a mano, so you have to employ a different strategy. With insightful thinking you can not only survive, but thrive. You have to roll up your sleeves and start the hard work of analyzing your marketplace, then defining and refining your strategy. You have to find a way to win.

All you have to do is find a way to make people believe.

Chapter Four

BIEBER IN A BLENDER
If They Feel, They Believe

Back in the late 1960s, Bobby Orr was turning the National Hockey League on its head. This phenom from Parry Sound, Ontario, was redefining what a defenceman was capable of. He led end-to-end rushes past puzzled veterans, controlled the game's pace at will and became the only defenceman in NHL history to win the league scoring title. As kids, we watched Bobby Orr with forensic fascination. We noticed he had only a single strip of black tape on his hockey stick. As we discovered, Orr liked the feel of the puck on a bare blade. But the league had a rule then that all sticks must be taped. So Orr adhered to that regulation by employing the absolute minimum—one solitary strip of black tape. He also didn't wear socks in his skates—a stunning revelation to us kids who were never privy to dressing-room rituals. But one night as a junior, Orr had forgotten his socks and realized he loved the feel of his bare feet in skates. The direct contact of his toes to the leather sole was like a system of levers and pulleys he could employ to prove, as sportswriter Cathal Kelly once said, that physics is just a concept.

Many years later in 1988, Wayne Gretzky was sent to the Los Angeles Kings in a trade heard around the world. When he got there, he asked his new wingers how they preferred their passes—hard or soft? They looked at him like he was speaking Klingon. They had never been asked how they wanted a pass to *feel*. But Gretzky was the ultimate playmaker and those small details were important to him. In the heat of a frenzied moment, he was capable of personalizing the feel of a pass to his teammates.

The subject of feel is critical in so many endeavours.

Think acting. I once worked with Tony Roberts, a terrific actor who has appeared in many of Woody Allen's movies. I asked him if Woody was the best director he ever worked with. He said yes, but felt his best acting moment was in the Sidney Lumet movie *Serpico*. Roberts was playing a scene where honest cop Frank Serpico (Al Pacino) was telling friendly cop Bob Blair (Roberts) about the corruption in the police department. Serpico believed Blair was someone he could confide in, but in that critical moment, we realize instantly Blair can't be trusted. While filming the scene, Roberts kept making a small facial expression to suggest the deception. Lumet leaned over and whispered to Roberts, "Don't show it to me." In other words, don't convey the duplicity physically. *Feel* it, don't show it. By not seeing it outwardly, we, the viewers, feel Blair's inner motivation profoundly in that pivotal scene. Roberts considers it the finest acting moment of his career.

One of the most important aspects of a movie script is the subtext. In most instances, it is the subtext that draws an actor to a film project. Reciting a line is relatively easy for a good actor, but the real feat is making the audience feel what is going on within a character without saying it. Subtext is the invisible language. It reveals a character's true motivation in a story.

Take the scene in *The Godfather* where Michael Corleone has dinner with police chief McCluskey and mob rival Sollozzo. We know the purpose of the meeting. On the surface, it is to negotiate a truce. But in reality, we know Michael is there to kill them both.

The subtext in the scene is riveting. To that end, director Francis Ford Coppola has a large portion of the scene spoken in Italian. But he does this for a reason: he wants us to concentrate on Michael's churning feelings, not the dialogue. Michael has never killed before. And Michael knows there is no going back after he does. The subtext is so powerful it creates an almost unbearable tension. We, the audience, feel the invisible language as clearly as if it had been spoken.

Think of a doctor's bedside manner. So many doctors seem to lack the empathy that's needed when relaying difficult news, and opt instead for an antiseptic, clinical message when a heartfelt one is called for. They have no feel for the moment.

Think music. At a recording session in a new studio, a sound engineer once set up a screen to put between Frank Sinatra and the orchestra. Many recording engineers do this, by the way, believing the vocalist should be isolated. But Sinatra ordered him to take it down. Ol' Blue Eyes needed to feel the sound of the orchestra hitting him in the chest. It affected how he placed himself into the music, and the sound washing over him helped Sinatra make his lyric more expressive. Music plays an enormous role in movies and television shows. As any director will tell you, music tells you how to feel. A sensitive scene becomes emotional when the music cues that feeling. A suddenly tense piece of music, long before we see an actor, tells us to feel anxious. When directing commercials, I always assigned music a role, treating it as another actor in the scene.

Now, think marketing.

Many years ago, British Rail was looking for a new advertising agency. It contacted several London shops, and one agency in particular, named Allen Brady & Marsh, responded by inviting the clients to come to their agency at nine o'clock on Monday morning to hear their pitch. So at the exact time on the given day, three highly polished British Rail executives walked into the agency's reception area—and couldn't believe what they saw. The lobby was filthy; it looked like it hadn't been cleaned in months. There were empty coffee cups, overflowing ashtrays, layers of dust and bits of newspaper strewn about. The receptionist ignored them while she chatted to a friend on the phone, then abruptly, without looking up at them, told the clients to sit down and that the creative director would come out to get them when he had a moment. The very proper British Rail executives looked around the dirty lobby, wiped their chairs before sitting down and waited to be greeted by the creative director.

And time started ticking by. They sat in that lobby for twenty minutes, then thirty, then forty. After fifty full minutes, the British Rail clients were so outraged, so appalled, they got up to leave. At that precise moment, the creative director appeared and said, "Gentlemen, you've just experienced what thousands of British Rail customers experience every day. Let's sit down to see if we can figure out a way to change that."

Okay, that's got to be one of the biggest pitch gambles I've ever heard in my career. But guess what—the agency won the business.

Why? Because they made the British Rail clients *feel* the problem, not just understand it. (In other words, the railway company had to change its ways before any new advertising could be effective.)

So much marketing and messaging is pure information. Just reams of rational logic, slathered with cold facts, topped with a research cherry. Don't get me wrong, there is a place for hard data. It just can't be the thrust of your marketing. The reason is simple: People won't *act* on your message if it's just pure information. In a world where people are pummelled with messages on an hourly basis—Eric Schmidt, ex-CEO of Google, says on a single day modern society generates more information than all of civilization created before 2003—people just tune out to survive. Flat information is too easy to ignore. People will even ignore information that is critical to them. Twice a year, we're told to "change the batteries in your smoke detectors when the clock changes." Important, potentially life-saving information.

No one does it.

See, straight information is seductive because it seduces the person dispensing the information into thinking that a mere data dump is effective. But the key—the true secret to influencing someone—is to make them feel your message in their gut, not just intellectually understand it.

Emotion is the differentiator.

One of my favourite television campaigns from my youth was for Timex watches. From the mid-fifties to the early seventies, ex-NBC newscaster John Cameron Swayze conducted a series of Timex Torture Tests. In each instalment, the watch would be placed in a perilous situation to test its water and shock resistance. In one of the most memorable commercials, a Timex was strapped to the propeller of an outboard motor. The motor was put in a tank of water and turned on. The watch spun through the water at 4,500 revolutions per minute. When the motor was shut off, the watch was pulled out and a close-up revealed the second hand was still ticking. In another test, a Timex was attached to the tip of an arrow and was shot through a pane of glass into a tank of water. In yet another, a Timex was attached to the hull of a boat that was crashing through roaring rapids. In each case, when the Timex was recovered, it was still ticking. Not bad for a watch that retailed for $9.95.

The Timex campaign had one of the best tag lines of all time: "It takes a licking and keeps on ticking." So why did that campaign run for twenty years? Why did it make Timex the number-one watch brand in America by 1967, accounting for one out of every three watches sold?

Because viewers could *feel* the toughness of those watches in their gut. It's one thing to say a watch is shock resistant and waterproof, but it's quite another to show the watch surviving extreme torture tests. People didn't just intellectually understand that message, they felt it. You also have to put this campaign into an era-specific context. In the sixties and seventies, products failed all the time. I remember my father's cars constantly breaking down. My mother's appliances always needed service calls. Toys inevitably broke a week after purchase. It was a different time, when quantity trumped quality. But when Timex demonstrated its durability with tests that made your stomach jump, people marvelled at the distinction because they knew few products they owned could pass a punishing test like that.

If people feel, they believe.

Timex understood that and was adamant about authenticity. In one live commercial—the first time Timex attached the watch to the boat propeller—the testers pulled the motor out of the water and the watch wasn't there. The wristband had been ripped off and the watch had been lost. Did Timex trash that commercial? No, it aired it, with Swayze saying they were going to try it again in another commercial to prove that Timex could survive. The next time, they used a more secure wristband and when they pulled the watch from the water, it was still ticking. The failure of the first commercial made the success of the second one even more believable.

A twenty-first-century campaign that owes a great debt to Timex is for Blendtec, a line of kitchen blenders. In a series of very popular videos you can easily find on YouTube, founder Tom Dickson puts a shocking variety of items into his blenders to demonstrate their power. The infomercials are part of a series called *Will It Blend?* The title says it all. In 2006, Dickson did his first video by blending fifty glass marbles. He used the slowest speed on the machine—the ice cream mode—and reduced the marbles to a fine dust in seconds. Next, he ground an entire wooden rake handle to splinters in only ninety seconds. (This you have to see!) He blended his metal golf driver right down to the clubface. He blended hockey pucks. A can of Coke. A fifteen-foot garden hose. As time went on, Dickson's videos got even more fun and outrageous. He blended "bad guy" action figures along with a Chuck Norris doll (hilariously, the Chuck Norris doll rises from the bad guy dust). He blended his iPhone and his iPad. He blended his snow skis. He even blended a Justin Bieber doll, CD and DVD.

The videos have generated enormous sales for Blendtec. As of this writing, the nearly 150 videos have attracted over 250 million views. They are incredibly persuasive, just as the Timex commercials were in their day. Paired with Dickson's charming stiffness, Blendtec's tests make an emotional impact. You laugh, you smile, your stomach jumps and sends a purchase Post-it note to your brain. The outrageous degree to which the blender surpasses expectations leaves you with no choice but to believe.

When the creator of True Religion jeans was struggling to generate sales, he thought about the fact that salespeople at clothing stores were the gateway to many customer decisions. So he gave the salespeople free jeans. In no time, his jeans were selling out. When the salespeople wore the jeans, they felt good in them. Then they started recommending the jeans to customers.

As psychologists will tell you, we make decisions using our heads 20 percent of the time and our hearts 80 percent of the time. Yet most advertising is aimed solely at the head. ("A better way forward"!) Most advertising is dull price-and-item, full of boring details and legal print. But even if people understand your message, they won't necessarily act on it.

If people feel, they will believe.

Laser eye surgeons often have difficulty persuading customers that eye surgery is safe. People are incredibly protective of their eyes. All you have to do is swing something sharp near someone's eyes to see them flinch. So to overcome that resistance to laser surgery, one doctor gave potential patients his talk, which was all fact-based. Then he would say "see," and point to a basket of discarded eyeglasses. In that moment, his patients could feel the benefit of the procedure. They wanted to put their glasses in the box, too. That desire was the emotional core of his pitch.

At the end of the day, the most important function of marketing is to persuade people to actually buy the product. For that miracle to take place, you need people to act on the advertising. And they will only get up off the couch and search you out if your message has emotional content. That kind of content can take many forms. A message can make people smile, it can make them laugh, it can make them worry. It can surprise them, move them to tears, make them empathize. Or it can make them look at a product in a completely new way. So if you're creating a marketing message, evaluate it based on that criterion. If your message is just straight information, think twice. If it doesn't provoke a reaction, it's invisible. There is a reason you can't tickle yourself—there is no element of surprise. I always say the only two products that can survive on straight information alone will be the cure for cancer and a solution for baldness. Everything else needs a mighty dose of persuasion.

Here's the good news. Emotion can be added to virtually any product or service—no matter how incidental or boring the product may be. Let me prove that to you.

A few years ago, a journalist named Rob Walker, who wrote the Consumed column for the *New York Times Magazine*, wanted to conduct an experiment. His hypothesis: "Stories are such a powerful driver of emotional value that their effect on any given object's subjective value can actually be measured objectively." In other words, he wanted to see if a story could increase the value of an object.

As Walker says in *Significant Objects*, the book he and Joshua Glenn eventually published about the experiment, stories make objects more meaningful. Stories make us treasure childhood toys, family heirlooms and otherwise incidental items. There is a one-dollar bill tucked away in the drawer of the desk I'm sitting at while I write this. It was the first dollar I ever earned as a copywriter. It has significance because of that story, not because of its inherent value of a hundred cents. Walker wanted to see if stories could make us value an item far beyond its rational "market" value. He wanted to know if a story has a magical ability to increase desire when all else is equal.

So here's what Rob Walker did. He went out to various flea markets, thrift shops and yard sales, and purchased a hundred plain, boring or kooky items at an average price of about $1.25 each. Next, he recruited some of the best writers he knew to write short fictional stories about those objects. All Walker asked was that the stories add significance to the thrift-store finds. Then he listed all the items on eBay, and used those stories as the item descriptions.

The results were startling. For example, one item, a meat thermometer, featured the following story: "Everything had a temperature in those days. Cheese was cold. Avocados were warm. My heart was a piece of hot meat pierced by love's thermometer."

What the hell does that mean?

Walker purchased that meat thermometer for seventy-five cents. After it was posted on eBay, with that story, someone bought it for fifty-one dollars. It's fascinating, isn't it? Another item was a red wooden mallet. It was tiny, the paint was chipped, and the photo was slightly out of focus. Here's the story a writer composed for the posting: "On September 16th, 2031, at 2:35 am, a temporal rift—a 'tear' in the very fabric of time and space—will appear 16.5 meters above the area currently occupied by Jeffrey's Bistro, 123 E Ivinson

Avenue, Laramie, WY. Only the person wielding this mallet will be able to enter the rift unscathed. If this person then completes the 8 Labors of Worthiness, he or she will become the supreme ruler of the universe."

The original price of the mallet was thirty-three cents. Price paid after it was posted on eBay, after a bidding war: seventy-one dollars.

The thrift store items Walker purchased for a grand total of $128.74 eventually sold for a whopping $3,612.51 on eBay. Many of those $1.25 items sold for over fifty dollars, some for over a hundred. It all resulted in a very interesting observation. Walker discovered that once you start increasing the emotional energy of an object, an unpredictable chain reaction is set off. This proved true even when the stories were negative, or made the items less—not more—attractive. They still generated a big increase in value because the stories stirred emotions.

This I know: When you add emotion to an object, people *feel* something. If you insist on using straight information in your marketing, chances are people will feel nothing.

EBay is a perfect metaphor for marketing in the twenty-first century. There is massive clutter. The endless litany of items comes with flat, boring photography and bone-dry descriptions. Like advertising in general, most of it is terrible. Yet the items Walker posted, with those short, odd stories, jumped off the page. While everything else on eBay was just Sahara-dry information, or a breathless forest of exclamation marks—Don't miss out on this item!!!—the stories of a heart being pierced by love's thermometer or a mallet that could transform the owner into the supreme ruler persuaded people to pay, in some cases, 2,700 percent more than the item was originally purchased for. The stories made buyers feel something, and that feeling stoked desire.

When you create a message with emotional content, it attracts people. Leadership consultant Edwin H. Friedman puts an even finer point on it, saying, "People can only hear you when they are moving toward you, and they are not likely to when your words are pursuing them." Emotion pulls, it doesn't chase.

I've always been a fan of humour in advertising, and most of the ten-thousand-plus commercials I've directed over the last twenty-five years were humorous. All marketing is an intrusion. It piggybacks on the real reason people have focused their attention—watching television, listening to radio, perusing a newspaper or surfing online. They are there for the content, not the advertising (though the Super Bowl may be the one exception to this rule). So if advertising is an interloper, how do you make that interruption the most polite or, at minimum, the least intrusive message possible? Even more, how do you give something back in return for the loud knocking? Humour is one answer.

It's important to understand the difference between humour and comedy. Humour is giving, it's generous. Comedy subtracts and is usually sarcastic or biting. That's why humour is better suited to marketing. To make someone smile, or laugh, forges an emotional connection. Humour gathers people. Think about people you know. The ones who make you smile are the ones you most want to be around. Humour doesn't pursue, it pulls.

Not long ago, I attended a talk given by filmmaker Richard Curtis at the Cannes advertising festival. Curtis is a very successful screenwriter and director whose credits include *Mr. Bean*, *Blackadder*, *Four Weddings and a Funeral*, *Love Actually*, *Bridget Jones's Diary*, and *Notting Hill*, to name but a few. Not a bad resumé. He was in Cannes to unveil a new marketing campaign he was spearheading to tackle extreme poverty and climate change. The campaign was going to begin with a cinema ad that would be shown on the same day in every movie theatre in North America and Europe. It would be the first global cinema ad ever done. When Curtis previewed the ad during his talk, the press was surprised that its treatment of extreme poverty and climate change was humorous. Didn't the subject matter call for a more serious tone?

Here's what Curtis said: In his early days as a writer on *Blackadder*, he realized the only way to get the audience to remember an important plot point was to attach it to humour. So if Sir Nigel Ridgley was coming for dinner, few people would remember that beat. But if Sir Nigel Fatbottom was coming, no one forgot. Humour made it stick.

Now, humour isn't the only answer to effective marketing, but it illustrates the rule. Emotional content makes people care. That said, most learning institutions put much more value on intellectual reasoning than they do on emotion. Yet emotion fuels the world. Even in a math-and-science-driven institution like NASA, the decision to go to the moon wasn't driven by rational facts. It was propelled by the emotion of John F. Kennedy's challenge of landing a man on the moon by 1970 to prove American superiority. Throughout the 1960s, NASA continually marketed the moonshot with emotion. It signed an ongoing contract with *Life* magazine to feature full-colour stories on the astronauts and their families; it framed the new satellite communications technology and even the small RCA cameras the astronauts took onboard as innovations that would have a beneficial impact on the daily lives of Americans. Maybe the most emotional pitch was the one that warned of letting the Russians (read: Communists) control outer space, dropping bombs on America "like kids dropping rocks from a highway bridge." That pitch alone persuaded the government to keep signing those big cheques.

The space organization needed the support not only of Congress, but also of the American public. Landing men on the moon was going to be the most expensive endeavour America had ever undertaken, totalling over $170 billion in today's dollars (and by the way, there was an expensive war going on in Vietnam). If the decision to go had been based strictly on logic, it never would have happened. Emotion made the difference. America felt invested in the outcome.

When companies like Duncan Hines marketed instant cake mixes after World War II, all you needed to do was add water and two eggs. It was a big hit with homemakers, but then in the 1950s, sales started to drop off dramatically. As time wore on, women stopped enjoying the quick baking mix. They felt unfulfilled by the process. It was too easy. It felt like they were cheating their families. The product that was created for ultimate convenience became too convenient.

So what did brands like Duncan Hines do to turn sales around? The secret was to make homemakers feel like bakers. It was literally the icing on the cake. The company showed cooks (read: women) how to add decadent frosting—not just to the top, but also between each layer and all around the cake. That suggestion made them feel like they were truly baking. With that, cake mix sales soared again. As a matter of fact, the photo of a frosted cake became one of the defining advertising images of that era. Once women felt invested in the process of baking a cake, they couldn't buy enough cake mixes.

In his fascinating book *Creativity, Inc.,* Pixar CEO Ed Catmull says the definition of superb animation is not just movement, but intention. Put another way—emotion. As of this writing, Pixar has had fifteen number-one movies in a row. The trick isn't just outstanding animation, it's that you tear up when a robot named WALL-E no longer recognizes his robot love, EVE, due to a programming reboot. It's a cartoon, it's about robots, and you need a box of Kleenex. If people feel something, they are invested. They will pay more, they will stay longer, and they will spend more time seeking you out when they are emotionally moved by storytelling in marketing. When Walt Disney started marketing the first Mickey Mouse toys, he realized that when people took a piece of Mickey Mouse home with them, they stored him in their hearts.

I mentioned earlier that the quality of products was less than desirable in the sixties and seventies. It's completely different now. Today, we take quality for granted. How often do you need a service call to fix your washer? When was the last time your car left you stranded on the highway? Product quality, more or less, is the great equalizer today. Brands are much more alike than they used to be. What matters now is differentiation—the personality of the company behind those products, the company's purpose and how the company treats you during and after the purchase.

Each of these elements is steeped in emotion.

To ignite a positive response in people, you have to inject emotion into information. Adman Jeremy Bullmore points out that the rational ingredients come from the product itself—things like performance, price and distribution. But the emotional ingredients come from communications—the advertisements, packaging, tone of voice, the social media conversation.

You can also get people to act on your messages even when they aren't positive, as long as they provoke an emotion. Yekaterinburg is the fourth-largest city in Russia. The streets in that city were littered with potholes so big you could almost lose a Volkswagen in them. The people of the city complained constantly about the road conditions. The politicians promised to fix them but never did. Politicians didn't seem to care enough about the problem. So here's what a Russian communications company did to get the politicians to act. First it identified the three worst potholes in the city. Then, in the middle of the night, it painted the faces of three politicians around the potholes, positioning the holes in place of their mouths. The paintings were perfect likenesses. Next to each face it spray-painted a quote from each politician citing their promise to fix the potholes. For example, the vice-mayor had said the holes would be fixed by the end of April. It was July. The next morning the drawings became a news sensation. (See Fig. 4.)

Everyone was talking about them. They got mentioned by three hundred media outlets and garnered over seven thousand social media mentions, reaching far beyond the Russian border. Then guess what happened? All three holes were fixed the next day. As a matter of fact, over 7.6 kilometres of road got repaired immediately after. The reason that idea worked was that it made the politicians feel the one thing politicians hate the most: humiliation. It was an effective lever. It made the politicians suddenly care enough about a problem they were ignoring. Or at least it made them care about their images, which then translated into fixing the problems. A simple, smart idea that ignited behaviour change.

When film producer Brian Grazer was looking to cast the role of real-life commander James Lovell in *Apollo 13*, he initially dismissed the choice of Tom Hanks because he didn't think he looked like an astronaut. But *Apollo 13* had an interesting marketing conundrum. How to you get moviegoers to pay for a story when they already know the ending? So Grazer asked himself, Which actor would moviegoers most want to see rescued? The answer was a full-circle moment: Tom Hanks. It was probably the same reason director Robert Zemeckis chose Hanks five years later to star in the movie *Cast Away*. With Hanks in the lead role, people felt invested in the jeopardy. They already cared about the lead character.

Apple makes us care because it disrupts entire industries to give us more user power. Nike makes us care because it encourages us to make an important decision. Michelin used to make us care when it made us realize that four small patches of rubber were all that was between our families and the road. My local electrician makes me care because he's willing to come on a Sunday morning to fix something that could have waited until Monday.

Why does all that matter? Because I'm willing to pay more for an Apple computer. All things being equal, I prefer Nike running shoes. I never complain about a bill from my electrician. And a movie starring Tom Hanks always attracts my attention. There is nothing intellectual about any of those decisions. It's pure emotion. Each of those companies and people provoke a feeling in me.

Remember the TV series *Star Trek*? Spock was cold, rational logic. Captain Kirk was all emotion. Both were necessary for the success of the Starship *Enterprise*. But who was in command? Kirk. Emotion is the basis for all decision-making. As a matter of fact, Spock's monotone logic emphasized his alienness. Kirk's empathy made him the better emissary to lead a mission to meet other life forms in deep outer space. *Star Trek* creator Gene Roddenberry understood that dynamic. He was writing scripts that commented on topical social issues, disguised as science fiction.

He understood the power of storytelling.

Chapter Five

STEINWAYS AND AUTOPSIES
Tell Me a Story

One of my advertising heroes is a man named James Webb Young. Not only did he create incredibly effective advertising for ad agency J. Walter Thompson between 1912 and 1928, but he was also a wonderful essayist. He thought carefully about his profession, and he was endlessly curious about human nature. Young became a professor at the University of Chicago's new Business School in the thirties, and while there, he gathered a series of his lectures and compiled them into a book titled *How to Become an Advertising Man*. But it was during the war years that he published a series of diary entries, called, appropriately, *The Diary of an Ad Man*.

That book is a gem.

Even though written in the 1940s, nearly all of Young's observations are insightful and haven't aged a day. I'm a sucker for advertising books written in that era because they are all about selling with integrity. They are about understanding the subtleties of human nature and are not sidetracked by award competitions, corporate takeovers, ad agency stock price fluctuations or the vanity of the creators. These books are about the profession of advertising.

Back the 1930s, Young found himself on the border of Tibet, walking through a street market. As he looked at the various wares the merchants were offering, something suddenly caught his eye. It was the most luxurious, colourful hand-embroidered bedspread. The Tibetan trader who was selling it spotted the sparkle in Young's eye. He waved him over, and carefully draped the stunning bedspread across his arms. As Young's eyes and fingers ran over the fine fabric and its intricate design, the trader told him the history of the bedspread. It had been made for the bed of an Indian princess. But it had been stolen and spirited away from the castle, and somehow, over the miles and over the years, it had found its way to this street market. Young loved the bedspread and paid a small fortune for it that day.

See what happened there? Young didn't pay for the bedspread, he paid for the story.

The advertising industry realized a century ago that storytelling moves people profoundly in ways that other advertising techniques cannot match. A great story isn't just information, because a great story is aimed at your heart, not your head. The reason placebo sugar pills work 30 percent of the time is because pharmaceutical companies tell rich, emotional stories around a drug's potential benefits during the research phase, and those stories make people believe. One of the ad industry's leading creative directors, John Hegarty, maintains that what the heart knows today, the head will know tomorrow. Information enters through the heart. We are meaning-seeking creatures.

Logic is always valued above emotion in organizations, and certainly in business schools, but as Hegarty rightly points out, emotion is where a brand's true value lies. The intangible parts of a brand are the most important. Last chapter, I tried to persuade you that people have to feel your message, not just understand it. I could have said that four hundred times, and you may or may not have absorbed the message. But I'm willing to bet you will remember the British Rail story, because that story gives meaning to a marketing lesson.

Whether your company is big or small, whether it employs ten thousand people or the payroll is simply the person reading these words, your brand must differentiate itself from the competition. The brain is not interested in sameness, it is only interested in the different, the unusual. If you were to meet me, you would probably describe me as being on the short side, bald and devastatingly good-looking. You wouldn't say I had two arms, two legs and a nose. What makes us different makes us memorable.

Your customers have a lot of options. Their reasons for patronizing a place of business are varied: it's close by, it's cheaper, it offers free parking, their brother-in-law likes it. So if you're going to trump all those personal, almost invisible reasons people have for choosing your competition, you have to stand out from the pack. You have to present a well-defined and utterly compelling identity.

If you offer a product or service to the marketplace, you are a brand. Many people don't like that word. They feel it's demeaning, or clichéd or empty. I have a lot of respect for the word "brand." I believe strongly in branding and I know firsthand how hard it is to brand a company well. I study branding, I follow it through the decades, I watch organizations flourish when they do it well. I watch organizations struggle when they don't. People who think it's easy don't get it. People who don't respect it rarely succeed. Organizations that are obsessive about branding are almost always market leaders.

One of the biggest problems I see in many organizations when they are building their brands—and in particular, in smaller businesses—is an inconsistency in the marketing. They have friendly advertisements but are unfriendly when you're in their store. They project a moderate-price image but you discover steep prices when you get there. The website doesn't look like the store. The store doesn't feel like the advertising. The signage is different from the business cards. Their phone message says your call is important to them. But they leave you on hold for seventeen minutes.

Of the many marketing philosophies I hold dear, my shish kebab theory might top the list. Simply put, a shish kebab consists of a piece of beef, a green pepper, a piece of chicken, a yellow pepper, a tomato and a mushroom, all pierced by a skewer. Your marketing should mirror that concept. A website, a business card, a radio commercial, a print ad, a social media account—all skewered by a consistent strategy and tone of voice. In other words, it should all feel like it's coming from the same place. The trick is to maintain a consistent voice as you move from medium to medium. Your business card should feel like your signage. Your website should feel like your newspaper ad. Your radio commercial should feel like your on-hold messaging. The tone you strike on Twitter should feel like your website posts. Potential customers won't see all of your branding, they will only connect a portion of your dots. People build brands in their heads like birds built nests—with scraps and straws. That's why you have to be in many places, and why the skewer is the key. One of the best ways to ensure a solid skewer is via storytelling. Because what is a brand, but a story?

Apple's storyline was hatched during that *1984* television commercial. It is an explosive story of "us versus them"—a promise of personal empowerment. Everything Apple does is about taking power from corporations and giving it to you. Want to carry a thousand songs in your pocket? No problem, let us just disrupt the greedy recording industry for you. Want to take vivid photos with your phone? Give us a moment to disrupt the camera industry for you. Want to text free between iPhones? Let us bypass the phone carriers for you. Every commercial or ad that Apple creates contains the DNA of this story. Again, take the popular "I'm a Mac and I'm a PC" television campaign, where a nerdy guy tries to be as cool as the hip, good-looking guy. (See Fig. 5.)

The frumpy guy represents the stiffness of Microsoft, and the cool guy is the hipness that is Apple. Nerdy guy is always behind the times, his offerings are outdated or clunky and he is awkward beyond belief. Cool guy is relaxed, always has a better solution, and in a brilliant stroke of genius, is always nice to nerdy guy. He kind of throws an arm around him out of affection and sympathy, masking how vicious this campaign really was. (Watch the "2007 D5 Convention" conversation between Steve Jobs and Bill Gates on YouTube, where Jobs tells Gates that the campaign was all in fun— then watch Gates's reaction!) In another poster campaign, Apple shows silhouettes dancing with abandon to great music; the only colour is the white of the earphones coming from the white of the iPod. Again—the joy of personal computing power. Two different campaigns, one storyline.

Your storyline should really emanate from your company's purpose, its core mission, its attitude and its view of the world. The story flows from the founder's original burning desire to discover a better way. If your business has lost its way, for whatever reason, you can reverse-engineer to rediscover your story. Drill down to find your elevator pitch. Reduce, prune and refine the reason you are in business. Then put your shish on the kebab.

Obama's 2008 presidential campaign team decided his imagery should take on a shape-shifting quality, so the brand would appeal to a diverse range of voters. To achieve that, they created subtly different logos for each constituency. Each logo was a slight variation on the consistent theme of hope. But the "hope" skewer remained firmly in place.

For many decades in the first half of the twentieth century, Steinway Pianos ran a long series of beautiful print ads. Each ad featured a different classical composer and told the story of why that composer chose to play a Steinway. The headline of each ad was the same: "The Instrument of the Immortals." One day, a man walked into the Steinway store on West 57th in New York and said he wanted to buy a Steinway piano. There just happened to be a man from Steinway's advertising agency in the store that day, and he overheard the customer's request. The adman introduced himself to the customer and said, "May I ask you a question? What convinced you to buy a Steinway piano?" The customer thought for a second, then replied, "It was the advertising." Which, of course, thrilled the adman to no end. The adman then asked, "Which ad in particular?" The customer said, "Well, it was an ad I saw twenty-five years ago. It just took this long to be able to afford a Steinway."

I love that story because it demonstrates two important aspects of marketing. First, stories ignite desire. Second, compelling stories have a remarkable shelf life. (See Fig. 6.)

Years ago, I was doing some research for a screenplay idea I had. It was a procedural police thriller. As part of that research, I wanted to spend some time at the Coroner's Office to ask questions and get a sense of how forensic coroners look for clues. One of my neighbours happened to be a homicide detective, so I asked him if he could pull some strings and arrange for me to spend a few hours talking to a coroner at the morgue in Toronto. So he arranged it, and when I walked in that day I was greeted by one of the older, experienced coroners.

He began by explaining to me how forensic coroners do their jobs. What their thinking process is, how they look at a crime scene. A few minutes later, he showed me slides of actual crime scenes and asked me to guess what had transpired. So I'd stare hard at the photo, and say, "Okay, I think the following happened . . ." To which he would say, *wrong*—then he would take me through the crime scene again the way a forensic coroner would look at it. It was fascinating. Then he asked me if I wanted to see a video of an actual autopsy.

I said, O-kay . . .

So he rolled the tape, and there on the table was a middle-aged man. As the autopsy progressed, I was surprised that it had little effect on me. The coroner did all the things coroners do during autopsies, and I sat there completely unmoved. It was all very clinical. That's the best word I can use to describe it: clinical.

Then something happened. The coroner started to tell me about the man on the table. He was forty-one. He had a wife and two children. He had been working on a construction site, digging a hole. The ground had fallen in and he had suffocated. At that moment, the autopsy started to bother me. I had to stop looking at the screen. I'd started to care about the man on the table. The story the coroner told made that man meaningful to me, even though I did not know him. I had only a few scant details of his life, but it had an effect on me.

That's how powerful stories are. They can resound for years, like with Steinway, or they can penetrate in mere seconds.

The running storyline of *Under the Influence* is a backstage pass to the advertising industry. I spent my career in the industry, and in every episode we produce, every talk I give and every website post I write, I stick to that mission. The show is ostensibly about advertising, but it's really about life through the lens of advertising. Advertising is the study of human nature. Put another way, I'm telling people stories about themselves.

With all this in mind, there are many ways to use storytelling in your marketing. You can literally create an ongoing series of stories, like Steinway did. Or you can tell a completely different story each time out, as long as the skewer remains in place, like Nike does. Or you can tell the same story in a variety of ways, like

Apple does. The great thing about storytelling is that it is one of the most affordable techniques in advertising; great stories are already baked into your business. In other words, you can harvest great stories from within, rather than paying someone to dream them up from without. This is a critical point. The best marketing is genuine, real and organic. When I talk about storytelling, I'm not talking about fabricating a tale. I'm talking about relaying stories that already exist. I'm talking about plumbing your company DNA for your narrative.

Every product, or the company behind the product, has an interesting history, or a fascinating philosophy, or a unique understanding of its customer's needs that can be expressed in a story. If you've put the sweat time into developing your elevator pitch, you've already unearthed many of these stories. Why was the company established? What does the product do so much better than the competition? How was it developed? What are some of your best customer service stories? What are some of the most fascinating problems the company has solved?

Tell those stories. We want to know.

These stories are so important because they can be fertile ground for years of advertising and marketing ideas. Nike's "Just Do It" skewer has spawned thirty years of standout commercials that have gobbled up market share. But stories also deliver another very important benefit.

They add value. Value creates margin. And margin creates profit.

"Value" means people start attaching a secondary meaning to your product beyond its basic function. If that secondary meaning captures a customer's imagination, then any concerns about the price of the product often evaporate. But if your customers don't *perceive* value, price is everything. When you just shovel straight information at people—without building value via storytelling—you are just a commodity. That is the worst marketing position to ever find yourself in.

When customers *feel* something about a product or a company, it recruits other aspects of the decision-making process. Not just the purely rational part. It makes a beeline for the heart. Just as we saw with the Rob Walker eBay experiment, stories fuel desire. James Webb Young, a highly paid New York creative director who should have been immune to the bedspread story, still paid handsomely for it. As he later said, that story not only gave him great pleasure when he bought the bedspread, but it also gave him ongoing pleasure for years afterward whenever he retold the story to houseguests.

That is the power of storytelling.

Millions pay a premium for Apple products. The man in the Steinway store that day could have chosen a cheaper piano down the street or bought a lesser piano years before. But his heart was bound by the stories in Steinway's beautiful advertisements over the years. Storytelling is like a Swiss Army Knife. It has many different functions, depending on the task at hand.

In the early seventies, Honda was the right product at exactly the right time. The OPEC oil crisis was in full swing and fuel prices were surging. And here was Honda with a small, affordable, fuel-efficient car. Sales exploded. With that success, Honda decided to take advantage of the moment and launch its new line of motorcycles. It put the bikes into its dealerships and sat back to count its money. And no one came. Honda clearly had a problem, but it didn't know what the problem was.

So like all smart marketers, the Honda team went to research. They organized a series of focus groups with motorcycle owners so they could root out the problem. For each session, they parked a shiny, new Honda motorcycle at the front of the room and began asking questions. First, they asked the group if they liked the design of the bike. The respondents got up, looked at every inch of the bike, sat on the bike, and collectively said, That is a good-looking bike. Then Honda showed them a chart of performance statistics, demonstrating the bike's ability to go from zero to sixty miles per hour, how it cornered, braking distances, fuel consumption, and so on. The group collectively said, Very impressive. Then Honda revealed the price of the bike. The groups unanimously said, You know what, that is a very reasonable price for that bike. Then Honda said, With all you now know about the bike, would you buy one? And the group said absolutely not.

Honda was stumped. What do you do when the public likes the design of your product, likes how it performs, thinks it's well priced, but don't want it?

There happened to be a very smart moderator in those focus groups. She asked, "If price were no obstacle, which bike would you buy?" The answer was a resounding Kawasaki! Then she asked the most counterintuitive question. She said, "If Kawasaki were a celebrity, who would it be?" (Remember this was the early seventies.) They all said: Clint Eastwood.

The moderator then asked, "Okay, if Honda were a celebrity, who would *it* be?" The resounding answer: Ron Howard, a.k.a. Richie Cunningham of *Happy Days* fame.

With that answer, the fog lifted. Honda instantly defined the problem. Motorcycle owners had a perception that Honda bikes weren't tough. In other words, they weren't cool. Understand that there was nothing wrong with the bike, Honda didn't have to change one bolt. The problem was the *perception* of the bike.

By asking the right question, the company suddenly had a workable answer. Honda now knew exactly what it had to do in its marketing. It had to recalibrate its storytelling. The bikes were tough, but Honda had never featured that aspect in its advertising. Further research revealed that people had a residual image of

Honda scooters from the 1960s, which clouded their current image of Honda motorcycles. But once Honda started building stories around the toughness of its bikes, the cool factor kicked in and the line on its sales chart began to spike north.

Storytelling can also invent the future. Google Creative Lab produces beautiful documentaries and product demonstration videos for products that don't exist yet. Often, those videos and short films influence Google's engineers. They give engineers a sense of how a potential product could look and feel. Many times, they will be inspired to pursue the product in the story.

Storytelling can also help sell intangible benefits like trust and confidence. Product features you can't hold in your hand. Trust and confidence are so important in business, and doubly so in service industries. But I've always believed the one thing you should never say out loud is "trust me." The second someone says "trust me"— the first thing you think is, "I trusted you right up to the moment you said 'trust me.'" There's a reason soap operas love those two words so much. Because when you hear a soap opera actor say "Trust me, Daphne," you know what that really means. It means I'm going to poison you and marry your sister.

So instead of saying "trust me," tell stories about trust. Tell us stories about how your company demonstrates confidence. We'll get the message. Loud and clear. By telling a powerful story, you'll ignite those feelings without ever once having to say "trust me" out loud. Trust is meant to be felt but never stated. Like excellence, quality and reliability, those compliments shouldn't be self-referential. Stories, on the other hand, can help you sell the invisible.

It's also interesting that nowadays we trust perfect strangers when we buy items on eBay, rent homes with Airbnb and accept rides via Uber. Yet we are so suspicious of the companies on Main Street. Maybe it's because the sharing economy pivots on daily report cards of transparent feedback and ratings. Reputation is everything. In the bricks-and-mortar world, reputation is important, too, but it hasn't been built on minute-by-minute public scrutiny. In the Internet era, marketing has to be the custodian of trust.

Smart marketing is like a book. It has many chapters. It has a consistent through-line (skewer) and a compelling plot idea (elevator pitch). Every chapter has a specific task (tactic), the writing is infused with emotion (feel), and every chapter gets you closer to the climax (goal). In Honda's case, one chapter had to be dedicated to the cool factor of its bikes. That chapter still had to feel like the rest of the book, but it also had to address a specific issue. It still moved you closer to the moment of purchase, just as all scenes in a good movie progress the plot. But that underlines a point I will be making often. If your brand storyline is clear, it can easily absorb a new, necessary chapter. James Webb Young once observed that products tend to remain static, but markets tend to be highly dynamic. That means marketers find themselves forced to react when the market presents an unforeseen speed bump—or opportunity. You have to be nimble, but rooted in integrity.

Smart storytelling also has another goal: to create not just an ongoing campaign—but an entire world. Think Apple for a moment. Through its storytelling and its visual aesthetic, you walk into a universe. The Apple stores, the retail employees, the Apple products, the Apple commercials, the Apple posters, the Apple website—it's a fully realized experience. The last time I purchased something at an Apple retail store, the staff showed me how to download an Apple Store app that let me pay without talking to anyone in the store. I just picked up the item, paid through the app and walked out of the store. It seemed weird, and wrong, and half of me expected store security to tackle me in the middle of the mall. But it's Apple saying, We trust you. It's all part of the universe Apple has created.

Coke has created a world. Nike has created a world. Retail store Roots has created a world based on the founders' love of camping in Algonquin Park. Surprisingly, I would say that Microsoft hasn't. Even though it's one of the most valuable companies in the world, I don't see a Microsoft universe I can identify and step into. It's an exception to the rule. (Some companies succeed in spite of their marketing, but only if their product is remarkable.)

None of the major North American car companies has created a world you can immerse yourself in. But think about the world Volkswagen created in the 1960s. The tonality was utterly unique, the humour self-deprecating and the advertising absolutely consistent. It was remarkable for a small, unattractive car. Search Volkswagen print ads from the sixties and you'll see a breathtaking skewer of humorous and joltingly honest ads. When you purchased a Volkswagen Beetle, you stepped into a world of humour and reliability. (Heartbreakingly, that universe has exploded with the recent VW scandal.)

Storytelling also creates community, and there was no greater community than VW owners. Volkswagens were small, cheap, ugly and slow. What's not to love? But the stories told by advertising agency Doyle Dane Bernbach about the humble and dependable car attracted millions of people who loved the brute honesty of the marketing. In a breathtaking jeté, they capitalized on the car's perceived disadvantages.

Think of the incredibly challenging context in which Volkswagen appeared in the United States: It was an odd-looking German car, originally championed by Hitler, its diminutive size was clearly "anti-Detroit," and it was trying to find a market in post–World War II America! Yet it wasn't just liked by millions, it was loved.

When Disney considered cars for the lead role in what would become *The Love Bug* movie, the VW Bug won because it was the only car so loveable the inspection crew wanted to pet it. The VW Bug became so adored that the public played Punch Buggy or Slug Bug games, punching each other in the shoulder each time they spotted a Beetle on the highway. No one was doing that with Ramblers. By 1967, total import sales reached 700,000, with Volkswagen selling 430,000 of those. More than the sales of all other imported cars combined and more than any American brand except Impala, Mustang and Plymouth.

Volkswagen used plucky wit and humour to survive being squashed by the Big Three. As Simon Sinek would no doubt agree, VW became a famous brand by selling what it stood for, not what it made. And may I point out that Doyle Dane Bernbach made the languishing VW famous without a single design change to the car and did it while working with the same VW marketing department the previous ad agency dealt with.

They did it all with storytelling.

One of my favourite VW television commercials shows a blizzard and a lone VW coming to life as a headlight pierces the snowy night. The Bug begins to make its way slowly through the snow, the only vehicle on the road in the pre-dawn darkness. As it arrives at a big shed, a voiceover says, "Have you ever wondered how the man who drives the snowplow *drives to* the snowplow? This one drives a Volkswagen, so you can stop wondering." We see a snowplow come to life, it pulls out of the garage and starts pushing snow as it passes the parked VW. So simple, so persuasive, so in keeping with VW's consistent storyline of humble dependability.

VW print ads had headlines like "Think Small" and "Lemon" (the most toxic word in the car business), yet the underlying story was one of high standards. The "lemon" in that ad was a VW with a blemish on the glove box chrome. Not good enough to be sold. The headline in another print ad said, "It takes this many men to inspect this many Volkswagens." The photo showed over a thousand white-coated inspectors and one single VW. The copy began as follows:

> There are really only two things that stand
> between you and a new Volkswagen:
> $1799.
> And 1,104 inspectors.
> The money is your problem.
> The number of inspectors it takes to okay
> each and every Volkswagen that leaves the
> Volkswagen factory is ours.

It goes on to say that every single VW part is inspected three times, so before a VW makes its way into your hands, it is inspected sixteen thousand times. Further, it states that VW pulls an average of 225 Bugs off the assembly line each day.

As marketing strategist Kevin Kelley says, great brands impose a view on you. If all your customer touch-points are hanging handsomely on your skewer, if every public element of your business is surprising but still feels like it's coming from the same source, you are imposing a view on your customers. It's your universe. If it's genuine, you have a brand that is hard to ignore. VW was a brand that was hard to ignore.

Like in a book, storytelling in marketing needs an arc. Bruce Springsteen summed this notion up nicely during an interview in *Rolling Stone*. He said, "The one thing I keep in mind is that I'm in the midst of a lifelong conversation with my audience, and I'm trying to keep track of that conversation." Consistency in storytelling is as important as consistency in look and feel. You have to be aware of the stories you've told, because your audience is incredibly adept at spotting holes and contradictions. That's why sitcoms and soap operas create "bibles" of their programs. They catalogue every character nuance and plot beat. So if Lance Handsome mentioned he used to be an airline pilot in an episode eight years ago, he won't have a fear of flying in a later episode. Every link in the chain holds. The same is true with marketing.

So ask yourself: If your brand story was a book, would you read it? Storytelling, by the way, doesn't just live in advertising. It lives in meetings, over lunches and in presentations. You just have to look for the best opportunities to tell the story.

Chapter Six

FINDING YOUR INNER BROADWAY
What Is Your Greatest Area of Opportunity?

Back in 1996, Procter & Gamble created a spray that made bad smells disappear. It was colourless, odourless and could eliminate smells on any surface. The offending odour was drawn into the spray's molecules, and when the mist evaporated, the scent was gone. It was an incredible breakthrough. P&G stood to make billions. All it had to figure out was how to market it.

The P&G team called the new spray Febreze (a mash-up of the words fabric and breeze) and decided to give free samples away in a few cities, observe how people used it and base a marketing campaign on the results. Which they did, but the results weren't spectacular. The sales of Febreze started off small—and got smaller.

The product was failing.

P&G decided to do more market research. One day, a group of researchers were visiting a woman who owned nine cats. They could actually smell them before they went into the house. When they walked into the living room where the cats lived, the smell was so overpowering that one of the researchers gagged. "What do you do about the cat smell?" they asked the woman.

"What cat smell?" she replied.

That same scenario played out in dozens of smelly homes. Suddenly, P&G realized its marketing problem. The people who needed Febreze the most didn't know they needed it. People become desensitized to bad smells when they live with them every day. That's why Febreze wasn't selling.

So P&G made a momentous decision: it decided to add a scent to Febreze. Now the spray that was developed to destroy odours was transformed into a spray with a pleasant odour. It dawned on P&G that the majority of the public doesn't crave scentlessness. On the other hand, millions crave a nice smell after a cleaning routine. P&G had realized its greatest area of opportunity: The pot of gold lay at the end of a cleaning chore, not at the beginning. Febreze could almost be a treat. It wasn't to get rid of bad smells, per se, it was to leave behind a pleasant smell when the cleaning was done. With that change in marketing focus, Febreze sales doubled in two months. Within a year, sales were $230 million. Today Febreze and its spin-offs account for over one billion dollars of revenue per year.

The lesson here is interesting. Until you identify your greatest area of opportunity, you will be wasting money and vastly under-achieving. When I talk to marketers with limited budgets, I notice it all the time. They try to do too much with too little. Most identify multiple marketing needs or opportunities, then formulate advertisements or marketing tactics to go after them. The overriding problem is going a mile wide and an inch deep. No one thing gets the proper attention; no one market gets the appropriate amount of media budget. I always recommend to dive deeply into a small, warm pond instead.

Let me give you an example. Several years ago, my company was approached by the Wine Council of Ontario. It wanted to increase sales of its VQA wines. VQA, which stands for Vintners Quality Alliance, is a designation assigned by an independent authority to wines that are made from 100 percent fresh, Ontario-grown grapes.

Furthermore, a VQA wine must adhere to origin verification, extensive laboratory testing and tasting by an independent expert panel, and the winemaker must adhere to rigorous winemaking standards. In other words, a VQA-designated wine is the best wine from the Ontario region. The Wine Council wanted to increase its VQA sales. When we asked how it proposed to do that, the answer was to attract new customers.

As we sat there listening to that marketing request, and then in subsequent meetings, understanding how a wine is made, learning about appellations and terroir, soil conditions, winemaking processes and how strict VQA standards were, it occurred to us that this much knowledge was going to be a difficult sell in the thirty- and sixty-second world of broadcast advertising. Clearly, new customers would have to appreciate new knowledge about VQA wines in order to desire VQA wines. The problem, as we saw it, was that marketing wasn't the place to do the teaching. Telling an in-depth story takes one critical element: time.

It takes time to tell a layered story within a message, and it takes years to unfold that story. That also meant it was going to be expensive. Gaining new customers is a ground-zero proposition, and it's the most expensive form of marketing. As we sat there rolling this over in our minds, we wondered if there could be a greater area of opportunity. So we asked the Wine Council what would happen to its sales if current VQA customers bought one more bottle a year. Their team said it would have a dramatic effect on sales. That's when we said, well, that's our strategy. We want to convince existing VQA fans to buy one more bottle of VQA wine this year. Surely, that had to be achievable. We weren't asking customers to buy one more bottle per week, or per month, we were asking them to buy one more bottle *per year*.

At that time, research revealed that Ontario wine drinkers were hesitant to bring a bottle of Ontario wine to social gatherings.

In other words, they were happy to enjoy a VQA wine in the privacy of their home, but defaulted to a California or Italian wine when they went to a party. The reason was interesting: they felt judged. No one questions a California or Italian wine. But eyebrows are raised when you put an Ontario wine on the table. There was the task. Convince existing VQA wine lovers to bring one more bottle to a party sometime this year.

The way to do this was to arm them with stories. The VQA wines all had great winemaking stories behind them: the weather conditions, the microclimates, how the roots of a grapevine dig into the soil, and the kinds of soil and stones the roots encountered all affected the taste of the wine. Every vintner had its own winemaking methods, each interesting and unique.

We created a campaign aimed at current VQA customers. We assumed awareness of VQA, so our starting point, instead, was to tell stories about how certain grapes were grown and how the wine was made. We wanted to arm VQA fans with persuasive stories, so that when they plunked a bottle of Ontario wine down at a party and someone raised an eyebrow, they could confidently say, "Wait until you hear the story behind this wine . . ." By equipping them, we gave them licence to buy at least one more bottle a year for a social occasion, instead of confining purchases to their own dining room tables.

The key to this strategy was to target existing fans. Put another way, it was a warm call, not a cold call. We already knew this customer base liked to buy VQA. All we had to do was convince them to share that love with friends. It was the Wine Council's greatest area of opportunity. With a limited marketing budget, we could focus on an existing customer base instead of a new, uninformed one. That difference is such an important distinction, one that allowed us to start the race halfway down the track. The Wine Council could have gone after brand-new customers. As a matter of fact, most businesses choose to put all their resources into attracting a constant flow of new clients. But that is not always the greatest area of opportunity. The return on investment may be hiding in a different target.

That's why formulating a marketing plan necessitates playing a What-if game. It was our favourite idea-starter in the Pirate writing room. Essentially, we would blue-sky notions and directions. What if we put a bottle of VQA wine on every doorstep? What if we told current VQA buyers not to listen to our commercials? What if we could create a party game that required VQA wine? What if we convinced current VQA fans to buy one more bottle a month? Or just one more bottle per year? What-if games can't have rules. You need the freedom to explore every possible option, even the ones that seem ridiculous and unlikely. By asking "What ifs," you trigger a search for solutions under new rocks, and by expanding your search perimeters and ignoring conventional thinking, you may find a hidden solution that will have an enormous impact on your business. Asking what the greatest area of opportunity is sounds like an easy question. But in my experience, marketing solutions almost never come easily. And the greatest leaps are made when you ignore the status quo. It requires many more questions and thoughtful answers to get you there. Asking "What if" is one way to bridge these gaps.

Back in 1980, New York City was in a bad way. The city was broke. There were garbage strikes. There was record-breaking crime. You wouldn't walk in Times Square during the day, let alone after dark. The city was at one of its lowest ebbs. No one, and I mean no one, wanted to vacation there. Tourism was at an all-time low.

The city was desperate to rebrand itself. So it began with what all smart marketers do when beginning a large communication campaign—with research. The city's marketing team gathered potential tourists into focus groups, asked them if they would consider visiting New York and got a resounding *no* in return. Which just confirmed the problem. They started asking people about different aspects of New York. The restaurants. The fashion shopping. The hotels. The sites. How safe they felt. How expensive it was. Almost all triggered negative responses.

But when tourists were asked about visiting Broadway, their attitude changed dramatically. They were completely positive about Broadway shows. They loved them. So the take-away from the focus groups was: Hate New York. Love Broadway. All the research came back to that same insight about Broadway. Over and over. As all good marketers know, one of the indicators that you're uncovering an essential marketing truth is when subsequent research keeps pointing back to the same place. But that research also uncovered a blinding flash of the obvious: It was pretty difficult to visit Broadway without visiting New York.

So New York's advertising agency built a campaign around that insight. They asked, What if we sold Broadway instead of New York? The first commercial featured all the casts from the most popular Broadway shows at the time, singing a very catchy "I love New York!" tune. The voiceover talked about Broadway Show Tour packages.

A lot has been written about this campaign, but I include it to make an important point. It's a story about discovering your greatest area of opportunity. If I had asked you yesterday what the "I love New York!" campaign was about, you'd say, "It's about New York, Terry." But it wasn't about New York, was it?

It was about Broadway. Research showed the city that it could leverage Broadway as a way to entice people back to New York.

"I love New York!" became the skewer that research kept pointing to. Again, your greatest area of opportunity is never easily found. It is always buried in the details, but it pays enormous dividends to dig for it. New York's marketing team had to ask dozens of questions and play a big What-if game before they discovered Broadway was the thing that could save them. Why did people respond so profoundly to Broadway? Because Broadway tells stories—stories about the human spirit and challenges and redemption.

That's the power of storytelling.

The phrase "I love New York!" was not just an external battle cry, it also became an internal rallying cry, because it persuaded New Yorkers to feel proud about their city again. And once New Yorkers started to feel good again, paired with the newly awakened interest from tourists, New York couldn't lose. That campaign turned around a deeply embedded perception that New York was not tourist friendly. Even after 9/11, when New York was facing a very different reason for the same problem—namely that no one wanted to go there—what did New York do? It returned to its greatest area of opportunity. The city aired a commercial with all the casts of the Broadway plays singing "I love New York!" in the middle of Times Square. The final line of the commercial was extremely important. It was beloved actor Nathan Lane saying, "Let's go on with the show . . ." Rallying all the Broadway performers from every Broadway show to sing their hearts out in Times Square was New York's way of saying it was open for business. That it could not be broken.

The "I love New York!" campaign has been running for over thirty years now. Extraordinary. Which underlines my belief that a great marketing insight can provide a platform for a very long time. No one wanted to visit New York in 1980. Last year, 54.3 million people visited New York City, a new record. And the city began that repositioning by pursuing its greatest area of opportunity: the love of Broadway.

When you begin thinking about your greatest area of opportunity, it may involve targeting a certain type of customer, timing your message perfectly or adjusting the media you employ. Your opportunity may even depend on how you choose to distribute your product.

When *People* was first published in the 1970s, the circulation department wanted to find a unique way to launch. The magazine shelves were crowded, and the category was cluttered. What *People* needed was to find its greatest area of opportunity. The editors knew that women were the ideal market for this type of magazine. So they asked: Where do women shop most frequently? The answer was grocery stores. So the folks at *People* did some research into the grocery business. They discovered tomatoes were the ideal grocery item. They had an eleven-day shelf life and stock had to be turned over quickly, a quality grocery stores loved. From that thinking, it was determined that *People* would be a weekly magazine—which meant it had a seven-day shelf life. Even better than a tomato.

Next, the circulation department approached grocery store chain Winn-Dixie to try a one-week experiment: place *People* magazine at the checkouts, and see what happens. In those years, magazines weren't part of the typical grocery store offering, let alone placed at the cash register. After one week, *People* completely sold out and Winn-Dixie doubled its order for the next week. The rest is *People* magazine history. When other publications like the tabloids and *TV Guide* saw that success, they insisted on cash register placement, too.

People's success was based not just on its unique editorial mix of celebs and civilians, but also largely on the leveraging of its greatest area of opportunity. Had it not been for the grocery store strategy, it might have got lost in the sea of magazines that clutter corner stores and may eventually have disappeared as so many magazines have. But by pushing for a unique distribution model, *People* thrived. And if you do your shopping in grocery stores, you'll still see *People* at the cash, over forty years later, front and centre beside the tabloids.

Sometimes, your greatest area of opportunity can be found in the oldest media. The number of kidnappings in Colombia has always been high. By 2000, it was estimated that 3,752 people had been kidnapped in the South American country. While the number has dropped dramatically over the last ten years, the rate of kidnappings in Colombia is still one of the highest in the world. And that number includes hundreds of missing police officers and military personnel. The government of Colombia wanted to figure out a way to communicate with its kidnapped soldiers. The goal was to boost their morale and to tell them not to lose heart, and to assure the soldiers that the government was coming for them. How they chose to communicate this was remarkable.

Radios are commonly played in the jungle camps of the kidnappers. Radios can run on batteries, they can tune in distant signals, and they are a simple way to provide a distraction as well as a method to hear breaking news. Knowing this, the government devised a way to talk to the kidnapped soldiers via radio—without the kidnappers knowing. They used a code hidden in a song.

First, a contemporary song was written. Titled "Better Days," the message of the lyric was that even though you feel forgotten and alone, better days are coming and we will see each other again soon. While the tune was catchy, the arrangement contemporary and the lyrics uplifting, those three elements alone wouldn't have got the attention of the kidnapped soldiers. Something else would do that. Morse code.

All military personnel are trained to decipher Morse code. So a message in Morse code was created that said, "Nine people rescued, you're next, don't lose hope." The Morse code was then recomposed as a music element inside the song. To the untrained ear, the code felt like a part of the percussion arrangement. But while the lyric sent out one message, the Morse code tapped out the real one.

It was an extraordinary solution. For the first time in a decade, the Military Forces of Colombia broke through enemy lines and reached their soldiers with a message of strength and hope. And they did it by leveraging their greatest area of opportunity—radio. The military harnessed the medium's remarkable portability, and sampled it with twenty-first-century thinking.

Sometimes your greatest area of opportunity is weather-related. Sears spotted a pattern in its auto parts department. It realized car batteries more than five years old tend to die after three consecutive nights of sub-zero temperatures, so it began to place ads on the day after the third freeze. Battery sales jumped. By watching the forecasts, Sears can spend tactical money and trigger big, almost predictable sales, instead of spending money during the long winter months with inconsistent returns.

By partnering with the Weather Channel, Pantene hair products "bought" humidity, for example. So when women checked their Weather Channel app on their smart phones and saw a humidity warning, they would also see an ad for a frizzy-hair-taming product. Conversely, in a low-humidity location, when hair might go flat, Pantene would advertise a hair volumizing product on the app. Pantene also provided coupon codes and addresses of nearby drugstores using location data—giving women a timely product, a money-saving voucher and directions to the nearest store. All born of a great opportunity.

In the twentieth century, marketers looked at weather simply as four seasons and made decisions accordingly. But the twenty-first century has taught us that there is a much greater opportunity to be had. Using predictive technology, the Weather Channel helped increase revenues for Michaels arts and crafts stores. Michaels traditionally increased its advertising during rainy days, as many people stay indoors and look for things to do. But the Weather Channel convinced Michaels not to advertise *on* rainy days, but rather three days ahead of a rainy forecast. Michaels got an instant sales lift.

Rain and cold snaps force people indoors, so smart retailers create marketing messages just ahead of the bad weather to persuade people to use their holiday gift cards for ordering online. The purchases often include items beyond the gift card amount, so the stores win twice just by leveraging an opportunity.

Negative moods caused by bad weather can sometimes make consumers respond better to negative messaging. On dark, gloomy days, a dental floss manufacturer told customers to floss or they might get gingivitis. It ignited more sales than messages telling people flossing would give them brighter smiles. Even though rainy summers kill barbeque sales, they present other opportunities. Lawn mower and grass trimmer sales go up—because the grass grows faster in wet weather.

The Spin Neapolitan Pizza chain came up with the idea of offering its customers "crummy weather vouchers." The kicker—discounts could only be used on bad weather days. Not only did it drive sales on rainy days, but the increased traffic spilled over onto good weather days.

Weather Trends International is another company that helps marketers profit through weather. It publishes a fascinating list called "The Profit of One Degree." It's a list of how the change of just one degree in temperature can affect sales.

For example, when the temperature drops one degree colder in the fall and winter, soup sales go up 2 percent. And one degree colder in the fall equals a 4 percent increase in children's apparel sales and a 25 percent increase in mousetrap sales.

When the temperature goes up one degree in summer, beer and soft drink sales go up 1.2 percent. It also translates to a 10 percent increase in sun care products and a 24 percent increase for air conditioners.

If you're a retailer, your greatest area of opportunity may very well be the weather, and having a weather strategy can pay off handsomely. In the UK, supermarket chain Sainsbury's conducts strategic weather forecast meetings every day, which lets it plan at least eight to ten days ahead. The chain knows the first sign of frost kicks up demand for bird seed, milk and cauliflower (which is used for soup). When the temperature is forecast to increase just a few degrees in early spring, Sainsbury's knows sales of two disparate products will shoot up: hair-removal products surge by 1,400 percent, as women decide to bare their legs, and barbeque sales rise 200 percent.

In Scotland, a temperature of 20°C, or 68°F, will prompt barbeque sales to triple. But in London, the temperature has to be 24°C, or 75°F, to see the same result. Interestingly, supermarkets in the UK realized they sell more ice cream on a sunny, cool day than a cloudy, hot day. When the temperature reaches 25°C, or 77°F, ice cream sales plummet. The reason: shoppers worry it will melt before they can get it home.

This kind of information helps merchants identify patterns that lead to their greatest areas of opportunity, allowing them to streamline their inventory, control their marketing spend and maximize profits.

There are many ways to interpret your greatest area of opportunity. Often, a client would hire my company to create a radio campaign, then they would plan a media buy to air the commercials. Instead of airing the radio commercials lightly across ten stations, I would recommend airing them heavily on, say, three stations. Again, my strong preference is to always go narrow and deep, instead of wide and shallow. It takes repeated airings to get noticed. One rule of thumb is that it takes twelve exposures to a commercial message for it to be noticed and registered by a listener or viewer. On radio, for example, the most listened-to times are the "drive times"—meaning the times people travel to work in the mornings from 6 to 9 a.m., and the times they travel home at the end of the workday, from 4 to 7 p.m. These two parts of the day are also the most expensive. So spend your money on the handful of stations that deliver your target audience best, and buy those stations heavily. To determine which stations, look at their ratings, what listeners they deliver and what their commercial time costs. You want the stations that will get your message to the audience with the most potential, giving you the best return on your investment. While I'm using radio as an example, that principle applies to any medium.

In Toronto, there is a radio show that airs on Sundays from 9 a.m. to 9 p.m. on rock station Q107, called *Psychedelic Psunday*. That show, which plays music from 1965 to 1975, has one of the largest audiences of people aged 25–64 during that timeslot on Sundays. Retailer Bay Bloor Radio, which specializes in audio and video equipment, has been advertising on that show for almost twenty years. It's an interesting media buy. *Psychedelic Psunday* is a twelve-hour radio show with a loyal audience. That audience loves music. Its most popular host, Andy Frost, who sits in the chair during the noon to 6 p.m. shift, is a music aficionado, and listeners love his passion for the era.

As an avid radio listener, I don't hear Bay Bloor Radio advertising on many other stations. Yet it is one of the biggest and most successful sound equipment retailers in the city. Owner Mark Mandlsohn voices his own ads and he has an endearing personality. His commercials always talk about his love of music and the best sound equipment for enjoying that music. He believes in talking to one specific audience often and well. Clearly, Mandlsohn has decided that sponsoring one radio show consistently is a great area of opportunity. It delivers a big audience, that audience loves music, and the store spends what must be a substantial chunk of its marketing dollars sponsoring that one program year after year.

In other words, it chooses to go narrow and deep. If I was in the market for excellent sound equipment, Bay Bloor would come to mind first. Because I'm a dedicated *Psychedelic Psunday* listener, it's at the top of my list and I've made many purchases there over the years. For two decades, Bay Bloor Radio has stuck with that decision because it works.

This is an important aspect of marketing when you have a limited budget. I often see smaller marketers spending money in too many places, trying to reach every single segment of their potential market. But because they are spending lightly, that market isn't hearing them.

Much better to spend wisely and focus on the greatest area of opportunity. If you pick the influencers, they will spread the word for you. Like VQA wine drinkers, they are your heaviest purchasers and they become your evangelists, carrying the message to new customers. You simply have to arm them with the right message. But before all this can happen, you have to get everyone in your company onboard, or you have to convince your clients you have the right idea.

And that takes presentation skills.

Chapter Seven

START WITH THE END
How to Make a Persuasive Presentation

In business, persuading people to buy your ideas is a fundamental necessity. Whether you're in marketing or justifying a job quote, or if you just have to stand up in a meeting and convince someone to do something, knowing how to present effectively is a powerful skill set. It's do-or-die time for your proposal. Maybe your idea is big, or maybe it's small. Maybe the future of a brand depends on it. Or this is the meeting that will determine if the client is going to hire you—or fire you—so a lot is riding on the presentation. I suspect the ratio of good ideas versus *sold* ideas is probably 10:1. I may be optimistic there. Boardrooms are the Bermuda Triangle of business. I've seen so many great ideas disappear there because they were badly presented. Once an idea is served up ham-handedly, it is virtually impossible to pull that meeting out of the skid.

Early on, I realized that a long career in advertising requires two things: the ability to generate ideas and the ability to sell them. Plenty of talented people can fulfill the first requirement, but only a handful can deliver the second. Many talented marketing people are shy, so they have to rely on other people to sell their ideas. That rarely works. If the presenter doesn't have an umbilical connection to the work, the degree of passion required to persuade will be missing. It's a delicate thing, that passion. If someone else is doing the selling, it's a bit of an acting job. Someone once described a presenter by saying, "His voice was hot, but his face was cool"—meaning the words *sounded* passionate, but he was acting. His face betrayed him.

Then there's the other kind of presenter. They created the work, but they are awkward in the boardroom. Instead of setting up their idea as the inevitable solution, they are sowing seeds of doubt. Their nervousness registers in the client's mind as a lack of confidence in the idea. Their uneasiness is like a pair of red socks in the wash—everything in the presentation gets a little stained by it. It may be a good idea, but the presentation has hamstrung it. Then comes the really dangerous part of a presentation—when clients start to ask questions or post objections. As someone wise once said, the selling doesn't really start until someone says no. That's when a good presenter really earns their money.

In my career, I'd say I've seen maybe half a dozen great presenters. And I've witnessed or participated in thousands of presentations. That number of presentations is no big deal in the advertising business, by the way. Every idea you generate requires three or more presentations; one internally to the creative director, another to the account people on the brand, then at least a couple externally to the client, depending on how many levels of approval are required. If you've been in the ad biz for more than twenty-five years, your presentation count is easily in the thousands. Thousands of presentations, only a half-dozen good presenters. That's ugly math. But people are rarely taught *how* to present. You are expected to pick it up by osmosis, which is what I did. I watched good presenters control a room with words and tone and body language. I watched terrible presenters fumble their way with Spirograph logic and snatch defeat from the jaws of victory. Colleagues will often critique your style in a post-presentation meltdown, but you rarely hear about what went right.

First, let's talk about what can go wrong. 'Tis a long and hilarious list.

In one famous speakerphone presentation at a Toronto agency, the presenter was waiting for the client to come on the line and whispered to his colleagues that the client was an idiot. The client was already on the line. The best part was he never let on, then after a minute or so, announced he was present, heard the presentation, responded, then asked the presenter to hang on the line after everyone else left. You can only imagine that conversation.

In an elevator on the way up to make a new business pitch to IBM, a creative director once said, "Don't seat me beside a computer geek in the pitch, it's depressing." The CEO of IBM was standing at the back of the elevator. The agency didn't get the business.

These examples are grenades that go off before the presentation even starts. That's how perilous the moment is. You can lose before you even step into the boardroom. Once inside, the grenades turn into endless landmines.

In an amusing book titled *The Real Madmen*, Andrew Cracknell tells a story of an ad agency pitching a big airline account back in the 1960s. When the agency was about to begin its pitch in the airline's boardroom, they announced they wanted to start by showing a reel of their best commercials. Agencies often do this to set the tone and to show off their best work. This particular presentation was before the days of VCRs and DVDs, so the reel was on film and a projector was set up. As the lights dim, the signal is given, the projector is turned on, and—to the agency's horror— the film begins playing backwards. The agency folks jump up, lights are turned back on, throats are nervously cleared, apologies are made, and the two film reels are quickly switched. Then the lights are turned off again, the signal is given, and the projector is turned back on. This time, the film starts running upside down. Nervous laughs and coughs. Lights go on again, film is reloaded, lights go off, signal is given, projector is turned on, and the film just smoothly spools onto the floor.

With that final humiliation, the ad agency politely got up, thanked the airline reps for their time, packed their projector, and left. After all, what was the point of continuing? As the forlorn agency folks were getting into their car in the parking lot, there was a tap on the window. It was the director of marketing for the airline, who told them they had won the account. When the shocked creative director genuinely asked why, after the disaster in the boardroom, the client said, "Because it's obvious you're not slick salesmen."

You never know what will win you an account.

Cracknell tells another story about an agency pitching the Volvo account. The Swedish carmaker was pretty new to North America at the time. Throughout the agency's entire pitch, which included dozens of print ads and signage ideas, they misspelled the word Volvo as *Valvo*. Must have been a pretty good presentation, because they still managed to win the business.

In a book humorously titled *Pickett, Plunkett and Puckett*, adman Larry Postaer tells a story about pitching the Luxor Hotel account in Las Vegas. He decided to put together a video of snippets from other hotel commercials to show the Luxor clients just how predictable most casino advertising was. The video showed clichéd scenes of swimming pools, blackjack tables, showgirls and slot machine winners—all set to Elvis Presley's "Viva Las Vegas." Halfway through the video, Postaer notices something. All the toes are tapping under the boardroom table.

In that moment, Postaer knew he had blown it.

The Luxor clients were loving the video. They did not see clichés, they saw their exciting lives flashing before their eyes. They saw Vegas greatness. Which is not what they saw when Postaer presented his alternative campaign idea.

Adman Fred Goldberg recounts the story of wanting to get his ad agency on a list to pitch a courier account called Airborne Express. To impress the courier company, Goldberg decided to send in a package of his agency's best ads. A few hours later, Airborne Express sent Goldberg a note saying the ads were incredible, but the agency would *never* get a chance to work on the account. Confused, Goldberg asked why. The courier company said it was because the agency had sent the package . . . Federal Express.

You just gotta laugh.

There are basically two kinds of presentations in the advertising world. First, there is the new business pitch, where an ad agency is trying to win a new account. This is the mother of all pitches, as it involves a steep learning curve about the potential client and about three months of work compressed into a few short weeks. It is expensive, because hundreds of hours of labour may not be compensated if the agency loses the pitch. There are usually three to five agencies competing, so the heat is intense. As legendary creative director John Hegarty so correctly says, a new business pitch is all about redefining a brand's future. It's not an exercise in coming up with an exciting advertising campaign, it's about mapping out the brand's strategy for the next five years.

Before a new business pitch, smart agencies list everything they know about a company or a product before they begin to do research. It's the only time they can think like the general public. The more they immerse themselves in the product, the more they become like the client. A new business pitch is also a chemistry test. The clients are deciding which group of people they want to sit across from for the next few years. Tighten that screw with the fact that the potential account may be worth millions of dollars. Even if it's a small agency pitching a small account, the presentation is still a big deal to both of their businesses and can induce a variety of facial tics.

A subset of this pitch is when a client announces it is putting its business "up for review." That is code for we aren't 100 percent happy with our current agency, and we want to see what else is out there. Kind of like being married but still dating. It's an awkward moment for the incumbent agency, as the world sees a crack in the relationship and competitors jostle to get a foot in that door. In the world of public service, most government departments are required to put their advertising account up for review every three years, so it's standard practice. The incumbent has to choose whether to swallow their pride and repitch the business, or just walk away. Most try to win the business back, because the account represents a sizable chunk of revenue and pays a lot of salaries. Occasionally, the client will be convinced to stay with the existing agency.

The second type of presentation is the standard and much more frequent pitch to sell a new idea or campaign to an existing client. In this scenario, the agency already has a relationship with the advertiser. Day to day, the advertiser gives the agency marketing tasks, the agency comes up with ideas, presentations are scheduled. In most agencies, there are presentations going on every single day. Boardrooms are booked solid. While these frequent presentations may appear routine, there is so much riding on them. Big new brand campaigns are presented, which will eat up the biggest chunk of a company's marketing budget, so the anxiety in that presentation is huge. Maintaining existing campaigns and keeping them fresh is also a daunting task. It's one thing to have an idea turned down, but it's quite another when the deadline isn't changing to accommodate a return to the drawing board. Now the creative team has only two days to come up with a completely new idea. They had six weeks to come up with the first one. Many of those failures are the result of poor presentations, not bad ideas.

An idea is a fragile thing. When it only exists as a notion—a flicker of potential—the slightest breeze from across the table can extinguish it. Presenting a new idea requires poise, persuasion and gust protection.

The first rule is: Know your audience. You have to have a deep understanding of who you are talking to in order to be relevant. In a presentation, you need to know who is across the table. You have to understand the dynamic of the room. You have to understand the agendas at play and the differing personalities that will be judging your work. Maybe one client always asks how this idea fits in with past campaigns. So you are careful to include this explanation in your pitch. Maybe another client likes to interrupt with budget questions, so you head that off at the pass by incorporating those numbers into your presentation as you go. And just maybe you know your clients love typical casino marketing, so you are careful not to insult their taste.

It's also important to know where the power resides in the room. Will it be a group decision, or does the green light sit firmly in one lap? While you want to sway the entire room, it helps to know who has their finger on the trigger. In a presentation to a large group of Labatt executives once, a perceptive account director leaned over to me and whispered, "Sometimes you don't count the votes, you weigh them." Meaning that even though seven members of the client's marketing team may vote yes, the lone VP at the end of the table may vote no, and that's all she wrote.

Finding the clout in a room is not always easy when the headcount is high, especially when the relationship is new. Back in 1970, adman Jerry Della Femina wrote a dark but hilarious book titled *From Those Wonderful Folks Who Brought You Pearl Harbor.* The title comes from a headline Della Femina suggested for client Panasonic, the Japanese electronics giant. He wasn't serious, he was just trying to loosen up a brainstorming session, but it gives you an insight into the mind of Della Femina.

In that book, he tells a story about scoping a boardroom for the person with clout. An advertising agency was pitching a new account, and a meeting was arranged. The agency VP who was handling the bulk of the presentation arrived a few minutes late. He apologized, sat down, arranged his papers, and just before it was his turn to speak, quickly scanned the faces around the table looking for the person with the power. He spots one guy who looks like he's important and appears to be leaning in with interest. The VP decides he's the clout, and stares him straight in the eye all the way through the pitch. In his mind, the VP threw the rest of the people out of the room and directed all his powers of persuasion toward this one man. When the VP was done, he was convinced he had done a masterful job. There was a lot of handshaking, the clients said thank you and asked for a little time to think the pitch over. As the agency team was getting into their car, the VP noticed the client—the one he directed his entire pitch to—was climbing into the backseat with them. A few moments later, he realized he had been pitching to a new guy at his own agency. A lowly assistant media guy. He had pitched—no, he had laser-beamed—his entire presentation to one of his own staff.

Yes, there are a million ways to die in a presentation.

Then there are other times when pitching new business requires some brinksmanship. Paul Lavoie, the co-founder of the highly creative ad agency Taxi—named for Lavoie's belief that the number of people needed to service an account should be able to fit into a cab—was so successful because of his ability to make an indelible impression. When Taxi was pitching the Nike business, his account director told him that the Nike people don't look at your eyes in a presentation, they look at your feet. Which was interesting, because Lavoie was a die-hard Converse wearer. His team pleaded with him to leave the Converse sneakers at home the day of the pitch (this was before Nike bought Converse).

But on the big day, Lavoie strolled into the boardroom wearing bright yellow Converse running shoes. All Nike eyes followed his feet. At the end of the first of two presentation meetings, Lavoie put one of his size thirteen feet up on the table, and said, "Get me out of these shoes." There was a very short pause, then the clients erupted in laughter. In the next meeting, Lavoie wore one Nike and one Converse shoe. He said, "You're getting close."

Not long after, Nike arrived at Taxi with champagne and a brand-new pair of size thirteen Nikes. Taxi had won the business.

It was a bold pitch. Every other agency pitching the prestigious account was falling over themselves trying to impress Nike. Yet Lavoie made the Nike team feel *they* were pitching Taxi. He challenged Nike to convince him to take the business. His confidence was the deciding factor. To walk into a Nike meeting wearing a competitive brand took chutzpah. I can't think of many ad agencies that would have had the testicular fortitude. Even at our Pirate studios, when Coca-Cola was coming in for a short two-hour recording, we were ordered to remove all Pepsi products from our fridge. And vice versa when Pepsi was in the house. I noticed a tiny but telling moment in an early episode of *Mad Men*. As a meeting with Lucky Strike begins, the cigarette client sits down at the boardroom table and immediately sifts through the ad agency's ashtray looking for competitors' butts.

That's how seriously brands take their competition.

When Lavoie was pitching the launch of the BMW Mini, he told the client that they didn't need any advertising in their first year, because they would be the car launch of the decade. He then went on to say they wouldn't need any advertising in the second year, because they would still be highly newsworthy. But it was in the third year that they would need Taxi. Now I ask you, What other hungry advertising agency would pitch a big account by saying you don't need any advertising? But that calculated risk paid off. Mini parked its business at Taxi.

When Taxi pitched cellular phone company Clearnet (the precursor to Telus), Lavoie & co. walked into a presentation where Clearnet was expecting to see creative ideas. Instead, Lavoie sat down at the boardroom table with just a notepad and a pencil and said, "I have no answers, but I have ten questions. If together we can answer these ten questions, we can build your business substantially." Lavoie sensed the cellular clients would respond better to strategic thinking than to premature creative work. He was right. Clearnet called later to award them the business.

When I worked at Chiat/Day advertising, the LA-based agency was renowned for bold pitches. When Labatt was looking for an agency to launch a new brand, Chiat/Day was included on a list with four other agencies. As we worked on the pitch ideas, we had questions. That's when co-founder Jay Chiat (pronounced Shy-it) made the boldest suggestion. He said, "Why don't we invite Labatt to sit in as we develop pitch ideas?" Now, no advertiser ever does that. They brief each agency equally, they are available at arm's length to answer any questions, but they never "sit in." When Chiat invited Labatt's people to be a part of our development process, they said, "We can't do that just for you." When asked why not, Labatt said it wouldn't be fair to the other agencies. Chiat then asked, "Have any of the other agencies asked you to sit in?" Labatt said, well, no. Chiat smiled and said, "Then that's their loss." Labatt sat in.

There are two vital lessons embedded in each of those pitch moments. The first is the critical value of standing out from the competition. Lavoie knew how to make a big impression. Chiat knew that some rules could be broken. Dare and the world always yields.

The second is the persuasive power of confidence. I have often said clients could put their fingers in their ears and decide whether your idea is any good. Why? Because they can judge your confidence level just by watching you. Uncertainty puts a cramp in your body language and leaves a toxic aftertaste. It corrodes a presentation, especially when the work is unusual and fresh. The painful truism in marketing: The better the work, the harder the sell. Safe, solid work is an easy win. Bold, thought-provoking work makes palms sweat. You have to believe in your work. You have to have a deep conviction about it. You have to present with confidence and be able to fend off doubts when the arrows sail across the table.

When producer Brian Grazer was trying to sell the idea of *Splash* to studios, he kept selling it as a movie about a mermaid. No one was interested. But Grazer never gave up. He would keep coming back and presenting it again. One studio executive said, "I throw you out the door, you come back in through the window. I throw you out the window, you come back in through the chimney." But you have to admire Grazer's conviction. As he wisely notes, there is a lot of information in a no. So he began listening carefully to the rejections, and realized he was pitching it too much from the mermaid's perspective. In response, he recontexualized his pitch. Instead of being about a mermaid, Grazer pitched it as a love story—about finding the right love for yourself, as opposed to the love that people will choose for you. Same movie, different framework.

With that slight tweak to his elevator pitch, Disney snapped it up for its new film division called Touchstone. *Splash* was the first movie Touchstone made, it became the fastest money-making film in Disney history up to that date, and it made stars out of Tom Hanks and Daryl Hannah. *Splash* exists because Grazer had unshakable conviction and was willing to recalibrate his pitch based on the feedback. It took seven years to get it made.

I remember presenting a television commercial idea to the Hockey Hall of Fame once. The Hall of Fame wanted to attract kids, because if kids wanted to go, dads would come more often. But it was a tough sell because the hockey players in the hall were all retired, not active. Kids only love current stars. So the hall created a big area full of fun, interactive games that revolved around hockey, and needed a commercial to announce the news. The idea I was presenting showed a man walking up to an interactive machine, pushing a button, and being pelted in the face with pucks—to his utter shock. Then the machine stops, and says, "Welcome to the Johnny Bower exhibit." The man smiles, and excitedly pushes the button again. A voiceover then announces the Hall now features interactive games that are so much fun, "You won't know what hit you!"

Two things: the hall didn't *have* a Johnny Bower exhibit, and hitting a visitor in the face with a dozen pucks wasn't exactly neighbourly. Both valid criticisms. Nonetheless, I believed strongly in the power of that fun, and funny, commercial to drive business. The Hall of Fame, on the other hand, was so unsure about the idea that it made me present it to five different levels of executives, then finally to the board of directors (which was highly unusual). I had to present that commercial in no fewer than six meetings, and perform with all the vigour and excitement of the first presentation each time. At every stage, I was pelted with client misgivings. But I stood my ground, because I was convinced it was right. This commercial will work, I said. It's unexpected, it's fun, you want to see it over and over again. It's all about interactivity, and kids will love it. Yes, you have no Johnny Bower exhibit, but everyone will understand that. Count on the intelligence of your audience. It's a funny and memorable way to launch the concept of interactive games.

In the end, the hall approved the concept and held its breath. When the commercial hit the air, it was an immediate sensation. Noisy sports bars across the country would suddenly go quiet, watch the commercial, then laugh uproariously. When it was shown on the big screen at NHL hockey games, the crowds went crazy. Best of all, there was a line-up outside the Hall of Fame every morning. School buses full of kids started showing up. Ticket sales shot through the roof. The commercial went on to win numerous awards, and the actor was cited for best performance in a TV commercial that year. I had never sold a commercial as hard—or as often—as I sold that one. But my intuition was a burning ember. Always love, honour and obey your gut feelings.

This I know: A presentation is a piece of performance art.

Think of the famous presentations Steve Jobs did to introduce new Apple products. Pure theatre. My mentor, Trevor Goodgoll, was outrageous in presentations. He never sat down, he was always moving, and he employed the amusing technique of presenting an idea beautifully, getting the client all excited about it, then breaking the art board over his knee, tossing it on the floor and saying, "But it isn't good enough!" After two or three flamboyant knee strikes, Trevor would pull out the recommended idea and land his argument. It was a memorable performance. And it worked.

You want to fill a presentation room with energy, and most of all, you want your staff or clients to imagine the idea through the mist. You want them to *feel* the concept, to get caught up in the enthusiasm of the pitch. Early in my career, I would present ideas in a sober, business-like tone. I assumed the reserved businesspeople across the table from me wanted to hear from a reserved advertising man. My batting average was anemic. Then, every once in a while, I would lose myself in the performance. I would stand on a chair for a moment as I acted out the commercial; I would affect funny voices to approximate a child or a cop in a script. I would work up a sweat jumping around the room to demonstrate the physicality of the script (imagine that Hockey Hall of Fame presentation!). I came to realize that whenever I did that—which is to say whenever I got caught up in the presentation *myself*—my batting average skyrocketed. It took me a while to make that correlation, but when I did, it changed the trajectory of my career.

In one presentation, we brought two big easy chairs to Labatt's boardroom, sat the two clients down and gave them each a TV remote control. Just before we started acting out our television commercials, we said, "If you don't like our ideas, zap us." They were laughing before we even started presenting.

Energy is transferrable. Enthusiasm is infectious. Conviction is palpable. Clearly, a presentation is not just an exchange of information. It's an exercise in persuading and convincing. And because you want people to accept your idea, it's a meeting that demands a unique kind of effort.

To help, I've developed a list of tips that have survived the crucible of real-life boardrooms. These are six simple insights that have worked for me again and again. Together, they will help you steer a presentation through to an approval, while not driving with the parking brake on.

CREATE AN ATMOSPHERE OF APPROVAL.

From the moment you step into the boardroom, start to create an "atmosphere of approval" (like the easy chair idea we used with Labatt). Take control of the room with an easygoing, confident tone. Don't slip into business-ese or advertising jargon; just talk like a real human being. When you've got your clients smiling and comfortable and nodding their heads, the air in that room favours approval. Then casually transition into your presentation without a formal throat clear or a sudden change in tone.

PRESENTATIONS NEED STRUCTURE.

Like any good story, a presentation needs a beginning, a middle and an end. A well-structured presentation feels professional, feels smart and feels persuasive. It has an arc. The best presentations take people on a journey, so the trip has to feel like it's been carefully planned and thoughtfully arranged. Use the lead-up to revisit the initial brief, outline your thought process, tell the client not just what you've included but also what you've discarded, and frame your upcoming recommendation as the inevitable solution.

PREPARE THE END.

The most important moment in a presentation, without question, is immediately *after* you've revealed the ideas. Not the lead-up, as most people think, but the epilogue. Yes, the introduction sets up your idea. Quite a few people are good at that, but almost no one rehearses the end of a presentation. Moments after they've seen the work, your client's mind will be racing like a pinball machine— with equal parts analysis, fear, excitement, anxiety over what their superiors back at the ranch will think, and just plain angst about how consumers will react. As the presenter, here is your big chance to calm all that down while the cement is still wet. Your first line after the work has been exposed should be, "Now, let's look at what we've achieved here . . ." Then clearly explain how the idea has carefully answered all the briefing requests.

In many ways, the epilogue should mirror the lead-up. Where you initially said "You asked us for this and this and this . . ." you should now be tying the bow by saying, "As you can see, we've delivered this and this and that . . ." Explain why the idea is fresh and unique. How it differs from the competition by staking out interesting ground. Demonstrate how the campaign can easily be rolled out. How the core idea can migrate to other mediums. Most of all, explain—with confidence—why you feel this is the right idea. Period.

This is your chance to persuade your client to buy the ad. Your client already knew the lead-up—after all, they wrote the brief. It's this part of the meeting that is new. Eliminate all the obstacles to approval here and now. If you wait until a few days after the presentation, those small speed bumps will have grown into large walls.

NEVER LET THERE BE SILENCE.

Silence immediately following a presentation smells like fear. I can't tell you how many presentations I've sat through where the idea is presented, then there is a huge period of silence, until someone meekly asks the client, "So, what do you think?" Wrong. Silence can smother an idea. Keep talking, keep the energy up in the room. Use this time to persuade your client the idea is right, gently eliminating every obstacle they are forming in their head as they analyze the idea. Don't stop talking until the client finally says something, then roll with the ensuing conversation. When I say practise the epilogue, it means spend time anticipating every possible objection and formulate smart, thoughtful replies. That doesn't mean to be overly defensive, it means take the time to analyze your recommendation from all angles. That means never get caught flat-footed with a question. So if the client says, "Why didn't you reference our safety record in this campaign?" you can confidently reply, "We considered that, but we feel . . ."

NEVER TELL A CLIENT WHAT TO THINK.

Never, ever begin a presentation with "You're gonna love this!" Because the first thought your client will have is, No, I won't. You're setting yourself up for failure. Why work from a deficit?

SELL IT, THAT'S LUNCH.

When you get an approval in a meeting, it's time for lunch. I've seen presenters keep selling an idea past an approval, then start to buy it back. The client gets sucked into a conversation about the ad and finds something small that suddenly bothers them, then the next thing you know you're back at the drawing board. Don't be the kind of presenter who can't take yes for an answer. If it's sold, move on.

Of course, there will be times when you don't win. Sometimes the worst outcome is when a client approves the concept, but insists on major revisions that crush the original idea. John Hegarty tells the story of presenting a headline to a newspaper client that said, "Depth without Drowning." One client thinks "depth" looks like death. One hates "drowning" because he has a fear of swimming. So Hegarty turns to the third client and asks, "How do you feel about the word 'without'?"

A creative director I once worked for had a great line for moments like this. He simply said "This idea is no longer for sale." Rather than produce an ad we no longer believed in, he insisted we come back with a brand-new idea. There is no reason why you should have to live with a hamstrung idea. The best ad is an ad that both the client and the agency love.

Want to become wildly successful? Become a great presenter. More to the point, become a great presenter of surprising ideas.

Chapter Eight

PURPLE CHICKENS
The Joy of Counterintuitive Thinking

Chicken farmers in Nakuru, Kenya, own small plots of land. Raising their free-range chickens poses several problems, the biggest of which is predators. Farmers were losing the majority of their chicks within the first ten weeks to hungry eagles and hawks. So the farmers decided to try saving their chicks by employing some counterintuitive thinking. They hid their chicks in plain sight. They began painting the chicks purple.

The colour purple is not appetizing to birds of prey. As a matter of fact, eagles and hawks don't know how to process purple things—they don't recognize purple as food. It was a fascinating solution. The purple chicks run around the yard with no protection, and the eagles and hawks leave them alone. Even if a hawk lands near a purple chick, it doesn't attack. It just looks at the purple bird and thinks, What the hell *is* that?

The farmers developed a purple paint that is biodegradable and harmless to the chicks and wears off in ten weeks. By that time, the chicks have yard smarts and know enough to hide when a shadow appears overhead. The survival rate has gone from 20 percent to over 80 percent. A stunning reversal of fortune. That solution has also led to the formation of a new sub-industry—chicken painters.

They charge about three Kenyan shillings, or four Canadian cents, to paint each chick.

It's a powerful lesson in the power of counterintuitive thinking. Instead of incurring the cost of putting up protective netting or wire, or instead of hiring someone to watch the chicks every minute, the farmers figured out a smart, affordable way to solve a debilitating problem. Hide the chicks in broad daylight.

The solution led to another problem, however. Suddenly, farmers had to feed multiplying chicken flocks. Most Kenyan farmers can't afford that much poultry feed. So again they needed to think outside the proverbial box. The answer was insects. Chickens love to eat insects. As it turns out, about a ton of termites live under each acre of soil in Kenya. But accessing that source of chicken food was daunting. So a local NGO did some research and discovered a group of people living in another part of Kenya who ate termites. The NGO asked this tribe how they caught the termites and were told they used bundles of waste crop stalks soaked in water. The termites loved the stalks. They came up to the surface to feed and were easily captured. So that's what the Kenyan chicken farmers did. Each day they took crop stalks, which were waste anyway, soaked them in water and laid them on the ground. The termites surfaced, the chickens ate to their hearts' desire, and the farmers enjoyed a free source of chicken feed.

Neither of these two solutions cost much money, but each had a huge impact on the bottom line. Farmers had more chickens to sell, revenues rose and families got more nutrition.

The key to counterintuitive thinking is understanding human nature. Or in the case of Kenyan chicken farmers, understanding Mother Nature. The colour purple is rarely the colour of food, so animals don't see purple as dinner. The colour blue has a related effect on humans. Very few foods are blue—even blueberries are really purple—so when people diet, they are often told to paint their dining rooms blue, because it diminishes appetite. That dieting trick is based on a profound knowledge of human nature.

The city of Chicago is built on the lip of a great lake. As a result, Chicago roads have a lot of dangerous winding S-curves hugging the lakeshore—which led to many traffic accidents. Clearly, the city needed to do something to lower the vehicle mishap rate.

First, it made the lane markings much more distinct. Nothing changed.

Then it made the curve-warning signs bigger. No one noticed.

Then it added big flashing lights on the curve-warning signs. Nothing worked.

So the city decided to expand its thinking beyond the usual solutions. And here's what Chicago did. It painted new horizontal stripes on these roads—beginning evenly spaced as usual—but as they get closer to the curve, it painted the stripes closer together.

Why? Because it gives drivers the sensation they are driving faster. Why in the world would you want drivers to feel like they are driving faster when approaching an S-curve? Because the immediate instinct is to slow down. And when drivers slow down, fewer accidents occur. Make people think they are driving faster on S-curves to slow them down. I love that kind of thinking.

It was a perfectly counterintuitive solution to a persistent problem. If you've listened to my radio program, you'll know that I'm endlessly curious about counterintuitive solutions. I am fascinated by fresh, unexpected, took-a-left-turn-at-Albuquerque answers that not only fixed the imminent problem but also propelled the company as a result. (See Fig. 7.)

The difficult thing about counterintuitive solutions is that they are often difficult to swallow and hard to present, and are usually shunned by almost everyone initially. They don't look or smell like past solutions. They don't resemble yesterday's answers. They often seemed hare-brained. You want to paint my chickens *what* colour? Yet the click you hear when opportunity, creativity and counterintuitive thinking lines up is unmistakable.

To generate this kind of thought process, you have to shut out the status quo, standardized strategies and groupthink. Again, the phrase "That's the way we do it around here" is the death of marketing. If you want people to react to something in a new way, you have to communicate with them in a new way. If you want to solve a persistent problem, the answer just might have to be unorthodox.

There is a reason most beer advertising looks like other beer advertising, and why most car advertising resembles other car advertising. Those advertisers are letting the guardrails of their industry confine their thinking. I say those boundaries are artificial. Self-imposed. The key to generating counterintuitive solutions is to stop thinking within the confines of your category. Don't think like a car dealer, think like a great marketer instead.

Often, big companies are more entrenched than smaller, nimbler ones. Getting through a bureaucratic maze often crushes a novel idea. But thankfully, that's not always the case. Take Walmart. Even though it is the eight-hundred-pound gorilla in many retail categories, the company is still under immense competitive pressure. In particular, it is going head-to-head with Amazon online. Amazon now offers thousands of products, at very low prices, and often delivers those items for free. And in some cases, with next-day delivery. So to combat free shipping, Walmart began experimenting with same-day delivery. Now, with a company that has as many resources as Walmart, you can kind of imagine how it might pull that off—with a fleet of trucks and drivers and complex logistics. But instead, Walmart chose to push the guardrails back. It began experimenting with having its customers deliver the packages.

Yes, you read correctly.

Essentially, Walmart would ship online orders directly to its stores, invite customers to "rent out" space in their vehicles, and ask them to deliver the packages to other customers who happened to live on their route home. So instead of utilizing thousands of trucks, Walmart would employ its millions of customers. It's a staggering thought, isn't it? Customers would sign up, then be prescreened and vetted. They would be offered a discount on their next shopping bill in return for their time.

Let's analyze the strategic thinking at work here. Walmart has over eight thousand locations around the world it can use as warehouse hubs. Amazon only has eighty. Walmart has millions of customers. Amazon only has 150,000 employees. A crazy idea?

Walmart began experimenting with this service at twenty-five stores. It may work, it may not, but that freeform thinking will surely lead to more innovative solutions. Once you jump your fence in your thinking, once you get out of the cast-iron inflexibility of your category, then, and only then, can you start to see what is truly possible.

Let's stay with online shopping for a moment. One of the problems online retailers face is that people are rarely home during the day to receive their packages. Courier companies don't want to leave them on doorsteps for fear of theft or weather damage. Nor do they want to crunch them into mailboxes. Therefore, missed deliveries are the bane of online shopping. So the people at Volvo thought of an interesting solution. The carmaker wants to allow delivery companies to drop off merchandise to your parked car.

That's right—to your parked car. Volvo would give delivery companies the location of your car and provide GPS coordinates, as well as the car's colour, make and licence plate number. Then it would provide the delivery company with a one-time digital trunk key. The delivery person would press a button on their smart phone or tablet, and Volvo would unlock the car via its On Call technology.

Once the package is placed in the trunk, the car immediately relocks and you get a text confirmation on your phone that the delivery is complete. (See Fig. 8.)

A kooky, hypothetical idea? No, it's already being used in Sweden. It's a counterintuitive solution to a problem that is plaguing online shopping. Deliver the packages to parked cars.

That idea could only come about because Volvo was playing a What-if game. The purpose of "What if" is not just to lift boundaries but to trigger crazy connections. I can honestly say that all the big ideas I've been a part of have come as a direct result of the craziest suggestion of the day. That crazy suggestion was the stepping stone to a bigger thought. We would have never got to the big idea without the bridge provided by the kooky idea. Look for happy collisions. The rule is to be as loopy as you want while blue-skying possible marketing ideas. What if the product we were marketing actually made you better looking? What if we had the biggest budget in the world? What if we could only use a mime artist? What if our spokesperson was a duck?

One of the most successful radio commercials I ever wrote was triggered by a kooky "What if"—What if we plucked a duck? It was for a pillow made of soft DuPont fibres called Quallofil, which was being positioned as a cheaper alternative to down pillows. In the radio commercial, we plucked a cartoon duck—who was amusingly annoyed—saying there was no need to pluck ducks anymore now that there were soft fibre pillows. It sold more pillows than anyone was prepared for, and people actually called radio stations requesting the commercial, as if it were a hit song. DuPont offices as far away as Sweden heard about the commercial and asked for copies. It would have never been created if we hadn't played "What if."

We were once asked to help launch a beer in Portland, Maine. It was a new microbrewery and the founder, Bill Perna, wanted to brew a new beer called Sparhawk Golden Ale. When we asked him why, in God's name, the world needed yet another beer, his answer was interesting. He said everything in Portland, Maine, is geared to tourists. Everything. But Sparhawk was aimed at the people who lived in Maine. It was to be a beer they could call their own. That brief actually made sense to me.

Perna had only a small budget, so radio was chosen, because it's much more affordable than television and it offers more frequency than print. While we were throwing around ideas in the Pirate writing room, something occurred to us. How do we advertise a new beer on radio without tourists hearing the commercials? That led to a big "What if":

What if we never mention the name of the product in our commercials?

The idea was simple but outrageous. In the first commercial we aired heavily for the first two weeks, which would be broadcast just before the tourist season began, we would introduce Sparhawk Golden Ale, tell Mainers it is brewed in small batches for a better taste, and most importantly, that it is brewed for the people of Maine, not tourists.

Then we said the most unexpected thing. This commercial would be the last time people would hear the words "Sparhawk Golden Ale." From that point on, we would only talk in code so tourists wouldn't understand. Specifically, a code whistle. So when Mainers heard a specific three-note whistle, it was a secret signal that a new batch of Sparhawk had been brewed—and to come get it. We proposed creating a series of fake radio commercials for a car dealership, a jeweller, a funeral home and a lawyer's office. Typical radio advertisers in Maine. But at the end of each commercial, we would place our three-note whistle. That was our idea. We were really excited about it.

There was a lot of silence on the other end of the line when we presented it to Bill Perna. Then he finally interrupted and said,

"So you mean to tell me I'm going to launch a new beer, and you're not going to mention the brand name in the advertising?" Exactly!

You can only imagine what was going through his mind. But, like the Hockey Hall of Fame ad I described earlier, I truly believed in the idea. I also believe listeners are smart. I had no doubt that Mainers would get the idea quickly, appreciate it and play along.

Perna wasn't so sure. He wanted to sleep on it. But I bet he didn't get much rest.

He arranged another call, and this time, Perna invited a seasoned beer man to listen in. This gentleman had worked in the advertising department of beer giant Budweiser, and had lots of experience selling beer. Perna asked us to walk this ex-Bud man through the idea. Which we did. Then Perna thanked us and hung up. He called us back about an hour later. When we asked him what his Budweiser buddy thought of our campaign, Perna said his friend told him to "stay the hell away from that idea. What beer launches without mentioning its name?!"

A reasonable question. But thankfully, Bill Perna was a smart guy. He knew the idea was big, he knew it was fresh, and as we reminded him, he had a tiny budget. He knew he had to make a big splash. A new product only gets one launch. Only one first impression. Only one first kiss. In spite of all the alarms going off in his mind, the frantic arm-waving of his Budweiser friend, and the fact that we were pitching the idea over a phone and not looking each other in the eye, Bill Perna gave us the okay.

So we recorded the commercials and the first one hit the air. It introduced Sparhawk Golden Ale, told Mainers it was brewed for them not the tourists, and from that point on they would only hear a whistle. For two weeks, Perna got no feedback from the commercials. Nothing. Absolute radio silence. It was his worst nightmare coming true. Somewhere an ex-Budweiser man was patting his stomach saying, I told ya so. Then the funniest thing happened.

While filling up the Sparhawk delivery truck at a gas station, the driver heard a whistle behind him. A three-note whistle. When he turned to look, it was a guy at another pump, giving him the thumbs up.

The campaign exploded. People started ordering the beer by whistling at the bar. The local newspaper did a full-page story on Sparhawk. Mainers called the radio stations when the fake commercials aired, saying they knew it was really Sparhawk beer advertising and that they loved the campaign. Sparhawk Golden Ale was suddenly in demand. The beer was officially launched, on a shoestring budget, with its full name mentioned only in the first two weeks of an eight-week campaign.

It was a purely counterintuitive idea. A secret language tourists wouldn't understand. Born of a What-if game.

The success of that idea lay in its boldness. Maine radio listeners understood it immediately. There was an underdog tone they responded to. They wanted to support the beer and the brewery, and to jump onboard the advertising idea.

As the word implies, a counterintuitive idea is counter to one's normal instincts. It is often brazen, it ignores conventional wisdom and it takes the path less travelled. Sometimes never travelled. But if it's a smart idea (use a code), if it zigs when all else zags (no brand name mention), and if it is rooted in an insight (made for locals not tourists), it has a great chance of being noticed. Attention is the oxygen of all product launches.

Years before Sparhawk landed on our table, we were approached by a game inventor named Richard Fast. Actually, Fast was an ex-restaurant waiter with an idea. He had created a board game called MindTrap. It was a game of lateral-thinking questions. Example: "If you were in the Arctic and saw a naked man frozen under the ice, how would you know instantly that it was Adam, of Adam & Eve fame?"

Tick tock.

Answer: He has no belly button.

Fast wanted a radio campaign to launch the game. He had two goals: to sell a ton of games during the upcoming Christmas season when 80 percent of games are sold, and to get the buyer for Toys "R" Us to hear the commercials and want to stock the game (leapfrogging the usual lengthy protocol for getting into a big retail store).

When we played the game at the office, it was apparent—and surprising—how well we could answer lateral-thinking questions. Over time, we got into the slipstream of thinking in three dimensions. And when new players joined the game, we could beat them hands-down. As we played it, the overriding benefit of MindTrap came into focus—it was a game of one-upmanship.

The radio commercials we eventually produced were highly unusual because we never played the game in the ads. I dare you to think of one other game commercial where you don't see or hear people playing the game. But our insight was this: It's not the game, it's the benefit of one-upmanship. Richard Fast got it fast.

We created commercials that had fun with the idea of one-upping your successful brother-in-law. And your judgmental mother-in-law. And your credit-stealing boss who says, "Good work, Stan. Which is okay, except your name is Gretchen." It was a completely counterintuitive way to launch a game. But the humour was undeniable, and the insight was right.

After only a few months, MindTrap became the number-one board game in Canada. Toys "R" Us stocked MindTrap within a few weeks—which was unheard of. The commercials eventually ran across the United States and England. When the American distributor wanted to change some wording in the commercials, Richard Fast said, "You change nothing." Love that guy.

Counterintuitive thinking is like a coast guard icebreaker in the frozen thinking of marketing. It cuts through the usual hardened, conventional strategies of selling. While every other brand tries to squeeze into the same selling space, a counterintuitive idea sits there alone, in all its glory, with no congestion. Not playing MindTrap was the key to get people playing MindTrap.

In 1978, a married couple named Mel and Patricia Ziegler found five hundred old army shirts in a warehouse. They went to a flea market the next weekend and put them up for sale. They sold a grand total of ten. The next weekend, they made a strategic decision. They decided to double the price and call them Short-Armed Spanish Paratrooper Shirts.

They immediately sold a thousand dollars' worth of shirts. With that epiphany on pricing and presentation, they decided to open a retail store. Perhaps you've heard of it.

It's called Banana Republic.

Let's analyze their decisions for a moment. They had a product that wasn't selling in a very competitive low-priced flea market, so they doubled the price. Who doubles the price of anything at a flea market? I mean—really? Who does that? But by branding them as "paratrooper shirts" (which they actually were) and doubling the price, they made the shirts more desirable to consumers than they were the week before. Note, the product hadn't changed, only the strategy did. It was another perfectly counterintuitive idea. It went against all the conventional wisdom of flea markets, where the lowest price is the law.

Nothing will happen in business if an idea has to mirror past ideas. If sameness is the criterion, then results will always be incremental at best. Great marketing is about taking leaps. Clearly, one of the best ways to develop counterintuitive strategies is to consider doing the one thing that makes no sense. Like make drivers feel as if they are going faster in S-curves. Or double the price of a shirt at a flea market. Who does that? That's why counterintuitive ideas are hard to wrap your head around.

In Buenos Aires, the capital of Argentina, an ad agency had a client who needed a big advertising campaign to promote a new riverfront real estate development called Madero Este. It covered a seven-block area, and included a Hilton Hotel, a convention centre, an apartment building, three office buildings, a mall with an eighteen-theatre Cineplex, a sea museum and a 2,500-foot pedestrian street for outdoor events. It would be a city within a city, located in a historic area on the Rio de la Plata riverbank. But it had one big drawback—it was situated in a remote section of the city. So the advertising campaign had a clear objective: to generate awareness and drive traffic to this out-of-the-way complex. Budget: four million dollars.

As the ad agency was developing the launch campaign, something kept nagging at them. The typical recommendation—and the one the client was expecting—would have been a comprehensive, multi-media marketing campaign to launch Madero Este. The campaign would highlight all the features of the new complex and give people reasons to hike the distance. But the agency couldn't help but think that spending four million dollars on an ad campaign would be a mistake.

May I say, that's a highly unusual thought for an advertising agency.

Given its inconvenient location, the agency truly believed that no ad campaign could drive the level of traffic required for success. There were too many competitive malls that were far easier to get to. The obstacle of distance was too great. So they began to explore other ways to drive shoppers to the Madero Este complex. They conducted research to determine where the traffic would come from, what the most compelling reasons to shop there would be, and how people would get to the out-of-the-way location. It was while pondering this last question that they made a counter-intuitive leap. Instead of building an ad campaign, why not build something that would literally bring people to the complex?

In other words, why not build a bridge?

Their idea was to build an actual pedestrian bridge that would cross the river and provide easy access for the public. Then they pushed the idea one step further. Many of the world's major cities had famous landmarks. In Sydney, you have the Opera House, in Paris, the Eiffel Tower, in New York, the Empire State Building. But in Buenos Aires, landmarks were scarce. Instead of a utilitarian bridge, they suggested a world-class structure designed by a world-renowned architect.

So let me ask you this: If you were a CEO who had asked for an advertising campaign, and your agency came back with a bridge—what would you say? The Madero Este CEO sat there completely stunned. But he listened to the agency's idea and their thoughtful rationale . . . and bought the bridge. The project was a go.

Even though the press and the advertising industry both dismissed the idea initially, the stunning footbridge became a landmark and symbol of the new Buenos Aires. It eventually generated more publicity than any advertising campaign could have, and brought shoppers out by the thousands. It was an out-of-the-park homerun.

A creative director I once worked for, the legendary Lee Clow, once said that not all business problems can be solved with advertising. Even though an advertising campaign was the expected solution—the requested solution—the ad agency looked at the problem with fresh eyes. Fast Company co-founder Bill Taylor calls this "Vuja Dé." We all know what déjà vu is—looking at an unfamiliar situation and feeling as if you have seen it before. But Vuja Dé is the opposite: it means looking at a familiar situation as if you have *never* seen it before. That's exactly what the agency in Buenos Aires did. The job was to drive traffic. Who knew they would take that challenge literally. It was purely counterintuitive thinking. Interesting that the advertising industry originally poo-pooed the idea. But a truly fresh idea rarely has allies at dawn.

It reminds me of the Hans Brinker Budget Hotel in Amsterdam. If you've ever stayed at the Hans Brinker hotel, chances are you would remember it. It has been called "the worst hotel in the world."

The rooms are prison bare. They may, or may not, have toilet paper. The linens are stained. The walls are full of graffiti. Guests smell weird things, and the halls are filled with cigarette butts. The reception area is filthy. The food is barely edible. And the staff is grumpy. It's not just bad, it's terrible. But here's the thing: the Hans Brinker Budget Hotel is okay with that. (See Fig. 9 and 10.)

In the early 1990s, the hotel's manager said he was tired of hearing complaints from guests about how bad the hotel was. He wanted to "manage expectations." His thinking was that if customers expected nothing, they couldn't complain when they got it. So what do you do when your product has no benefits, no features and only the barest of essentials? You do the unthinkable—you tell the truth.

The hotel's ad agency rolled up their sleeves and went to work, creating a campaign that told customers the Hans Brinker Budget Hotel was "Everything you've *never* wanted in a hotel and more." The campaign hid nothing. It leveraged the luxury of complete honesty. The campaign would sometimes feature the things the hotel didn't offer. No whirlpool. No bellboy. No pool. No parking. No mini bar! One ad said, "Our maids work twice as hard, since we only have one." Sometimes the campaign would highlight what you did get: *Now*—a free key with your room! *Now*—free

FIGURE 1. Trevor Goodgoll, in front of one of his famous brown-paper strategy sessions.

FIGURE 2. The commercial that established Apple's rebel stance for all time.

FIGURE 3. A brilliant creative expression
of the fact the airline's fleet just got faster.

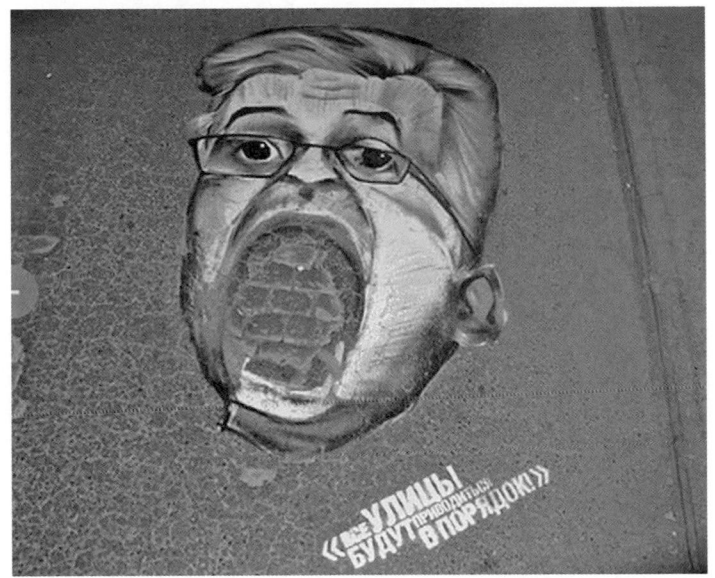

FIGURE 4. This ingenious solution made Russian politicians put their money where their mouths were.

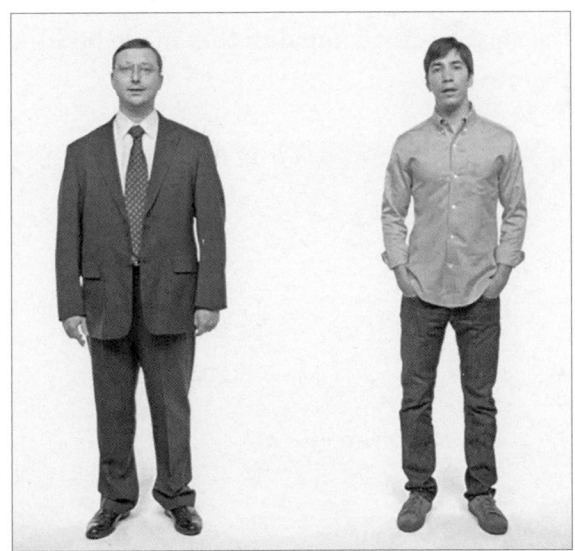

FIGURE 5. Actors John Hodgman and Justin Long weren't just personifying a PC and a Mac, they were personifying a Bill Gates and a Steve Jobs.

The Instrument of the Immortals

There has been but one supreme piano in the history of music. In the days of Liszt and Wagner, of Rubinstein and Berlioz, the pre-eminence of the Steinway was as unquestioned as it is today. It stood then, as it stands now, the chosen instrument of the masters— the inevitable preference wherever great music is understood and esteemed.

STEINWAY & SONS, Steinway Hall, 107-109 E. 14th Street, New York
Subway Express Stations at the Door

FIGURE 6. The classic print campaign that made budding pianists dream of a Steinway.

FIGURE 7. Note the horizontal lines that get closer together as they approach the curve.

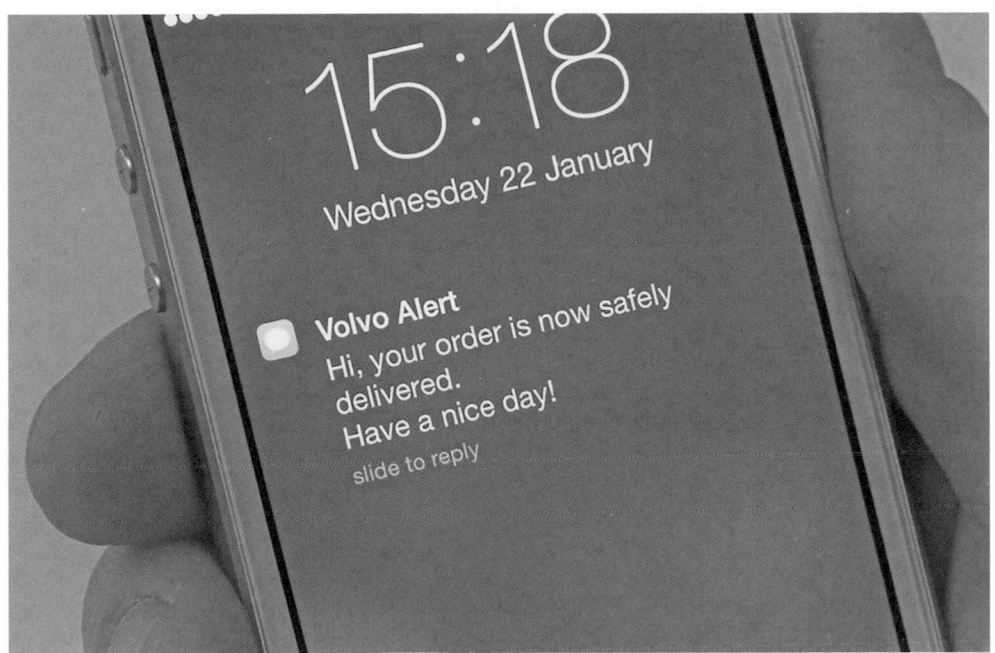

FIGURE 8. Volvo puts your junk in the trunk.

FIGURE 9. Proudly the worst hotel in the world.

FIGURE 10. Hans Brinker Budget Hotel promises you everything you never wanted in a hotel—and more.

FIGURE 11. The story fishermen all over the world couldn't pass up.

Figure 12. Marilyn Monroe's passing brought the Rapala company to life.

Figure 13. Not just a receipt but a recipe that could be used that very night.

Figure 14. This is what listeners saw when they Shazammed the Hudson's Bay radio ads.

Figure 15. I'll let you figure that Veet ad out on your own.

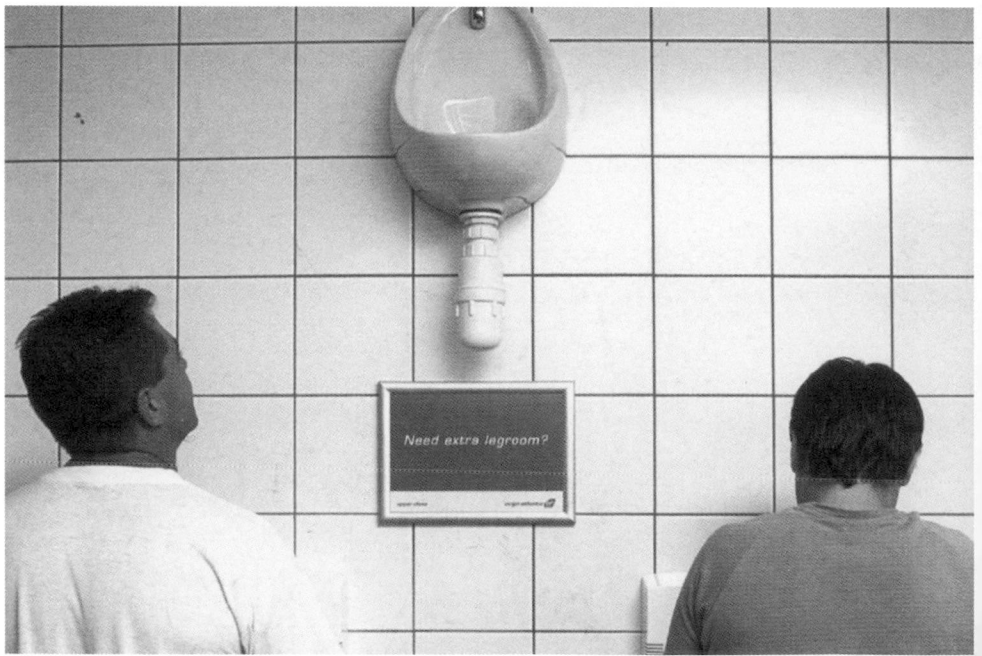

Figure 16. The right message aimed (!) at the right people at the right time.

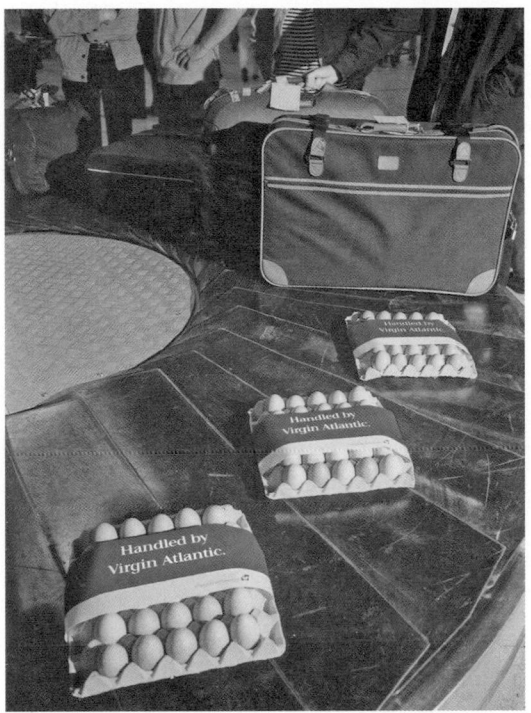

FIGURE 17. A beautifully timed message handled crack-free by Virgin Atlantic.

FIGURE 18. This tweet proved to be more memorable than Oreo's $4 million Super Bowl commercial.

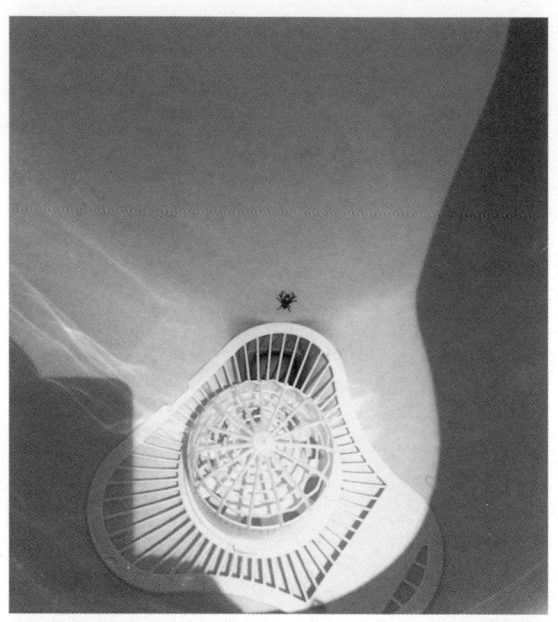

FIGURE 19. We aim to please. You aim, too, please.

FIGURE 20. Nudge, nudge, tip, tip.

FIGURE 21. Just look at the tweeter's face when Morton's showed up at the airport with a bag of food.

FIGURE 22. Before you can choose vitamins to improve your eyesight, you need better eyesight to choose your vitamins.

FIGURE 23. Viva Las Vegas.

FIGURE 24. The kind of surprise you like to find under a hotel bed.

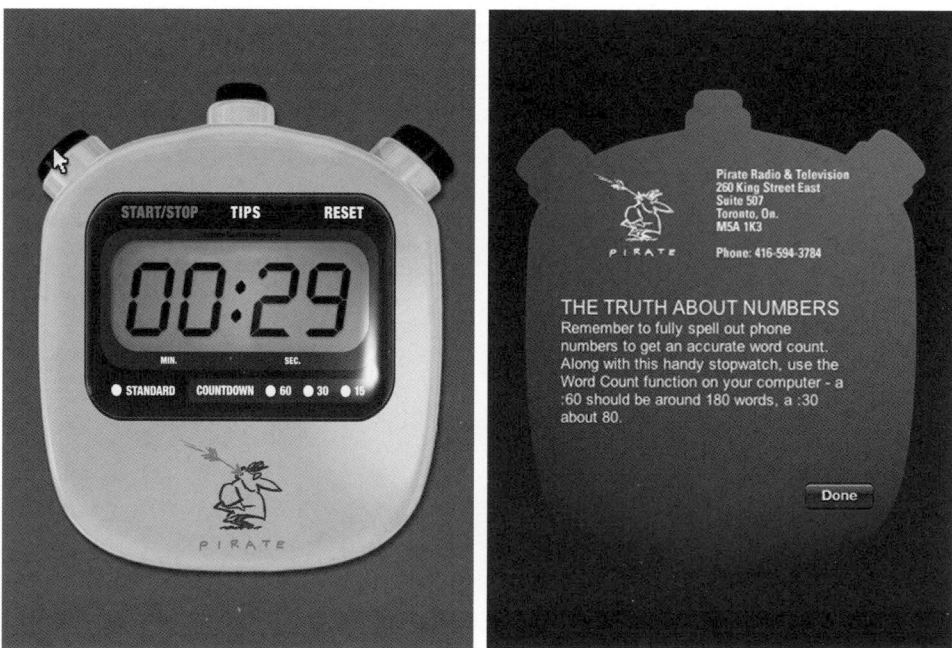

FIGURE 25. One of over two hundred tips loaded into the Pirate stopwatch. (And it only took eleven words to say it.)

FIGURE 26. Reid Miles set a new standard with his celebrated Blue Note album covers.

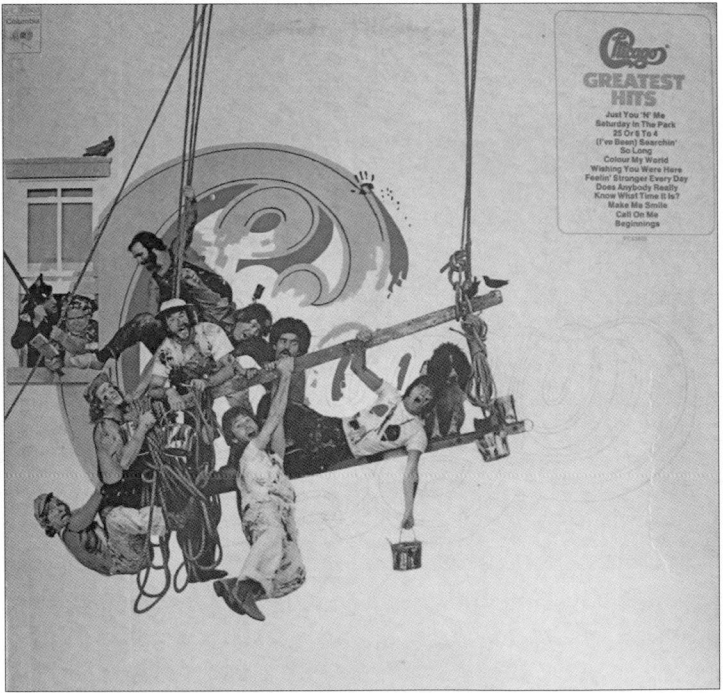

FIGURE 27. Reid Miles took the still out of still photography.

Figure 28. An art director and copywriter (me) on the run in Los Angeles, as photographed by Reid Miles, circa 1986.

You can't eat atmosphere.

Horn & Hardart. It's not fancy. But it's good.

FIGURE 29. Ed McCabe knew how to serve up a bold ad.

FIGURE 30. I nervously presented the idea for this Fiberglas Canada commercial in one of my first meetings at Campbell Ewald. Because I listened to my gut feelings, the idea got my boss's attention big time.

toilet flushing! *Now*—more rooms without a window! *Now*—even less service!

When a *New York Times* report stated the general public's immune systems were becoming weaker because of our obsession with cleanliness and Purell, the Brinker hotel jumped on the opportunity. It harvested a pile of dirt from its rooms and sent the cooties to a lab for testing. Sure enough, the results showed the hotel was swarming with all kinds of unpleasant microbes. The hotel then created this ad:

> **ATTENTION CLEAN FREAKS**
>
> You are making the world too clean. Your immune system is in danger. We need contact with dirt to build up natural resistance to harmful bacteria. For this reason, the Hans Brinker Budget Hotel is proud to be dirty and carry a wide variety of bacteria. Just one night's stay will give your immune system the boost it needs to remain effective. Visit before it's too late.

Here's the thing: bookings spiked.

Before the campaign started, the hotel had an occupancy rate that drifted around 45 percent. Within five years, it soared to 80 percent. And get this: guests pay a little *more* to stay at the Brinker than they could pay at the many other budget hotels in the area. They just want to see how bad it really is. The Hans Brinker Budget Hotel is doing a roaring business. And it is accomplishing this in the incredibly competitive landscape of budget hotels. Not only is it doing more business than its competitors, it's doing it at a higher margin. As its competitors fight it out for a patch of the budget hotel category, the Hans Brinker Budget Hotel is all alone in the *worst hotel in the world* category. Could there be a more counterintuitive notion?

While it's a strategy I wouldn't recommend, you have to admire its boldness—and the moat it built around the Hans Brinker brand.

Something else goes without saying here. To benefit from zigs when everyone expects you to zag, companies need to create a culture that is open to counterintuitive thinking. Most counterintuitive ideas sound unstructured and ill-conceived at first. It takes courage to suggest them. Can you imagine the moment someone at Walmart stuck their hand up in a meeting to suggest that customers deliver the packages? That must have taken some guts. But good on Walmart, it clearly wants new ideas. Same with the folks at Volvo. Why help online retailers deliver packages? Answer: They aren't helping online retailers, they are thinking about Volvo customers and trying to make their lives better.

The biggest gains in business are not found in statistics or facts or big data, but in dreaming what could be. Yes, you have to absorb all the research and the focus groups and the conventional wisdom. But then turn that part of your mind off, and let your intuition get a shot at the steering wheel. Because it is your intuition that is capable of the bigger leaps. Most corporations don't value intuition. It's seen as flakey, unquantifiable. As author Sam Sheridan says, intuition has become a banned substance.

But the best organizations know different. Every company needs the smartest number of people per square foot. So the most successful marketers try to create an environment of "systematic serendipity." Just like when we played What-if games while writing at Pirate. The rule was: at this stage, there are no bad ideas. I wanted to hear everything the writers were thinking, good, bad or terrible. I wanted everyone to feel free enough to yell anything out. Baked or half-baked. Reasonable or ridiculous. No one was judged. At best, we would stumble on a thread leading to a big idea. At worst, we all just had a good laugh.

A counterintuitive strategy is like a string of green lights, avoiding the traffic congestion of brands all trying to squeeze into the same parking space. All it takes is a little Vuja Dé. And good timing.

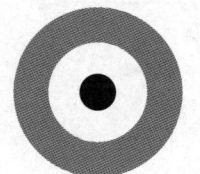

Chapter Nine

FISHING FOR MARILYN
Timing Is Everything

Years ago as a young copywriter, I wrote a print ad for an industrial plastic product made by DuPont. It showed a kayaker about to go over a gigantic waterfall, and the headline said it was the wrong moment to be wondering if the kayak was made of the right material. As an ad, it was arresting and it definitely got your attention. In the copy was a phone number to call to learn more. Unfortunately, we inserted the wrong phone number. Instead of DuPont getting calls, a small bakery in Wisconsin got hundreds of calls asking about industrial plastics.

Ha-ha (nervous throat clear).

Coming up with big, business-changing ideas is never easy, nor is it for the faint of heart. Fresh thinking attracts the most resistance and requires the best armour to survive. Plus, there are so many delicate petals to a compelling marketing campaign. Is the core offer meaningful? Is the target audience well defined? Does the creative idea express the offer in a memorable way? Is the language persuasive? Is the art direction fresh? Is the media buy effective?

But one of the most important questions you can ask of your marketing is this: Is it the right message aimed at the right person *at exactly the right time*?

There was a period when advertising was less intrusive and more relevant. When boomers first started watching TV and listening to radio, commercials were produced with one eye to the broadcast environment. Rock stations sold stereos and beer, Top-40 stations sold bubblegum and Pepsi. As researcher John Parikhal notes, boomers didn't need to put up any filters. But as they got older and mass advertising began to bombard them, boomers have had to turn on numerous filters. That requires energy, and it began to generate anger at commercial interruptions. Younger viewers, on the other hand, have always had to filter, so it doesn't bother them.

Believe it or not, overcoming advertising anger is an all-consuming task in the world of marketing. You wouldn't think that by watching an evening's worth of television, but it's true. It's just that most advertisers are really bad at it. Committees peck great ideas to death, lousy copywriters are enabled by lousy clients, and stock-price-driven companies hunt their customers instead of delighting them. The double-whammy is that an advertiser can still annoy the public with great advertising—if it's seen by the wrong target audience, for example, or by the right audience at the wrong time. A great TV commercial for acne cream repeatedly aired during a program watched by fifty-year-olds will become annoying. A highly creative car commercial watched by viewers who bought a car six months ago feels irrelevant.

The best way to be heard in the marketplace is to say something in a unique voice paired with exquisite timing. Timing really is everything. Big data algorithms are achieving that right now. Automakers, for example, can use cookies to track your car shopping online. They observe you visiting their site, looking at the features of a specific model. Then when you start to close in on a purchase and are searching for financing, they'll send you a rebate offer. You may be considering a rival brand, too, but this tempting offer just might tip your decision their way. The right message at exactly the right time.

Much well-timed advertising requires planning, and some of it requires spontaneity. And some perfectly timed marketing is just pure luck. One of my favourite stories of timing explains why movie goddess Marilyn Monroe is in a Fishing Hall of Fame.

Rapala lures are famous in the fishing world. They were first created in 1936 by a Finnish man named Lauri Rapala. An observant fisherman, he noticed big predator fish would dart into a school of minnows and attack the weaker ones that swam with a slightly off-centre wobble. So he carved a wooden lure that wiggled in the water like an injured minnow. The kind of small fish that big fish love to eat.

His Rapala lures worked so well, he started a small company in Finland to manufacture them, and he did okay business. But his biggest marketing success would come completely by accident.

In its August 1962 issue, *Life* magazine ran a small article with the title "A Lure Fish Can't Pass Up." It featured the original Rapala artificial minnow, and told the story of the lure's amazing ability to attract big fish. Little did Rapala know its world was about to be turned upside down. Unbeknownst to Rapala, this particular issue of *Life* had a photo of Marilyn Monroe on the cover. (See Fig. 11 and 12.)

The Hollywood sex symbol had just died, the country was mourning her passing, and the issue contained a large spread on her life and career. It happened that this edition broke all circulation records and became the biggest-selling issue of all time. That enormous readership had a dramatic effect on the small Rapala company. It immediately received over three million orders for lures. Which was a tad overwhelming, considering the US Rapala office had a staff of only two.

Needless to say, Rapala struggled to keep up with the orders. It was receiving more than three bags of mail a day, many stuffed with cash, begging for as many lures as the company could manufacture. That issue of *Life* launched Rapala lures into the stratosphere. Today, Rapala is sold in over 140 countries and holds more world records for catches than any other lure. It's all because Rapala had the right message aimed at the right people at—accidentally—the right time. And that's why, in 2008, Rapala inducted Marilyn Monroe into its Fishing Hall of Fame.

When Brian Grazer was producing a new series called *24*, starring Kiefer Sutherland, the first season was well into production when 9/11 happened. To be sensitive during the aftermath, the premiere was delayed one full month. But the producers needn't have worried. A series about a resourceful American agent battling terrorism after the Twin Towers tragedy became the right show at exactly the right time.

Back in 1979, the movie *The China Syndrome* opened. It was about the panic of a nuclear reactor malfunction. Twelve days after the film hit theatres, there was a real nuclear reactor meltdown at Three Mile Island, Pennsylvania. The news story gripped the nation, and eventually 140,000 people were evacuated. The studio didn't know whether to pull the film out of theatres or ride the wave of serendipitous timing. It did both, pulling the film for a brief period, then reintroducing it and reaping over fifty million dollars in ticket sales. Big money for that era.

The problem with luck is you can't harness it, you can't count on it and you can't summon it. Knowing that, many companies look to create a set of circumstances they can control, and part of that ability comes from having a deep knowledge of their customers. In other words, if you know your customers inside out, you can perfectly time when to talk to them.

In his book *The Power of Habit*, author Charles Duhigg tells another interesting story about how companies learn secrets about their customers. One day, a statistician who worked for the American retailer Target was approached by two colleagues from the marketing department. They asked him an interesting question. "Can your computers figure out which customers are pregnant, even if they don't want us to know?" As Duhigg points out, new parents are the Holy Grail for retailers. There is probably no more profitable, product-hungry, price-insensitive group of consumers in the world.

Most people don't shop for everything they need at one store. They'll do their grocery shopping at one store, then buy their books at another and their clothes at yet another. But since Target sells everything from food to diapers to lawn furniture, it is constantly looking for ways to convince shoppers that Target is the only store they need. Retailers know that once shoppers' habits are ingrained, it's extremely difficult to change them. But there are brief moments in a person's life when habits are susceptible to persuasion. Like when big life changes occur: graduation, marriage, a new job—or having a baby.

Someone buying new towels, sheets, silverware, pans and frozen dinners has probably just bought a new house. Or is getting divorced. Bug spray, kids' underwear, a flashlight and lots of batteries means someone is going camping. A garden hose, a bucket, car wax and a bottle of Armor All Tire Shine probably means someone just got a new car. By closely tracking people's buying habits, retail analysts can predict what is occurring in their homes. Target, like most other major retailers, tracks its customers' purchasing habits in a variety of ways. If shoppers use a Target-issued credit card, redeem a coupon that was mailed to their house, fill out a survey or purchase anything online, Target's computers notice, and those shoppers are issued Guest ID numbers.

New parents are so exhausted and overwhelmed, they tend to buy everything they can at one store. As a result, their shopping patterns and brand loyalties are in flux. Because birth records are public, the moment a couple has a baby they are immediately bombarded with offers, coupons and ads for baby items. It's part of the new hyper-targeting ability of marketing. As soon as news of baby is added to your data profile, stores start to market to you accordingly. So the key for a marketer is to be the *first* to reach you, before other retailers even know a baby is on the way. Timing is critical, because a coupon for a product that expectant mothers would only use before the due date is useless once it's passed.

The second trimester of a pregnancy is when most expectant mothers change their buying habits. Target's marketers knew that if they could start marketing to new moms as early as the fourth month of pregnancy, they stood a good chance of persuading those mothers to continue shopping with them. Target noticed, for example, that expectant mothers begin to buy large amounts of unscented lotions within the first twenty weeks. They also start to load up on supplements like calcium, magnesium and zinc. They buy extra cotton balls and an astounding number of washcloths. Target's people were able to identify more than twenty-five products that, when analyzed together, allowed them to assign a "pregnancy prediction" score to their customers. They could even estimate a woman's due date to within a small window based on purchases. That allowed Target to send coupons and online offers timed to specific stages of a pregnancy.

Target applied that program to every regular female shopper in its national database. It soon had a list of hundreds of thousands of women who were most likely pregnant, and began marketing to them. If only a fraction of those women started doing their maternity shopping at Target, it would add millions to the company's bottom line.

About a year after Target created its pregnancy-prediction model, a man walked into a Target store outside Minneapolis and demanded to see the manager. This man was angry, because his teenaged daughter, who was still in high school, had started receiving pregnancy-related coupons from Target. The father demanded to know if Target was trying to *encourage* his daughter to become pregnant. The manager apologized profusely. Still feeling bad a few days later, the manager called the man to apologize again. But the tone of that conversation was decidedly different from the first one. The father was much more low-key this time.

He'd had a talk with his daughter. It turns out she was due in August.

Target knew about her pregnancy before her family did. All based on her shopping patterns.

It eventually created an interesting problem for Target, because many women reacted badly to the fact the retailer was, as Duhigg puts it, "studying their reproductive status." So Target had to slow down its laser-like marketing. The retailer now sends pregnant women who are in their second trimester advertisements for lawn mowers, frying pans *and* diapers, so the baby ads feel more random.

Sometimes you can be *too* timely.

Facebook experienced some pushback when users noticed ads for pizza delivery started showing up in their feeds after they had mentioned wanting a pizza in their posts. Facebook tried to reassure users that no humans were actually reading their messages; rather, it was an algorithm that picked up on the words "hungry" and "pizza."

The world of big data and algorithms is not available to all advertisers, especially smaller ones. But any smart advertiser can create timely messages; it just takes an opportunistic eye. When the film *Top Gun* hit theatres in 1986, moviegoers were enthralled by the story of a rebellious fighter pilot training at an elite Top Gun school in Southern California. Star Tom Cruise played a pilot nicknamed Maverick (names say it all) who is trying to bury his father's ghost, win a girl and compete with his nemesis, Iceman, played by

Val Kilmer. The movie featured some of the most exciting aerial photography ever done, following F-14 Tomcat fighter jets as they executed breathtaking combat manoeuvres at speeds of over a thousand miles per hour. Those aerial dogfights coupled with cool fighter pilots thrilled audiences, and made *Top Gun* the number-one movie of the year.

The popularity of the film also led to a very interesting marketing strategy for the US Navy. It set up recruitment booths in theatres where the movie was playing. As a result, applications for the navy doubled. But it wasn't just the success of the movie that led to the surge in applications, it was the timing of the booths—attracting recruits just as they were leaving the theatres, while they were in a state of heightened desire to be as cool as the fighter pilots they had just watched on the screen. Timing was everything.

Smart marketing is not only designed to be informative and distinctive, it's designed to strike while a consumer is in a specific state of mind. A mindset when they are most open to a selling message. Timing really is all about receptiveness. Every potential purchase has a moment when there is a tipping point. Timing a message to hit that sweet spot is a nudge that can trigger a purchase. (More on nudging later.)

Recently, Dr. Scholl's placed the right ad at exactly the right time. It was a poster advertising Dr. Scholl's Fast Flats, designed to give women a quick slip-on option to their uncomfortable heels. The company placed the poster in the women's washroom at dance clubs. The headline said: "Ladies, are you really in here taking a break from your high heels? Just take 'em off and slip into Dr. Scholl's Fast Flats." Any women reading this right now instantly understand that ad. Most men won't. Dr. Scholl's understood that women wear very uncomfortable high heels when nightclubbing. And one of the biggest reasons they go into washrooms isn't to tinkle, it's to take their shoes off and rest their aching feet. That poster, in those washrooms, at that exact moment, caught women when they were feeling extreme discomfort. Which meant they were at their most receptive to receiving a comfort message from Dr. Scholl's. Seeing that message days later in a magazine would not have had nearly the same impact as seeing it *while* they were clubbing.

This I know: Timing is persuasion.

When you analyze the purchase cycle someone goes through when thinking about buying your product or service, consider the beats in that journey. When do they start looking? What prompts the search? How do they search? What is the deciding question they ask just prior to purchase? When caught between two good choices, what tips a decision in your favour? Probing those questions and timing a marketing message to intersect with those answers can have a big impact on your bottom line. Most small to medium advertisers only look for interesting advertising messages. Smart advertisers look for interesting timing.

Not long ago, Hellmann's Mayonnaise leveraged those same questions to put a message into the hands of shoppers at just the right time. Teaming up with a supermarket chain in Brazil, Hellmann's installed software in over a hundred cash registers that recognized when customers had purchased a jar of its mayonnaise. Then, remarkably, the software quickly created recipes based on the other items in the customer's cart—using Hellmann's Mayonnaise as a main ingredient. The recipes were printed right on the grocery receipt. (See Fig. 13.)

The Hellmann's recipe receipt was brilliant on several levels. First, a large percentage of households still think of mayonnaise as just for sandwiches, which limits the use of Hellmann's to lunches. The recipes extended the use of mayonnaise to dinnertime. Second, it took advantage of environment. Shoppers were in a grocery store and in the frame of mind to think about food. And third, it was all about timing. Ask any parent what the worst decision of the day is, and they'll instantly say, What to make for dinner. Just as they were struggling with that question, Hellmann's gave customers a custom-made solution, using the ingredients they already had in their shopping cart. So if you had purchased twenty items that happened to include chicken, parsley, curry powder and Hellmann's, your receipt gave you everything you needed to prepare a delicious curried chicken dinner.

Recipe. Ingredients. Cooking instructions. In-store signs near the cash registers said, "If there's Hellmann's in your cart, there's a surprise on your receipt."

Sales of Hellmann's increased 44 percent in the first month alone. It was the result of perfect timing, putting the right message in front of people who were receptive to that message at that moment. And as I mentioned, it was a double win for Hellmann's, because it also positioned the mayonnaise as a dinnertime solution, freeing it from its lunchtime prison.

Timing a message can have many upsides.

Not long ago, a Swedish advertising agency called Forsman & Bodenfors developed a Slow Down GPS app, sponsored by an insurance client. Because most drivers slip into a daydream state while driving, they unintentionally speed. The Slow Down app is like any other voice navigation app, with one critical difference. When you drive by a school, daycare or other area where there are children at play, the regular navigation voice instantly changes to a child's voice. As the agency says, we are all programmed to take care of children. Suddenly hearing a child's voice during navigation makes you acutely aware of your speed, and your attention sharpens.

The right message at exactly the right time.

A few years ago, we were working with retailer Hudson's Bay on its Christmas radio campaign. Every year, Hudson's Bay president Bonnie Brooks would record one commercial per day, starting in late November and leading up to Christmas Eve. Each spot featured a one-day sale, and Bonnie would describe the item and its special twelve-hour pricing. I was a fan of Shazam, the amazing app that can tell you the name and title of any song you are listening to when you hold your phone up to the source. The app detects the embedded code, then retrieves the title, artist, album, lyrics, music video and more. One day, I wondered if it could do the same with advertising. So we called Shazam, and asked if the app could work with a retail radio commercial. Shazam's developers told us they had never done it before, but it was certainly possible. Sure enough, Shazam figured out a way to code the commercials. The idea was that when Hudson's Bay's radio commercials aired, Bonnie would tell listeners to open their Shazam app at the beginning. When people did, they could instantly *see* the merchandise as Bonnie talked about it. (See Fig. 14.)

It offered a kind of breakthrough for radio, because for the first time, you could literally see the product in a radio commercial, in real time. This was very persuasive, as many of the retailer's fashion items were available in a variety of colours and textures. Not only that, but you could purchase the items via a link on your smart phone that took you directly to the Hudson's Bay website. And it all came about because we looked at the familiar Shazam app on our smart phone in a new way.

When President Obama was first inaugurated on January 20, 2009, the *Daily Telegraph* in the UK reported the story on its front page. At the bottom of page four was a big ad that said, "Goodbye Bush." The ad was for a product called Veet, a waxing and hair-removal product. (See Fig. 15.)

I'll bet no one from Veet asked the ad agency for an ad to say good-bye to the "Bush" era—more likely someone at the agency spotted a timely opportunity. The key to capitalizing on moments like this means you have to look at the world through fresh eyes and be willing to be nimble. In other words, you have to plan for the unplanned. There are endless occasions out there to surprise and delight your customers. Most of them cost very little. They just require you to spend creativity instead of money. That means being alert to opportunities, to connecting the dots between seemingly unrelated things (Veet + Obama) and looking at the world through a new filter.

Take the weather forecast, for instance. During the big winter blizzard that blanketed the east coast in early February 2013, dubbed Nemo by weather forecasters, Starbucks decided to stay in touch with its social media followers and stay relevant within the context of the impending storm. The coffee company geo-targeted the areas with the heaviest snowfall and sent out Twitter and Facebook ads with a "snow day" theme, suggesting people try and enjoy the forced day off with a cup of hot java. Then the company sent free coffee offers to areas where the weather had forced the local Starbucks to shut down, which customers could use when the stores reopened. In other words, the campaign moved with the storm in real time. It was a small gesture, but the timing made it unexpected and welcome.

Virgin is one of my favourite marketers, because the company has a history of bold messaging. That feisty attitude, no doubt, flows directly from its daring founder, Richard Branson. Virgin is particularly adept at creating singular messages with memorable executions, and for a big public company with deep pockets, a high percentage of those marketing ideas are surprisingly inexpensive.

For example, in one execution, Virgin wanted to tell travellers that it offers more legroom than other airlines. Now, it could have done that in a variety of advertisements, in a variety of predictable ways. But that's not Virgin's style. Instead, when men walked into the washrooms in certain airports, they saw a urinal on the wall about seven feet off the floor. A small, red sign under it read, "Need extra legroom? Fly Virgin." So inexpensive, so amusing, so memorable. But it was the timing that was genius—Where do passengers go immediately after getting off a long, cramped flight? Directly to the first washroom. Where they would be particularly receptive to that message. (See Fig. 16.)

In another execution, Virgin wanted to tell travellers they take more care with luggage than other airlines. So at luggage carousels, while people waited for their suitcases, cartons of eggs started coming down the chute. Not one egg was broken, and each package was wrapped with a red sticker that said, "Handled by Virgin Atlantic." So unexpected, so inexpensive and so well timed. We all stand at those carousels, not just waiting, but looking to see what damage our luggage has endured during the trip. As those travellers waited to see what shape their suitcases arrived in, Virgin communicated with them in a surprising way. It was the right message aimed at the right people at exactly the right time. (See Fig. 17.)

It has been said that with the emergence of social media, there is no weekend. Everyone is always on. But the twenty-four-hour nature of social media has presented marketers with enormous opportunities, because you can now react instantly. The Super Bowl, the biggest sporting event of the year, is ripe with opportunities. During the 2012 game, Coke created a website featuring its famous animated polar bears. Viewers who had both their computers and their TVs on at the same time watched in amazement as the bears reacted in real time to the Super Bowl action. Cheering when a touchdown was scored, moaning when a ball was fumbled. The funniest moment was when a Pepsi commercial came on—the Coke bears fell asleep. In real time.

But the 2013 Super Bowl raised the real-time stakes even higher. In the third quarter, the lights suddenly went out at the Mercedes-Benz Superdome in New Orleans. The blackout held up play for thirty-four minutes, and generated over 230,000 messages *per minute* on Twitter. But as viewers waited for the power to come back on, some smart brands took advantage of that small window of opportunity. Within minutes, Oreo cookies sent out a witty tweet that said, "You can still dunk in the dark," and included a beautiful photo of an Oreo cookie half-lit in a shadow.

How did Oreo put that response *and* an art-directed photo out so quickly? Oreo had fourteen of its key marketing people together in one room, which was set up to monitor the social media response to its new four-million-dollar Super Bowl TV commercial. Moments after the lights went out, the Oreo creative team came up with the idea, presented it to the Oreo marketing team, and—after waiting a few minutes to make sure the outage wasn't a terrorist attack—got a quick approval right on the spot. In other words, everyone who was needed to create and approve the message was in the same room. The "You can still dunk in the dark" message wowed fans, who then retweeted it over fifteen thousand times, while drawing over nineteen thousand Facebook likes—all in the first hour. With all the advertising smog that accompanies the Super Bowl, that Oreo real-time tweet was the big story of the day. It's still talked about as a milestone, and many marketers now refer to real-time marketing as "Oreo-ing." (See Fig. 18.)

As one marketing person later asked: Do you remember Oreo's Super Bowl four-million-dollar TV ad? Probably not—but millions remember the thirty-character tweet.

It proves you don't have to spend a lot of money to attract a lot of attention. You just need creativity, a modicum of good taste and a willingness to be fast off the mark. A number of other advertisers reacted quickly during that Super Bowl blackout, albeit without a great Oreo-like photo. Tide detergent tweeted: "We can't get your blackout, but we can get your stains out." Audi took a dig at rival Mercedes by tweeting: "Sending some LEDs to the Mercedes-Benz Superdome right now." PBS sent out a very cheeky reminder that if you were bored with the blackout, *Downton Abbey* was playing on its station.

All were funny, clever and timely. But it was Oreo that stole the show—because it wasn't just an all-type response, it was a witty line accompanied by a fully art-directed graphic. All done within minutes of the lights going out.

During the 2014 Super Bowl, retailer JCPenney started sending out tweets that looked oddly illegible. Almost as if they were being composed by someone who had been drinking. The first tweet said, "Who kkmew theis was ghiong tob e a baweball ghamle." About an hour later, JCPenney tweeted, "Toughdown Seadawks!! Is sSeattle going toa runaway wit h this???" Someone responded by tweeting, "Go home JCPenney you're drunk." Soon, brands started piling on. Coors Light hit reply with, ".@JCPenney We know football goes great with Coors Light but please tweet responsibly." Restaurant chain TGI Friday's took a shot, tweeting, "Go home @jcpenney, you're cut off." Maybe the most amusing was Snickers, who told JCPenney to "Eat a #SNICKERS, you're not you when you're hungry."

As it turned out, it was a brilliant Twitter strategy on behalf of JCPenney. The retailer eventually sent out a tweet with a photo of a new line of mittens it was promoting. The accompanying text said, "Oops . . . Sorry for the typos. We were #TweetingWithMittens. Wasn't it supposed to be colder? Enjoy the game!"

Smart, simple and attention getting. As *Advertising Age* magazine later said, JCPenney's tweets proved to be the most exciting real-time marketing at that year's Super Bowl. The retailer had taken advantage of a big event audience with a hashtag, and came up with a clever idea to promote its mittens—all inside the punishing 140-character limit of Twitter. As other brands took shots at it, it heightened the awareness of JCPenney's hashtag, so the retailer effectively harnessed the tweeting power of other companies to do some of its work. Then, the retailer sat back and patiently waited to reveal its mitten promotion. It didn't spend money, it spent creativity. And it did it in real time.

A few months before, the mighty Oreo learned a lesson in real-time advertising by getting one-upped by AMC Theatres. Oreo had tweeted the question: "Ever bring your own Oreo cookies into the movie theatre?" Within eight minutes, the cinema chain responded with a tweet that said: "Not cool, cookie." AMC, like most theatres, has a no-outside-food-and-beverage policy. Thousands of people witnessed the exchange on Twitter. Soon, the retweets were up to five hundred, and the exchange was picked up by news organizations. Then the retweets crossed the one thousand mark. AMC's witty retort was widely admired. The company had 136,000 Twitter followers at the time. It picked up 34,000 more as a result of that single tweet. Its quick real-time response ended up giving the company more publicity than many fully funded advertising campaigns would have delivered.

Just before that Oreo/AMC showdown, Taco Bell and Old Spice had a real-time Twitter dust-up. One day in July 2012, Old Spice tweeted: "Why is it that 'fire sauce' isn't made with real fire? Seems like false advertising." Minutes later, Taco Bell, the maker of Fire Sauce, shot back with a hilarious tweet that asked: "Is your deodorant really made with old spices?" Again, thousands saw the amusing real-time skirmish, and it attracted a ton of free press for both companies.

The public has been weaned on highly polished, tweaked-to-within-an-inch-of-its-life advertising, so to see brands react cleverly and lightning-fast gets big attention. It also says a lot about those companies. They are aware. Someone is monitoring their social media feeds. They are on top of their messaging. It's handled with just the right amount of wit and restraint.

Let's not forget that, monitoring hours aside, this type of marketing costs nothing. No expensive media, no production costs. The only caveat is to be careful about what you react to. There are reams of stories about smart brands having a lapse in taste in pursuit of a quick tweet. During Hurricane Sandy, as thousands of people lost their homes, and some even died, a home decor retailer tweeted: "STORM our site and get free shipping by entering Code Sandy at checkout." It got a lot of press—and it wasn't the good kind.

Shoe retailer Kenneth Cole tweeted an insensitive joke during the Arab Spring revolutions: "Millions are in uproar in #Cairo. Rumor is they heard our new spring collection is now available online." The brand quickly deleted the tweet and apologized. The boundary is pretty clear. Don't use social misfortune as an opportunity to sell. No exceptions.

But by using sensible taste, marketers can get attention even within the confines of Twitter, a Facebook post or a unique photo on Instagram. The key is to be interesting, surprising or clever, or share some information that is genuinely interesting to your audience. It doesn't always have to be specifically about your business, just a related, mutual interest. The other important thing is to be consistent in your messaging (remember the shish kebab theory?) and to post reasonably often. Frequency of good material builds an audience. Yes, it takes effort, but you'll soon discover that posting and tweeting is actually a joy, not a task.

If you follow *Under the Influence* on Twitter or Instagram (@terryoinfluence), for example, you'll see an eclectic mix of show promotion, amusing tidbits, the sharing and retweeting of interesting information and a genuine conversation with our listeners. Remember, it's social media, not selling media, so it's not the place to sell hard. It's a space to attract attention via shared information. This is a delicate balancing act. Just as a good movie disguises plot points as narrative, your posts should say a lot about you without saying anything directly about you. What you post is revealing. The comments you retweet reflect back on you. Your taste level and your resourcefulness are on full display. Let that work for you.

Because social media is virtually instantaneous, you can leverage breaking news, live sporting events, special occasions, weather, time of day, serendipitous sightings or whatever. When presidents George W. Bush and Bill Clinton came to Toronto to speak at an event I attended back in 2009, I tweeted during the talk. Word got out that I was live-tweeting (Bush was actually hilarious, which stunned the crowd), and I attracted a huge number of followers that day. It was kind of my coming-out party on Twitter. The beauty of Twitter is that you don't even have to have a lot of followers, because you can just jump onboard a timely item by using event hashtags. What's more, you can pan for gold on social media. Experiment to see what works best. What gets the most attention, the most retweets, the most follows. Back in the day, marketing couldn't be revised so quickly. A print ad needed a month's lead-time, a TV commercial could take up to two weeks to revise, a radio commercial at least a few days. But a tweet only takes minutes. An Instagram posting attracts immediate feedback. That's a gigantic plus for marketers, especially those with challenged marketing budgets.

It's a good idea to have a personal social media account and a business one. Separate the two. Your business accounts should remain on point with your brand. There should be shish on both kebabs, but the ingredients of both can be different. (Your personal brand is still as important as your business brand—more on that later.)

Being timely with your marketing is like added jet fuel. Yes, your message is interesting, but when hitched to a real-time opportunity, the message doesn't walk, it flies.

Consider it a welcome nudge in the right direction.

Chapter Ten

NUDGE, NUDGE (WINK, WINK)
The Power of Gentle Taps

The airport in Amsterdam, Holland, wanted to solve a persistent problem in the men's washrooms. Namely, faulty aim. So they etched the image of a housefly into the urinals near the drain. Overspray was reduced by 80 percent.

Why did that work? Because men just love to aim at things, and the housefly presented a target. It was a nudge to change their behaviour. Nudging is a relatively new aspect of behavioural economics. While the advertising industry has intensely studied how to influence behaviour for decades, the employment of subtle influence has recently taken a big leap forward. The classic definition of behavioural economics is to gently steer people toward certain decisions while still leaving them free to choose. Get them to take a little step in order to lead them toward a bigger one. That gentle ushering is based on both the social and emotional factors behind decision-making. In other words, the concept resides at the intersection of economics and psychology. (See Fig. 19.)

In an episode of my radio series titled "Colour Schemes," I talked about how colours gently influence purchasing decisions. In another, titled "Speed Bumps," I explored how slowing the buying process down by adding steps, instead of speeding it up, can lead to more sales.

But using a nudge is different.

Consumers are not always rational in their decisions. They will often make a poor decision even when provided good options. In many instances, the way a question is framed can influence a decision for the better. That's why behavioural economics has also been referred to as "choice architecture." It is the deliberate designing of choices in order to steer someone to a specific outcome. The term "nudge" was first put forth in a fascinating book of the same name by behavioural science professors Richard Thaler and Cass Sunstein. The stories they told influenced not only marketers, schools and charities, but also the governments of at least two countries.

In Britain, the government tried to encourage homeowners to insulate their attics to save energy costs by preventing heat loss. As part of that campaign, the government put forth compelling economic arguments to persuade the public to insulate. On top of that, generous monetary incentives and subsidies were offered. Nothing worked.

The public appeared to have no interest in insulating their attics and saving money. Which puzzled the government. But when it dug further, it stumbled upon the reason for the resistance. Apparently, UK homeowners simply didn't want to clear the junk out of their attics to make way for insulation. In the UK, attics are storage spaces, and just the thought of having to clear out their attics was enough for people to forgo the energy savings of insulating. Once the government had identified the obstacle, it got to work on an interesting solution. It teamed up with a local home improvement company and offered a very affordable attic-cleaning service. With that, the number of people who insulated jumped. The attic-cleaning offer was the "nudge" to get people to do the bigger thing— to insulate.

The British government soon began to experiment with other nudges. For example, through experimentation, it discovered that people who were behind in paying their taxes responded to handwritten notes far better than computer-generated ones. Did a handwritten note suggest that a real person was monitoring them—or was it the mere courtesy of a handwritten note that made people react? It was hard to say, but writing a note was the nudge that worked. People who were behind in paying their UK road tax were found to be more likely to respond when presented with a letter that included a picture of their car. The personalized photo was the nudge.

When British prime minister David Cameron saw the remarkable effect of nudges, he embraced the concept and set up an official Nudge Unit, making Britain the first country to adopt nudging as a mainstream change strategy on a national level. He strongly believed that nudging was not only a way to get people to make better decisions, but that it could also help the government accomplish much more for less. Because when small nudges scale up to include millions of people, the impact can be enormous. As one minister said, imagine if the government could improve what it did by 5, 10 or 15 percent every year using nudges. The resulting revenue or savings could almost fix budget problems and buffet the country in times of austerity.

Sensing a vast opportunity, Cameron doubled the size of his Nudge Unit, and attracted a waiting list of not only other government departments eager to work with it, but also other countries. The American government has set up its own nudge squad.

A well-timed nudge is a sophisticated aspect of marketing that is usually the exclusive domain of big advertisers. But small to medium marketers can also take advantage of nudges if you recalibrate your thinking to look for opportunities. There are endless reasons why people don't buy an item, even though they are teetering on the edge of making a purchase. Often, I've said if the dealership had just called me one more time, I would have bought that car. Or if a store had thrown in the speaker wire for free, I would have bought that stereo. Or if the salesperson had spent five more minutes with me, I would have bought two shirts instead of one. Online stores monitor abandoned shopping carts. I believe millions of purchases are abandoned on the floor as well, for lack of one tiny nudge. The key to designing an effective nudge is to isolate an obstacle to purchase. What is stopping the customer from making a decision? What is the hidden reason that is preventing a purchase?

When I was renting a car recently, the person at the counter asked if I wanted to take out additional car insurance. I said no. He then asked me to check off two boxes. One said I had declined the insurance. The other said, "I decline peace of mind." A nudge. A ham-handed one, but a nudge nonetheless. We've all seen tip jars in coffee shops, and they are rarely overflowing with coins. But at one particular coffee shop recently, the staff had figured out the perfect nudge to overcome tipping inertia. Beside the cash register stood two tip jars with a sign that said, "Which gender is the most generous?" "Men" was written on one jar, "Women" on the other. It was ingenious, because the challenge nudged people to tip more, and more often, than usual. Whether it was the inherent gender competition, or the slight sense of shame it ignited if you didn't support your sex, either way I suspect they had to empty the cups every few hours. The obstacle was inaction. People probably felt they were paying enough for their fancy coffee already. Ubiquitous tip jars become invisible. But that simple nudge changed their behaviour. It was amusing, unexpected and fun. (See Fig. 20.)

Recently, some New York City restaurants have added a digital tipping feature to their tablet and mobile payment machines. Calculating a tip is frustrating for many people. Research has shown that if you can lessen the amount of mental effort required to calculate a tip, it ups the chance of receiving one. So many companies are giving customers three digital options. The first is called "Basic" and leaves 15 percent. The second is called "Better" and leaves an automatic 18 percent. The third, "Best," leaves a nice, fat 20 percent tip.

The presence of those three nudges has resulted in more people leaving tips, and like at the coffee shop, the resulting amounts have been choco-lotta more than they were before. What if you could generate 10 to 15 percent more revenue with one simple nudge? What if you could nudge that number up to 25 percent? It just may be possible.

You are surrounded by profitable nudges right now; you just have to be attuned to notice them. Ever sit at a bar and indulge in free *salty* nuts? Guess what the purpose of that nudge is? In grocery stores, merchants will often group all the ingredients for a meal, because seeing them in one convenient place is a nudge for time-pressed shoppers. With 65 percent of purchases being unplanned, retailers hang handy gadgets and candy at the cash register. They know you will be waiting in line with nothing to do but stare at the shelf, so it's a nudge to grab a high-margin item just before you check out. Since most purchases are impulse-based, you can only imagine how successful that strategy is for grocery and hardware stores.

Psychologist and writer Dan Ariely talks about the power of a nudge when it comes to organ donation. In Denmark, 4.25 percent of the people are willing to donate. Yet in Sweden, 85.9 percent have opted in. The Netherlands is at 27.5 percent, but Belgium boasts 98 percent. Austria actually hits 99.98 percent. Why the discrepancy between similar countries? It's all in the way the form is designed. In countries where the rates are abysmally low, the form gives you a checkbox to opt in. In the countries where the rate is sky-high, the form gives you a checkbox to opt out. People will almost always default to the easiest option, which is to not check any box. So forms with an opt-in box go unchecked. Therefore, a form with an opt-out box also goes unchecked. It's the perfect nudge, as it takes a small effort to opt out.

Most people stick with the default positions on various equipment and components, like smart phones and computers. It takes too much effort to change them. I was once talking to a friend who owned the same vehicle as I did. It was winter, and I had started my truck with a remote from inside the house. He commented that he also used a remote starter, and said the only problem with the device was that it didn't turn the heater on, too. I told him it did and that it was a feature he could find by scrolling through the dashboard menus. I saw his eyes glaze over. I knew then that the remote feature would remain in the default position until he sold that truck.

Knowing that people tend not to bother, choice architects are careful to make the desired option the default. That is a profound insight. You can steer a certain choice by designating it to the default position. Think about your business for a moment. What are the built-in defaults? Are they the choices that benefit your business? If not, can those choices be reprogrammed to be defaults?

You see similar nudges in charity donation forms. Often you are given three donation options. The first will be small, let's say $10, the second will be about $50, and the third will be high, say $250. It's a Goldilocks strategy. The charity knows you won't send $10, because it's too small a donation for the effort required. The organization does not expect $250 donations. Yet that amount is there for a strategic reason—to make your eyebrows shoot up a bit. They are nudging you to the $50 box. That is the donation they want. Not too hard, not too soft, just right.

Charities have been at the donation game for a long time, and they are keen observers of human nature. They have clearly identified an obstacle to donations. If left to their own devices, people would send in, say, $20. When scaled up, that amount probably doesn't meet the charities' needs. So they did the math, and decided they needed $50 donations to continue their good work. So how do you prompt more $50 donations? By steering the decision-making process. Nudge left, then right, and guide the pen to the middle. Again, it's an exercise in identifying barriers. What is standing on the garden hose of your sales results?

A Virginia grocery store wanted to increase the purchases of fruits and vegetables. They wanted customers to make healthier decisions, and also, produce has crippling best-before dates. The store searched for a nudge and came up with an idea. A line of yellow tape was put across each shopping cart, dividing the cart in half. A sign in the cart asked shoppers to put fruits and veggies in the front half of the cart, and everything else in the back. When people finished their grocery shopping and saw how few fruits and vegetables were in the front half compared to the pile of less healthy items in the back of their carts, they were shocked.

Produce sales increased by 102 percent. The visual of the dividing line was the nudge.

In another grocery store, big green arrows were put on the floor directing shoppers right to the produce aisle. Nine out of every ten shoppers followed the arrows. In another nudge experiment, a glossy card was attached to carts, telling shoppers which produce most other shoppers were buying and which five fruits or vegetables were the biggest sellers. Because people are social animals and like to conform, produce sales jumped 10 percent by the second week. The store was so impressed by the results, it began duplicating the nudge in the rest of its 146 locations. Interestingly, the grocery store found its total sales remained the same, even though produce sales went up. In other words, people shifted their preferences to the other side of the store but still spent the same amount of money. So the store didn't lose revenue by nudging people, it just steered its customers to shop healthier.

But the art of nudging is a delicate one. Stores that used the green arrows on the floor *plus* an info card in the carts saw produce sales fall. The nudge became a shove. The very word "nudge" suggests a gentle tap. A small option that people can choose to employ or not. If people feel like they are being pushed, or if they feel the heavy hand of a marketer on their back, they won't respond. That means you may have to do some experimenting to find just the right nudge. It also means you have to excavate for the answer.

Insights are never first-level thoughts. My copywriting hero, James Webb Young, once said, "Exaggeration in movies and advertising is due, not to deceit, but a lack of skill in striking the true note. Admen and moviemakers live too much on the surface of their callings. They need to send their roots down into the subsoil of life." So very true.

The best marketers are thoughtful, observant and forever digging into that subsoil. The richest earth is found there, and the perfect nudge may just be nestled a few inches down in that loam. When you're looking for an obstacle, talk to your customers. Talk to people who don't shop with you or employ your services. Don't ever assume you know the answer. Nine times out of ten you will be wrong. I've sat through hundreds of focus groups, smugly thinking I knew the obstacles, and in most of those situations, I was incorrect. The obstacle was either completely different than I had expected, or bigger than I had anticipated, or more often than not, tinier. Sometimes so small, in fact, that we had dismissed it as a possibility. Yet when identified and removed, the floodgates of business opened.

This I know: You also have to be Switzerland when doing research. You have to be utterly neutral. Do not let your biases interfere with the feedback. If someone in your company is influencing the research results, get them out of there. Let your customers tell you the problems. Allow the obstacle to reveal itself.

Successful marketers are endlessly curious about their customers and their competition. Sam Walton, founder of Walmart, would convene a meeting with his top five hundred managers every Saturday morning. The meeting had two objectives: to go over sales aisle-by-aisle, and to discuss what the competition was doing. Walton expected his managers to visit rival stores constantly. He was endlessly curious about what was working for his competitors, wanting to know what Walmart should be aware of or should be imitating. He had no interest in what wasn't working, because that couldn't hurt him. When one of his managers met Walton for the first time, he said Walton "extracted every piece of information in your possession." That's how curious he was.

Understanding your customers should be an endless journey. Feedback should be a constant in your business. It's the only way to figure out what's working from your customer's point of view and to identify problems. From problems spring the possibility of nudges.

Political elections are compressed marketing campaigns, so they are the perfect environment for nudges. In his fascinating book *The Victory Lab*, Sasha Issenberg talks about how political parties are beginning to use nudging to remove obstacles.

He makes a very interesting observation: very few voters are undecided. That goes against a lot of conventional thinking in politics. I've noticed that in much of the Canadian election advertising I've been involved with over the years, a big effort is expended to sway undecided voters. But Issenberg states the real key to winning an election is to mobilize your existing supporters. A huge percentage of people are *infrequent* voters—meaning they support a candidate but don't make the effort to get to the voting booth on election day. These stay-at-home supporters can easily sway an election. Certain nudges have had great success in overcoming this inertia.

In 1998, voters in Connecticut got one of three different "Get Out the Vote" reminders. Twenty-five percent of people got a postcard, 25 percent got a phone call from a call centre and 25 percent got a knock on the door from a volunteer. And 25 percent got nothing, as a control group. The phone calls had no real impact, the postcards got a small reaction, but there was a massive response from the live door-knocking. Having a real person ask if you planned to vote was the nudge that got people to commit to voting, proving the ground game is essential in elections.

In another experiment, people were sent a formal letter from a politician saying, I see you voted three years ago, I hope we can count on your civic duty again, and I hope I can send you another letter thanking you after *this* election. The note got a substantial amount of people out to the polling stations. In another election, the strategy of shame was used. People were sent a letter saying: Here's your voting history, and here's your neighbour's voting history. Do you plan to vote in this current election? That nudge increased voter turnout by over 20 percent. It had the greatest response rate of any nudge by far. It also resulted in a few death threats.

Sometimes you can be too effective.

Team Obama understood the importance of getting his supporters to the voting booths, and put up billboards around the country that asked three questions:

> **1.** Do you know *when* polls open?
> **2.** Do you know *where* to vote?
> **3.** Do you know *how* you'll get there?

The signs featured this URL: barackobama.com/MakeAPlan. When voters typed that link into their browsers, the site helped them with all three questions. It's estimated that Obama generated 10 percent more votes with that billboard nudge alone.

Don't be afraid if a nudge requires a small amount of money to implement. A smart nudge is like good customer service; it doesn't cost money, it makes money.

In India, for example, luxury hotels were having trouble renting their high-end rooms during the post-2009 economic slowdown. Like airline seats and radio advertising space, hotel rooms are a perishable commodity at the end of every day. So one hotel decided to add a few nudges. It began to offer extra hours on checkout times, luxury car pickups at the airport, free Internet and white-gloved butler service. Each of these tiny benefits cost the hotel next to nothing to provide. But it sold 35,000 more rooms than the same period the year before. More importantly, while revenues grew 10 percent, net profit zoomed 145 percent.

Small nudges can yield big returns.

One of the critical aspects of nudging has to do with getting the wording or imagery of the nudge just right. John Caples, probably the best direct-mail copywriter of the twentieth century, lived from 1900 to 1990. In the era before big data, Caples was his own algorithm. He constantly tinkered with wording and could see the sales impact immediately, as direct mail meant direct results. If five thousand direct mailers were sent out and eight hundred people responded, Caples knew his rate of return to the penny. To underline that learning, he once told the story of swapping the word "fix" for the world "repair" in a headline. With that one-word nudge, the response rate jumped 200 percent. "Fix" sounded like work, "repair" sounded like a solution. Many decades later, an early website changed the word "Register" to "Continue," and sales went up 45 percent.

Language precedes behaviour change.

Words have different shades of meaning. The words "deep" and "profound" can both be applied to an insight, but to my mind each gives the reader a slightly different feeling. A deep insight suggests an understanding born of extensive research, whereas a profound insight suggests a penetrating, heartfelt epiphany that is undeniable and absolute. Same goes for the words "impact" and "result"—both can be used to describe sales, but they have different temperatures. Sales impact means the numbers have been affected one way or another, but a sales result generally sits in the plus column.

An Italian telecom company tinkered with its wording to retain customers. It offered to credit a hundred free phone calls to customers who called to cancel their service, in the hope that the temptation of free calls would change their minds. The response was tepid at best. So the company nudged the wording to instead say: "We have *already* credited your account with 100 free calls— how will you use those?" That one-word change persuaded a large percentage of people to stay with the plan. The addition of the words "already credited" made people feel like they "owned" the free talk time and they didn't want to give it up. A small nudge that probably saved the telecom millions of lost dollars.

Pollster Frank Luntz is another avid observer of human nature. In his book *Words That Work*, he tells the story of when Las Vegas needed to project a more savoury image to legislators, so the industry slowly changed the word "gambling" to "gaming." That subtle nudge in nomenclature suggested good, clean fun, and not organized crime and addiction. Gambling is a vice; gaming is entertainment.

When the US government couldn't get support for increasing welfare payments, a switch to "assistance for the poor" was a linguistic nudge that suggested benevolence, not handouts. Over the years, the beverage industry has changed its language, and "liquors" has evolved to "spirits." The evocation of "being liquored up" melted away; "spirits" connotes being in good spirits, with clinking glasses and pleasant social activity.

A nudge isn't confined to words, of course. Thaler and Sunstein tell the story of a city in California that gave its residents an accurate reading on their power bills, showing the average energy consumption of households in their neighbourhood. The hope was that when people saw that they were using more energy than their neighbours, they would scale back. It worked—but an unintended problem reared its head. While the above-average energy users dramatically decreased their energy consumption, the below-average energy users significantly increased their energy use to come up to the average.

The solution was to use emoticons instead of numerical averages. So if you used more than an average amount of energy, you got a frowning emoticon. If you used an average amount of energy, or if you used less than average, you received a smiling emoticon. No more numbers, just imagery. As a result, the big energy users reduced their energy consumption, but even more importantly, the problem of below-average users bumping up their consumption disappeared completely. Like gold stars on a school kid's homework, the emoticons were the perfect nudge.

One of the truisms of choice architecture is that the higher the stakes of a decision, the more nudgeable people are. In other words, we buy gasoline for our cars often, so nudges can be difficult to implement. But we're not so great at large financial decisions, because we don't get to practise those choices often enough. So mortgage nudges, like free valuations or free legal fees, can have a powerful effect. The same goes for education.

We usually make the decision to go to university or college only once in our lives. The authors of *Nudge* tell a story about a high school in Texas that wanted to increase the number of students that went on to college—as two-thirds of its high-schoolers never experience a higher education. But the school didn't have any outside funding to help with the problem. So it decided to nudge from within.

First, the teachers talked to the students in terms they would understand. They didn't try to sell the high-mindedness of college education. Instead, they hooked them with the universal symbol of teenage freedom: the automobile.

Teachers talked about how much money college grads earned compared to high school grads, explaining it as the difference between a Mercedes and a Kia. But the brilliant nudge they employed was yet to come, and it couldn't have been simpler. In order to graduate from the high school, students were told they had to complete an application to a nearby college. It was now a stipulation of graduation.

All that was required to gain acceptance to the community college was a high school degree and a record of having taken a standardized test. Teachers helped the students with the test, and made sure everyone filled out a college application, because completing the application was almost a guarantee of acceptance. In the end, that application nudge produced remarkable results. From 2004 to 2005, the percentage of students at that high school who went on to college rose from 11 percent to 45 percent. News of that successful nudge spread to schools all over the United States, and many have adopted it since. Just the simple act of filling out an application convinced 34 percent more students to pursue a college education. A small nudge that would affect the entire course of their lives.

In all these examples, the nudges are quite small. They are not elaborate, nor do they require a big outlay of cash. They are just smart and perfectly designed to overcome a persistent obstacle. The return on investment can be extraordinary.

Another lesson from these examples is to go with the grain of human nature. In other words, once you isolate the obstacle, use an understanding of human nature to create a workaround that plays into the path people are most likely to take. A nudge is always born of the obstacle. Want people to order more beverages? Offer them a welcome dish of salty nuts. Want them to decrease their energy consumption? Show them how to accumulate smiley emoticons. Want more people to become organ donors? Make it a small effort to opt out. Want people to tip more often? Set up a competition they can't resist.

A nudge can't feel like a stone in someone's shoe. It has to present an easy decision that doesn't create too much friction. Remember, too, that at the end of the day, a smart nudge still presents people with a choice. It isn't persistent, nagging or demanding. Male/female tip jars are amusing and you can still choose not to engage. You can notice green arrows on the floor of your grocery store and still choose to ignore them. You can spot a housefly in a urinal and still hit the wall.

Obstacles are opportunities to find new solutions. One of my most deeply held beliefs is that there is always a solution. And the solution is usually hiding inside the obstacle. Finding that nudge can prime existing customers to spend a little more, or it can increase the flow of new customers.

And once you have them, all you have to do is treat them well.

Chapter Eleven

WHAT TIME IS THE THREE O'CLOCK PARADE?
Why Customer Service *Is* Marketing

I am always pleasantly shocked when I get great customer service. It happens so rarely.

Let me tell you an amazing story. One day, a customer wanted to return some tires he had purchased. He brought them to Nordstrom; the clerk asked what he had paid for them, then handed him a cash refund with a smile, and the customer was on his way.

That doesn't sound like a particularly interesting story until you realize that Nordstrom doesn't sell tires. It is an upscale department store that specializes in fashion and home furnishings. But the store had a philosophy that the customer was always right, and it was renowned for the level of its customer service. Nordstrom did everything in its power to make that person happy, because a happy customer is a return customer. Even though it did not stock tires.

I'm not sure if that story is true or not, and Snopes.com, the website that investigates subjects of questionable origin, gives it the usual lashing. But not long ago, I was at a marketing conference in Dallas, and the speaker was telling a story about a retailer who sent a widowed customer five black dresses for a funeral. The store told her to try them all on and send the remaining four back.

When the speaker asked the audience what store it was, all four hundred people yelled out "Nordstrom!" And they were correct.

I found that astounding. Of all the thousands of retailers in the United States, the audience knew instantly which store would provide that level of customer service. Even if the tire story is just a tale, it proves the point about Nordstrom. Its customer service is legendary.

I firmly believe that customer service *is* marketing. It is not a separate department. What is marketing, but a way to put a face on a company and communicate its values? What is customer service, but a way to put a face on a company and communicate its values? Nothing tells customers more about a company than the way it treats them. It is a truer gauge than marketing could ever be. It is the company in action, not the company in theory. People are wary of a faceless corporation. That's why customer service is so critical. It all boils down to being human. It's not about the transaction, it's about making an emotional connection. It's about looking for opportunities to make that connection.

Ever walk into an Apple retail store, for example? You instantly notice something different. Beyond the stylish design and the fact that it's always crowded, there is something else in the air. It's the lack of a commission system. The Apple sales staff is not paid sales commissions. There's a reason for that. Steve Jobs wanted his sales staff to spend time with customers, not speed-date in order to pile up commissions. It's also the reason Apple created the Genius Bar, the tech support station in its stores. The Genius Bar isn't there to fix computers. It's there to restore relationships. When something goes wrong, or you can't figure out something on an Apple device, you get frustrated. You may even want to return the product. The Genius Bar is there to fix the problems, teach you how to use the technology and answer any questions you have. If you've ever tapped the Apple staff for a question, notice you never feel rushed, even though the store is buzzing with people armed with questions. The staff has been trained to take as much time with you as you need.

Apple isn't out to generate a transaction, per se, with the Genius Bar service. It wants to create a human connection. It's astounding how many companies never fully grasp this rudimentary point of doing business. But the best organizations do, and they always look for opportunities to prove it.

Recently, a businessman was getting ready to board a connecting flight that was the last leg of a long day of travelling. It was dinnertime, and he knew that there would be no food served on the two-hour flight and that he would be starving by the time he finally got home. Just for fun, he tweeted, "Hey @Mortons—can you meet me at Newark airport with a porterhouse when I land in two hours? K, thanks. :)"

Morton's steakhouse was one of his favourite restaurants. Imagine his surprise when he got off the plane two hours later at Newark airport to find a tuxedoed gentleman standing there, holding a sign with his name on it in one hand and a bag with a twenty-four-ounce Morton's porterhouse steak, shrimp, potatoes, bread, napkins and silverware in the other. (See Fig. 21.)

Let's analyze what just happened there. Someone at Morton's steakhouse read the tweet (meaning they were monitoring their social media). Someone had to get approval for the time-sensitive idea. A cook had to prepare the food. The food had to be driven twenty-three miles from the nearest Morton's to the airport. And someone had to track down the tweeter's arrival time and gate to figure out where to meet him.

The businessman then tweeted a shocked message with a link to the photo, saying, "Oh. My. God. I don't believe it. @mortons showed up at EWR WITH A PORTERHOUSE! . . . OMFG!"

Here's the thing. It wasn't just outstanding customer service, it was great marketing. The story was talked about and shared all over cyberspace. Morton's had taken the time to respond to a customer who loved its product even though the staff did not know him. Morton's steakhouse chose to take advantage of an opportunity, not even knowing if any more would come of it other than making one man happy that one night late at that airport gate. But look at the resulting power of that story. Morton's got more press and goodwill than any marketing campaign could have ever generated.

Customer service *is* marketing.

One night, a father and his kids camped out in front of Radio City Music Hall. The NFL Draft was happening there the next day, and they were hoping to be among the first in line to get wristbands so they could watch it. But the ticket window wasn't going to be open for another five hours. It was one in the morning, and it was freezing. Suddenly, a taxi pulls up, a man jumps out, drapes the family in blankets and hands them all cups of hot chocolate, then speeds off. As *Adweek* magazine noted, it wasn't an act of random kindness, it was caring customer service. The family had checked into the Ritz-Carlton before heading out to Radio City, and the night manager noticed them on their way out. He just wanted to make sure they were comfortable as they waited in the cold— even though they were on a sidewalk four miles from the hotel. So he sent the doorman to check in on them. They were his guests. He made it a point to care about them.

The Ritz-Carlton is a successful company, because it knows exceeding customer expectations can't just be a marketing campaign. It has to be an operating platform.

One thing is certain: That degree of client care can only happen if it starts in the executive suites of an organization. As famed management writer Peter Drucker once noted, the bottleneck is always at the top of the bottle.

Ad legend David Ogilvy had high client-service expectations for his staff. One of the things he insisted upon sticks in my mind. He said, "We don't walk our clients to the elevator, we walk them to the street." Think about that for a moment. After meetings, he expected his staff to walk their clients not just out to the elevator—but all the way down to the street, and probably help them hail a cab. If you've ever been to New York and stood on Madison Avenue, that is no small gesture. There isn't a building there that's less than thirty storeys tall. Escorting a client to a cab had to be a twenty-minute sojourn.

I would venture to guess Ogilvy & Mather was the only advertising agency in town that extended that courtesy in the daily course of doing business. But O&M believed in hiring people not just for their intelligence, but also for their manners. It was an extended shadow of the agency's founder and a vital aspect of the Ogilvy culture.

Why do so few companies make that kind of effort for their customers? Because that philosophy is so rare on the executive floors.

In another excellent book, *Small Giants: Companies That Choose to Be Great Instead of Big*, Bo Burlingham writes about fourteen small companies that rejected the pressure of endless growth and chose instead to stay small but great. He tells the story of restaurateur Danny Meyer, who owns several restaurants in New York, including the Gramercy Tavern. Meyer believes that all successful companies must have a soul. He regards traditional customer service—like being prompt, getting the food to the table while it's still hot, and cleaning up quickly afterwards—as a technical skill. You can teach people a technical skill, but Meyer wants his people to deliver something more. He wants them to make the customer feel like the staff is on their side. And that is an *emotional* skill.

It means Meyer has to hire people who already have that capacity. You can't instill empathy. You can't make people sensitive to the way their actions affect others. You can't give staff the desire to bend over backwards for customers. So Meyer hires for those innate emotional skills, and trains for the others. That means his interviewing process probes for kindness, generosity and warmth, not proficiency, speed and competence.

How does Meyer's philosophy look in action? Often, waiters see customers having trouble deciding between two desserts—so they'll bring the second one for free. One of his managers recently returned a handbag a customer had left behind, but chose to send it Federal Express, instead of just holding it for her at the restaurant. A maître d' recently put a rose on table 27 for a couple, knowing they always sit there on their anniversary. The couple only comes in a few times a year, but he makes it a point to remember that's where the husband proposed to his wife.

None of these acts of customer service are big. Just beautifully rare.

Meyer realized the difference customer service can make way back in 1995. In a New York restaurant survey, his Gramercy Tavern was ranked tenth for food quality and didn't even make the ranking for decor. But it was voted as the third-best restaurant in Manhattan. Clearly, people were coming for another reason.

That reason, as it turned out, was the incredible attentiveness and humanity of his staff. As Meyer says, you don't want clients to leave just satisfied, you want them to leave happy. That's a level beyond efficient service. It requires the restaurant to develop a relationship with its clients through individual, one-on-one contact. Think about how often you feel like you're just another number at a store or a restaurant. I would suggest that we all feel that way more often than not.

A supermarket chain in California called Nugget Markets recently received an astounding 10,400 resumés for 273 job openings. People love shopping there because the staff is so incredibly warm and accommodating. The CEO shares the same philosophy as Danny Meyer, saying, "We hire the attitude. We'll teach you the grocery business."

It takes an obsessive company to deliver standout service. And both Nugget Markets and Meyer's restaurants are obsessed with their customers' happiness. To achieve this, you not only have to like your customers, but you also have to be curious about them. Curiosity leads to questions, and questions let you understand your customers, learn a little bit about them and make a connection.

My wife and I have a favourite restaurant near where we live. It's a small pub. The menu is limited. The food is simple but good. The decor is rustic. It's not fancy, it's warm and cozy. We frequent that spot more than any other. Why? Because of the hospitality. The owner, Anna, and her staff learned our names and never forgot them. They always ask us what's new, and never forget the details. We always look forward to seeing them, and we're always greeted with big smiles.

In other words, we are loyal because of the customer service. Maximize the relationship, not the transaction.

There is so much shortsightedness in this department. Spend an extra few minutes with a customer, and be reprimanded for throwing the efficiency program out of whack. Suggest a customer service idea at a company meeting, be told there is no budget for it. But the smartest companies know that great customer service is a revenue generator. It is a way to differentiate your company from your competitors. It is a feature people will come back again and again to experience.

Why? I can't say it enough. Memorable, outstanding, go-the-extra-mile, I-can't-believe-you-just-did-that-for-me customer service is as rare as a winning lottery ticket. But if played daily, it is a winning lottery ticket for the company. The return on investment is ten-fold.

The Four Seasons Hotels chain, for example, is a great study in customer service. Founder Isadore Sharp tells an interesting story about growing up. He had three older sisters. When they travelled as a family, he noticed his sisters always packed small bottles of shampoo. So when he started his hotel chain many years later, he was the first to put small bottles of shampoo and conditioner in the rooms. A small touch, but now a staple of the hotel industry.

One of the ways Four Seasons ensures consistent customer service, hotel to hotel, is with its Guest History System. This system collects and files its guest's preferences, from what newspaper they like to read, to what kind of pillow they request, to their favourite drinks. In other words, every request is noted. Four Seasons uses this history to *surprise* its guests when they return the next time by putting their accustomed newspaper at their door, their preferred pillow on their bed and their favourite beverages in their rooms just before they check in. No matter what city they're in. It's a small thing, but it creates a powerful impact with the guests. It makes them feel like the hotel knows them and cares enough to remember.

Four Seasons managers also start every morning with a Glitch Report meeting. This is a summation of all the things that went wrong the day before. Every department must be present. They start the day with this list for one crucial reason: to look for ways to turn complaints into customer service opportunities. For example, one day an important fax didn't get to a guest in time for a meeting, and a complaint was registered. At the Glitch Meeting the next morning, the situation was discussed. The problem had originated at the front desk. As they talked about it, the hotel concierge mentioned that the same guest had made dinner reservations at a restaurant across town for later that evening. So the transportation department at the Four Seasons offered to make one of their town cars available for the guest and his wife to take them to dinner. A small thing, but that gesture made the fax glitch evaporate in the guest's mind.

Here's the learning: Turn pain-points into customer service opportunities. Front desk made the mistake. Concierge mentions he made dinner reservations for that same guest. Transportation department solves the problem. As Isadore Sharp says, "We are only what we *do*, not what we *say* we are."

So how can your company solve problems for your clients or customers? What are the big opportunities, and in particular, what are the small ones? Can one department solve the problem for another? What sticking points can you smooth out before your customers even mention them?

On the other side of the coin, great customer service doesn't always have to be problem solving, it can be about adding to a customer experience. Speaking of hotels, a woman was on a business trip and checked into her favourite hotel in Nashville. When she got to her room, she discovered framed pictures of her family on the nightstand. The hotel had gone to her Facebook page, replicated her family photos and had them framed. Now, I don't know how you feel about that story, but it's interesting on a number of levels. First, the photos were already public, as they had been shared on Facebook for the world to see. They weren't private, per se. Second, the hotel was looking for ways to utilize social media to make her stay more personalized. In other words, it was looking for customer service opportunities. And third, this business-woman *raved* about the photos when she told the story. She was amazed the hotel had made an extra effort to personalize her stay.

Another hotel uses Facebook to look up guest birthdays. So when guests check in on their birthday, they discover a small birthday cake waiting in their room. You may or may not be comfortable with hotels framing your family photos or doing a little research on your social media accounts, but it's a flash-forward into the world of twenty-first-century customer service and the new ways companies are expressing customer service.

Customers have never had more choices than they have today. People can sit in their pyjamas in front of a computer and, in a matter of minutes, survey all their options for any given product or service. You have a lot of competition. Quite often, the differentiating factor will be customer service.

According to a survey IBM recently did, 80 percent of CEOs believe their companies deliver superior customer service. The percentage of customers who agree: 8 percent. CEOs are wrong to the power of ten. And it's into that nasty abyss that customers fall and never return. That's why not just good but obsessive customer service is one of the best ways to trump the competition. The chances are great that your competition *isn't* obsessed with it. Amazon founder Jeff Bezos looks at his competition and says, "Your margin is my opportunity." The same can be said of customer service. Your competitor's lack of obsessive customer service is your opportunity. As writer Peter Matthiessen says, "Obsession that isn't crazed or criminal is always enthralling." So very true. It sweeps us up in its gales.

It's also interesting to note that when companies lose customers, most never try to get them back. They feel it's a lost cause. But one of the secrets of business is that companies are twice as likely to regain lost customers as they are to gain new ones. It's an extraordinary insight. Furthermore, it costs less to reclaim a lost customer than it would to generate a new one. You already have a relationship in the first instance, whereas in the second, you are trying to generate a brand-new one, and that is always the more expensive marketing proposition. The first is a warm call, the second a cold call. Mistakes are inevitable, no company is perfect, but organizations like Four Seasons turn glitches into opportunities to make their guests fall back in love with them.

They turn customer problems into customer opportunities.

Take the airline industry. I think you'd agree the level of service is pretty flat and standard across most brands. Except for Southwest Airlines. A few years ago, a man was en route from a business trip in Los Angeles to his daughter's home in Denver to see his three-year-old grandson for the last time. The boy, who was in a coma as a result of being beaten by his daughter's boyfriend, was to be taken off life-support at nine o'clock that evening so his organs could be harvested to save other lives. The grandfather's wife called Southwest to arrange the last-minute flight and explained the emergency situation to the airline. But on the way to the airport, the grandfather got held up by relentless LA traffic, and when he finally got to LAX, he encountered long line-ups. When he finally ran to the gate, a full twelve minutes after the flight was scheduled to leave—not board, but depart—he was shocked to see the plane was still there. Waiting at the gate was the pilot, who said to the grandfather, "They can't go anywhere without me, and I wasn't going anywhere without you."

There were a hundred business reasons why that Southwest flight should not have waited. Every five-minute delay on a major flight costs an airline thousands of dollars and dominos everything down the line. But that pilot knew his decision to hold that plane would be backed up by his company. It's the reason Southwest has shown a profit for forty consecutive years. It's the reason Southwest showed a profit through 9/11. It's the reason customers actually sent cheques to Southwest after 9/11, some for as much as a thousand dollars. They did it because they were worried the airline might go out of business. It's the reason the airline gets a hundred thousand applications when it has three thousand jobs to fill. It is constantly voted the top customer service airline.

No need to wonder why. Customers love Southwest because Southwest loves its customers.

Speaking of airlines, Virgin is known for great customer service, too. Again, it all starts at the top with Richard Branson. He is a CEO who is fanatical about customer service. And the smallest details. He elevates the experience for customers and employees to such a degree that other companies, even in other categories, use Virgin as a benchmark.

As Branson says, all airlines buy their airplanes from the same companies. Boeing or Airbus. They all start with the same product. Airplanes, terminals and schedules. But that's where the similarities stop. Virgin began offering amenities other airlines did not, like mood lighting, leather seats, in-flight Wi-Fi and super-advanced in-seat entertainment systems. Those things might entice people to try Virgin once, but it is the quality of the interaction with Virgin staff that makes them want to come back.

Like all the great companies I'm talking about, Virgin is very selective in its hiring practices, choosing about one out of every hundred who apply. Virgin searches for positive, friendly people. It values a magnetic personality more than proficiency. As Danny Meyer said, you can't teach people to be friendly. You can't teach people to love interacting with other people. But if you find the type of person who enjoys making people happy, you can empower them to look for client-service opportunities.

For example, I read recently that there was a fog delay one day in San Francisco. So the Virgin flight crew wheeled the first-class drink cart all the way up the ramp and out into the waiting area, and served everyone cocktails while they waited. How often has this happened to you when your flight has been delayed? Does the word *never* come to mind? But the Virgin staff knew it was an opportunity to go above and beyond. Upon hearing the story, Branson called each one of the flight crew personally to thank them for being so creative in keeping their customers happy.

By the way, Virgin responds to its customers on social media 24/7. To positive messages or negative ones. All Virgin America planes now have Wi-Fi, so it's not unusual for passengers to be texting. If they contact @virginamerica during their flight, there's a good chance they'll get a response before they land. Virgin doesn't use social media to simply pitch marketing messages, it uses it to engage its customers with fun, genuine and helpful conversations.

Have you ever read Virgin's mission statement? It's the best I've ever seen. I saw it once—it's hard to find, but I kept a copy of it. Here's what it said:

> *Everybody wants the next great thing.*
> *Even us.*
> *So we are a music store, who became an airline,*
>   *who became a soft drink company, who became*
>   *over 200 different businesses all over the planet*
>   *united by one simple common thought:*
> *We want to do what's never been done before.*
> *We want to create stuff that's valuable.*
> *And honest. And is worth making in the first place.*
> *We want to have fun while we're doing it.*
> *And we want our competitors to find us really,*
>   *completely irritating.*

Don't you want to work for a company that believes in that manifesto? This harks back to an important point I made earlier. In order to create great marketing and superlative client service, you have to encourage a customer-service-oriented culture. Your people have to know they are empowered to look for client-service opportunities. They have to believe that when they break a rule to help someone, management will back them up. They need to know they will be celebrated for it. Just as Branson did that day he called the flight crew.

It always comes down to culture. Companies have to be obsessed with client service.

One of the most obsessive organizations in the world is one you've known since you were a kid. The Magic Kingdom at Walt Disney World is a model of customer service. This attention to detail comes, not surprisingly, from the founder. Walt Disney's mantra was, "Give the public everything you can give them." From that simple statement, everyone at Disney strives to exceed customer expectations every day.

I read an interesting article on Disney World titled "What time is the 3 o'clock parade?" I'll explain that title momentarily. Customer service at the Magic Kingdom is both an art and a science. For example, Disney houses its lockers and wheelchairs to the right of the park's entrance, because staff have long observed that the majority of the visitors go to the right when they come through the gates. So by observing, they make their guest's experience better. A Disney study showed that people who bought hard candy with a wrapper took about twenty-seven steps before tossing the wrapper on the ground. So Disney placed a garbage can every twenty-five steps. You may not think of that as customer service, but it is. It keeps the park immaculately clean.

The best learning can be found in one of Disney's key philosophies, which states: "It's not my fault, but it's my problem." Which means that even though visitors may approach a Disney employee with a random question or a predicament, the employee is taught to "own" the problem and stay with the customer until it is solved. So when visitors ask, "What time is the 3 o'clock parade?" Disney employees are never sarcastic, but answer instead by saying: "The parade starts at 3 p.m. at Frontierland, but it will be at Main Street

USA by about 3:20. You can wait here in the shade if you like." Think about how rare it is for someone at a big store to stay with you until you find what you're looking for. Or for a helpline person to stay with you until your problem is solved, instead of passing you off to someone else. Every ride, show and train at Disney runs right on time. If the train is a minute late leaving the station, the conductor gets on the speaker and explains why it was delayed and how long it will be before the train gets going.

Disney staff are trained to be "assertively friendly." They are encouraged to seek contact with visitors. For example, they will actively approach someone who looks confused instead of waiting to be asked for directions.

Disney's grasp of customer service was so exemplary, its customer satisfaction ratings so high, that other companies began approaching Disney for instruction. That led to the formation of the Disney Institute in 1986. It's a Florida-based division of the Walt Disney Company that teaches other companies how to exceed customer expectations. Those companies have included Delta Air Lines, IBM, General Motors, Chrysler, and even the IRS.

The basic message at the Disney Institute is something that Walt Disney himself discovered decades ago: *People remember people, not products.* The key is to encourage employees to be consistently attentive, without seeming overly rehearsed or robotic. To extend basic human kindness and genuine attention. For example, the Miami International Airport came to the Disney Institute for help. Surveys ranked its customer service among the worst in the country. As a result of taking the Disney course, four hundred Miami airport staff learned to put "It's not my fault, but it's my problem" into action.

The Disney Institute's lessons are transferrable to any industry. A Chevy dealership in Massachusetts watched as customer satisfaction levels jumped 85 percent after studying with Disney. A staffing service company took the course and saw its revenues double in a year. By implementing Disney's best practices, the Orlando Magic basketball organization introduced a new service-oriented culture to its seven-hundred-person staff, and its customer satisfaction levels jumped above the ninetieth percentile.

The list is endless. What's the lesson? Customer service equals profit. When customer satisfaction soars, so do revenues.

A legendary example of great customer service is a company called Zappos. It's a US retailer that began as an online shoe store. Selling shoes online is a crazy idea. Who in their right mind would buy shoes without trying them on first?

But Zappos decided to brand itself as a store that cared about its customers. The first thing it had to do was take the risk out of buying shoes online. So Zappos allows its customers to order, say, eight pairs of shoes, try them all on, keep the one pair that fits, then return the other seven pairs at no charge. It also offers free delivery, and its return policy is 365 days.

Yes, you read right. You have a full year to return shoes.

See, Zappos realized what its key advantage was, and it wasn't having the largest selection of shoes, as the founders initially believed. It was creating the most amazing relationship possible with its customers. This was its greatest area of opportunity. Offer a higher degree of customer service than any other online retailer. Get a load of this: 40 percent of all orders are returned. That stat alone would scare most companies away. But here's what you need to know: the biggest returners are the most loyal, highest-spending customers. Interesting, isn't it?

By being open to returns of 40 percent, Zappos makes more money. Its culture is all about creating relationships, because happy customers are repeat customers. And the company goes to extraordinary lengths to keep its customers happy.

It begins with the hiring practices. For example, during the four-week training course, Zappos offers people a thousand dollars to quit. It's unheard of. But there's a reason—the company wants to weed out people who don't share its philosophy of empathy, kindness and humility.

In 2007, 3 percent of the candidates took the money. In 2008, 1 percent did. In 2009, no one took the money. So Zappos upped the offer to two thousand dollars.

Even the Zappos job application form is unusual. The first question is a crossword puzzle. Why a puzzle? Because the company is looking for problem solvers. At every step of the job training process, Zappos is trying to see if its values line up with those of the applicants. It's the same philosophy Danny Meyer uses in finding people for his restaurants. They are searching for untrainable skills.

Most companies who rely on phone centres to do business mandate strict time limits, insisting their staff process a certain number of calls per hour. Not Zappos. Zappos fields over five thousand phone calls per day, and there are no time limits. As a matter of fact, CEO Tony Hsieh (pronounced Shay) recently announced a new record for the longest customer service phone call ever: eight hours and twenty-seven minutes.

True story. I e-mailed the Zappos head office and asked. They responded immediately (of course) and confirmed the story. Hsieh couldn't be prouder of that record. Zappos's 1-800 number is the first thing you see at the top of its website because, as Hsieh says, the team actually wants to talk to their customers. He believes the telephone is one of the best branding devices out there. The way he looks at it, if you have your customer on the phone, you have their undivided attention for five or ten minutes. And what smart marketer doesn't want that?

He also firmly maintains his staff should look for every opportunity to wow their customers. Not only is shipping free, it's often done overnight. Which means that if you order before midnight, your shoes will be on your doorstep when you wake up in the morning. That kind of service creates a definite wow factor. More importantly, it creates emotional impact. As a matter of fact, people are so amazed, many of them scream out loud when their package arrives. UPS delivery people say they had to get used to that reaction when it comes to delivering Zappos packages.

Zappos stopped delivering to Canada, and you can guess why. The border put an intolerable kink in its promise. It can't deliver as fast as it wants to.

If an item is out of stock, Zappos staff will search three other competitors' websites to find the product and direct customers there. *Even though they will lose that sale.* But there is a reason they do that: they are not trying to maximize the transaction. Like the Apple Genius Bar, they're trying to maximize the relationship. What other company do you know of that would not only suggest another store, but help you find the product at the other store? The customer may buy that one item from a competitor, but they will come back to Zappos.

One last Zappos story. Hsieh once took some clients out for a night on the town. They ended up getting back to their hotel at two in the morning. One of his clients had a yearning for a pizza, but it was 2 a.m. and the hotel kitchen was closed. So Hsieh suggested she call Zappos to see if customer service could find her a pizza. You have to appreciate what he just suggested: He told his client to call his company, a shoe retailer, at two in the morning—and ask for a *pizza*. So his client picked up the phone, called Zappos and asked for a pizza. There was a short pause on the other end of the line, then the Zappos operator found three pizza stores near the hotel that were still open and ordered the pizza. That moment floored the clients, but I bet it didn't surprise Tony Hsieh. Because he has instilled in his company an overwhelming, all-encompassing desire to make customers happy. That's why Zappos reached one billion dollars in sales in only its eighth year of business.

There's another lesson here, too. Seventy-five percent of Zappos's customers are repeat customers. They call more often, and they spend more money. They keep shopping at Zappos because they've never been treated so well in their lives.

Customer service doesn't cost money, it makes money. It ignites loyalty, it attracts more customers and it achieves all this because it fuels the most powerful advertising of all: word of mouth. Nothing spreads faster than stories of outstanding customer service. Except, maybe, stories of horrid service. Most companies can't afford to find new customers every day. That means you have to rely on repeat customers. And the best way to ensure repeat customers is by exceeding their expectations.

Take Mr. Disney's mantra to heart: "Give the public everything you can give them." It's the reason the Ritz-Carlton delivers blankets and hot chocolate at one in the morning. It's why Morton's delivers a steak to a stranger in an airport. It's why the Gramercy Tavern sends a lost purse back to its owner via Federal Express. It's why the Zappos shoe store doesn't blink when asked to find a pizza at 2 a.m. And it's why a Southwest pilot can hold up an entire airplane to wait for one late passenger.

Every customer. Every time. No exceptions. No excuses.

It's a big promise. But do it right, and you'll discover that making people happy makes you happy. It's a wonderful, reciprocal experience. And delivering consistent, superlative, standout customer service is one of the best ways to cause your competitors to find you "really, completely, irritating."

It's all a game of inches.

Chapter Twelve

GOING THE EXTRA INCH
The Value of the Small Gesture

Not long ago, I was buying winter boots at the Australian Boot Company. When I asked about weather protector, I was told, "Don't worry, we'll apply it for you right now." When I asked how long that would take, they said twenty minutes. My mind did some quick math. The boot store was about as small as a retail store can possibly be. I'm sure when they put the key in the lock in the morning, they risk breaking a window. Just as I wondered how I was going to possibly kill twenty minutes in that tiny store, the nice sales clerk handed me a coupon for a muffin and a coffee and pointed to a little bakery across the street. She told me to go have a treat on the house and to come back in twenty minutes.

So I crossed the street, discovered a lovely little bakery and realized the boot company had just given me something I rarely get. The gift of time. I sat back, enjoyed my coffee and muffin, and relished twenty relaxing minutes. That little detail, that the boot company was a good host to my time, made me fall in love with it. I'll be back again. Little details create loyalty. The coffee and muffin offer was completely surprising. That's what made it so special. I'm sure the boot store had made a deal with the bakery: give us a discount on these coupons, and we'll send lots of new customers your way. And I was one of them. Both the boot store and the bakery got a new customer that day. The smallest gesture drove new business to both companies.

When I buy something from a store, and the cashier smiles while saying thank you, I don't consider that good customer service. I call that a given. And I can't pat someone on the back for delivering a given. To me, good customer service—or dare I say it, great customer service—is about surprising your customers with unexpected kindness or thoughtfulness. It doesn't have to be elaborate. As a matter of fact, the smaller the detail, the more intrigued and impressed I am.

Call it going the extra inch.

Smart businesses search for ways to deliver the smallest touches to make an experience memorable. Here's the big insight: I believe paying attention to the smallest details is a tremendous competitive advantage for small- or medium-sized marketers. While you can't compete with big marketing budgets, you can compete with personal service. The big boys can't bend down far enough to see the small opportunities, let alone take care of them. But smaller companies can, and it is a powerful way to level the playing field.

Attention to detail is one of the biggest reasons why people choose to become loyal customers and not just occasional customers. As a matter of fact, if you have a lot of occasional customers, ask yourself why that is. I would suggest that with even the smallest attention to detail, you can convert a large proportion of them into loyal customers. Whenever I'm shopping or dealing with a service company, I quietly observe how that company treats me and its other customers. I don't look for the broad strokes. I look for the little, unusual things. The tiny touches that make all the difference.

Let me give you an example. Because my wife and I live in the country, we do a lot of driving back and forth to the city. So we decided to buy a hybrid. One day, I was passing a Whole Foods store.

I had never shopped there before but decided to try it out. When I got into the underground parking lot, it was full. As I did the slow, skulking drive around the lot looking for a spot, I suddenly saw an open space. Not just any space, the perfect space. Right at the door. My first reaction was that it must be a handicapped spot. But as I drove up to it, the sign said: "Reserved for hybrids." Imagine my surprise. So I pulled right in. Even though Whole Foods can be expensive at times, that little touch made price issues evaporate that day.

That's the thing with small gestures. They can help you overlook big not-so-good issues.

Speaking of parking spots, many churches reserve the best parking spots for new members. It's a small but meaningful way to welcome new people to the congregation. To make them feel special and valued.

Our Pirate recording studios are situated in downtown Toronto. When clients drive to our office, they struggle to find parking. When we opened our doors in 1990, our building was surrounded by parking on all corners. Those lots have since given way to condo developments. So as a small detail, everyone at our company had a sign-off at the end of their e-mails that asked, "Need Parking Suggestions?" with a map showing all the closest parking lots. A small touch to be sure, but a useful one our clients always commented on.

As I mentioned in the last chapter, eliminating pain-points is one of the best ways to endear customers to your company. It's not one big annoyance that gets you, it's a nasty series of small irritants. The tricky thing is that these pain-points are often invisible to you. But to your customers, they are tiny, recurring thorns in their paws. Some will just put up with annoyances, because they love doing business with you. Others will take notice and move on to your competition.

Because pain-points are often hard for a proprietor to spot, you need to check in with your customers frequently. I would often ask our clients for the top three things they loved about working with us. Then I would ask them for the three things they hated most. I began with positives—not to coax compliments, but to use it as a nudge to be honest with the criticisms. People find it easier to be candid if they can balance the positive with the negative. And casually listing three things that bug them will probably render at least one good insight.

When you gather that information, look for patterns or recurring points made using different language. I guarantee the list will surprise you. Again, looking at your business from a customer's point of view is always an unnerving experience. It's like standing on a ladder in your house, and thinking, wow, everything looks so different from up here. But a customer's view is clear-eyed and vital. You have no objectivity when it comes to your own company. You are an inmate. I used to tell new employees that their objective opinions were valuable to our company for only one month. After that, they were indoctrinated and their impartiality was surrendered.

Here's the other thing I've come to realize: the list of pain-points will be overwhelmingly composed of small nuisances. Big problems have horns on them and are easy to spot. Small ones are camouflaged and often go unremarked upon. They are usually hidden inside something else that seems to be working. Like finding a seed inside a seedless grape. But while these problems are tiny, the opportunities to solve them are big. The trick is not merely to identify the problem, but to find the source of the issue.

For example, at the grocery store a little while ago, I approached a large display for Jamieson Vitamins. The type on the back of vitamin bottles, or any medication for that matter, is very small, which is a pain-point for many shoppers. Most vitamin bottles are not big, so the available space for print is challenging at best. That's when

I noticed something. There were magnifying glasses hanging on cords from the shelf. They were branded with the Jamieson logo, so clearly they were provided by the vitamin company. (See Fig. 22.)

People weren't buying enough Jamieson vitamins because they probably weren't sure which vitamins were right for them. That was the stumbling block. The information people were seeking was printed on the back of the bottles, but the font was too small. Installing magnifying glasses was the brilliant solution. Brilliant, because one of Jamieson's largest markets has to be seniors, who must appreciate those magnifying glasses more than you can imagine. A small touch, but a surprisingly handy one.

When companies embed thoughtful touches, customers notice. Those touches speak to the inventiveness and attentiveness of the company. They invoke warm feelings from customers, and because they are so rarely done, they inspire word of mouth. And word of mouth generates sales.

Here's another example. I was shopping at a local Home Hardware a while ago, and when I grabbed a shopping cart, I noticed it had a map of the store attached to the handle. It was a colour-coded directory of the departments, and I could see in an instant what aisle every product category was in. A surprising and much-appreciated detail. It eliminated the pain of roaming the aisles looking for smaller items that are never where you think they will be.

A mall in Century City, California, installed red and green bulbs over every parking space so people can instantly see where a space is available, cutting down frustrating time in a parking garage by 80 percent.

A company's every act is a marketing act. Every touch-point is an essay on how the company feels about its customers. Does it value its shoppers? Does it look at the process of shopping from a customer's point of view? Does it listen to feedback or ignore it? Does it constantly strive to eliminate shopping friction? Does it want you to come back?

Often, when using the drive-through at Tim Hortons, I'll order my usual carrot muffin and drive up to the window to pay, only to be told they don't have any carrot muffins left. Why not tell me that when I order? It happens too often to be a quirk. It's a pain-point Timmys could solve if it wanted to.

But not all small gestures have to be about making a sore point go away. When I brought my car in for servicing recently, I asked my mechanic how long he needed my car, then asked where the closest vehicle licensing office was. I had to renew my sticker that day. He said, "Take my car," handed me the keys, and explained where the licensing office was. Pleasantly surprised, I killed two birds with one stone that morning. That mechanic went the extra inch.

There's a pizzeria in New York City called Pizza by Certé. Its pizza boxes are 100 percent recyclable, which is nice. But that's not all. For starters, the lids on the boxes are designed to easily detach and separate into four squares, each serving as an individual plate. Then once the lid is gone to create those four serving plates, the bottom half of the box folds into a smaller, more convenient box to store leftover pizza easily in a refrigerator. Handy, smart and sustainable.

There is an opportunity hiding inside everything.

Because I travel a lot for work, I notice small details in hotels and airports. For example, like many business travellers, I want to make sure my phone and computer are charged up before a long flight and especially between connecting flights. So I appreciate power outlets in the waiting area at gates. A few airports have even installed handy charging poles. Clearly, someone at these airports is thinking like a passenger. I also like the little touch of being able to plug my computer into an outlet on the plane. On many of my longer flights, while everyone else is turning out their lights for a nap, I'm writing my radio show. So I appreciate the ability to charge as I write.

When you fly Virgin airlines to an international location, there's a nice routine just before landing. The flight attendants ask if you have any change in your pockets. Change becomes a nuisance when you travel, as it can't be used in a foreign country. So Virgin collects it in a basket and gives it to charity. A small touch, but a meaningful one.

When I stay in hotels, I like to have several easy-to-find electrical outlets so I can plug in my computer and phone. I don't want to pull a bed out from the wall or reach behind a heavy dresser. (You don't want to look back there, trust me.) I can't tell you how many hotel rooms have no available sockets. Or if there is one, it means unplugging the TV or the lamp to charge my stuff. I also prefer an outlet near the desk (for my computer) and another near the bed (for my phone). Many of us set wake-up alarms on our phones, and we don't want to leave them on all night, losing their charge. So we prefer the outlets to be within easy reach on the night table, not halfway across the room. Then there are hotels that have anticipated the issue and have made it a point to make power outlets available all around the room, or have a row of nicely designed outlets available on the desk. Love that touch. It's a little thing, but an appreciated thing.

A few years ago, I was judging an international advertising award show in Las Vegas, and was put up at the Encore Tower Suites hotel. After a long day of listening to hundreds of radio commercials, I came back to my room exhausted. When I looked at my pillow, there was a small note from the hotel there, tied with a ribbon. All it said was "Nighty Night." Not "Good Night," but "Nighty Night." It made me laugh. The next evening, there was another note on my pillow; this one said "Dream Big." Tiny things, but delightful things. (See Fig. 23.)

I stay at more than thirty hotels per year, and no other hotel I've stayed at has taken the time to add a personal touch like that.

While staying at another hotel in Niagara-on-the-Lake, I noticed there was a CD player on the nightstand. Beside it was a blue book, titled *Deep Sleep 101*. Inside was a CD of soothing music, which the book suggested I put on one hour before bedtime. The book, subtitled *A Guidebook Proven to Conquer Insomnia*, was full of tips that promoted sleep. A nice little touch for weary travellers, or for those who have trouble sleeping in a strange room.

A guest at another hotel tweeted a photo of a small card he found peeking out from under his bed. It simply said "Yes, we clean under here, too!" So funny, so smart, so memorable. (See Fig. 24.)

Recently while on vacation, my family and I were dining at a beautiful outdoor restaurant by the ocean, after dark. The only light on the table was a single candle, and we wondered how we'd be able to read the menus. But when the menus arrived, we were delighted to discover they were on leather-bound iPads. A novel idea that made for a memorable moment. The restaurant found a way to maintain the nighttime ambiance and still make the menu moment unique.

Which speaks to another insight: Find a way to make a mundane aspect of your customer service memorable. Ordering off a menu is par for the course at a restaurant, but ordering off backlit iPads at night made it special. This isn't about solving a pain-point, it's about enhancing a touch-point.

In the commercial recording business, clients spend many hours in a studio. Inevitably, lunchtime arrives, and in all the studios I've recorded in across North America, you get handed a binder of take-out menus. You try to agree on a restaurant, everyone places their orders, and the food arrives in greasy bags forty-five minutes later. At Pirate, we saw this as a customer service opportunity. We designed a beautiful kitchen and brought in five-star catering every day. When lunchtime rolled around, a delicious meal of varied dishes was beautifully arranged in the kitchen. Clients were notified, and they wandered out to enjoy a memorable lunch on china with silverware. While Pirate was known for its creativity, many clients joked that the reason they kept coming back was for the food. We weren't insulted. Our food was a competitive advantage. We were almost alone in preparing catered lunches for studio clients in the recording studio business. Even in the big studio meccas, like New York and Los Angeles, take-out menus were the norm.

Pirate also served breakfast to clients and our staff every day. First thing in the morning, we laid out a healthy breakfast of fruit, cereals, breads, yogurts and muffins. Most Fridays, the staff at Pirate would take turns donning a chef's hat and we would serve hot breakfasts, with pancakes, crepes, bacon and eggs. We did it for two reasons. First, a family that eats together stays together, and that was important to our company culture. Second, we wanted to create a unique experience when clients came to Pirate. An experience not confined to the level of creativity we brought to the recordings, but including the overall feeling of being there. From the moment you walked through our doors to the moment you left.

Another little touch we incorporated had to do with scripts. Specifically, helping copywriters time their scripts. The single biggest problem with radio scripts is that most are overwritten. Thirty seconds is a cruel mistress, and most scripts I directed clocked in at thirty-seven seconds. Which meant I spent most of the recording session trying to find ways to whittle it down without dismantling the idea, instead of spending it trying to record the best performances possible. So to help that problem, Pirate offered a virtual stopwatch. (See Fig. 25.)

Copywriters could download it to their computers, install it on their docks, and use it when working on a script. It offered three timing options—zero to 60/30/15 count-ups, and 60/30/15 to zero countdowns. The stopwatch also featured one more unusual button, labelled Tips. When you clicked it, the watch flipped around and a radio-writing tip would appear on the screen. Hundreds of writing tips from Pirate's radio seminars were loaded onto the stopwatch, so it was not only a way to time scripts but also a repository of advice and insights to draw on when writing. A small thing, but a handy thing that copywriters valued. And it was one more piece of shish on Pirate's kebab.

My wife and I recently donated money to a charity. About two weeks later, I got a call from the organization. Sensing it was a follow-up request to ask for more money, I started to blow them off, saying, "Look, I just gave to your charity a few weeks ago . . ." At that point the nice lady on the other end of the phone said, "We know you donated money, we're just calling you to say thank you." I stood there a little embarrassed, but a lot impressed. It was a small gesture, but I had never received a thank-you call from a charity before.

By the way, thank-you cards are almost solely the domain of women. Yet a handwritten thank-you note says so much, especially in this age of impersonal digital messaging. Not nearly enough thank-you notes are sent in business.

Yes, I'm looking at you, gentlemen.

Little touches can have an outsized impact on a company's revenues. In the homebuilding trade, some contractors understand that connection. One builder sends dozens of cardboard boxes to his customers just before they move into their new home. Just a small, helpful thing, to help them pack. Another homebuilder sends families a big pizza at the end of move-in day, knowing they will be exhausted and hungry. A tiny gesture, but one the family won't forget.

Typical word-of-mouth referral rates in the building trade hover around 8 percent. But builders who are obsessed with customer service experience rates of around 48 percent. Look at the range between those two numbers. Staggering. But not surprising.

When renowned actor John Neville was artistic director of the Neptune Theatre in Halifax, he made a point of giving free tickets to taxi drivers and their families. Cabbies, who are rarely shown much kindness, were immensely thankful, and would invariably talk up the plays to their passengers. As a result of that word of mouth, the theatre's operating deficit was soon gone and subscriptions doubled. Giving free tickets to cab drivers was a small act— but a powerful marketing idea. Even when you throw a small pebble into the lake, the water rises.

It's shocking how few businesses understand this. They see small gestures as beneath them, or unnecessary, or too costly. Our friend Laura recently bought a new Volkswagen and was excited to pick it up. When she got to the dealership, the car wasn't clean, paper sheets were still on the floor, and the keys were handed to her in a very mundane manner. It was a deflating experience. Later, she called the manager at the dealership and told him how disappointed she was with the experience; while he may be used to selling new cars every day, getting one was still a big deal to his customers. After she hung up, she told everyone at her office never to buy a Volkswagen from that dealership. The next day, a fellow worker bounced into the Laura's office with a big smile on her face. She had just bought a new Mitsubishi. The dealership had left a couple of new DVDs on the front seat for her kids and presented the keys to her along with a big bouquet of flowers. She was over the moon, and she couldn't say enough about that dealership.

Let's be conservative for a moment. Say, for example, that each of the twenty people in that office repeated those two stories to three other people. And let's say those sixty people passed the stories along to one more person each. In the blink of an eye, Mitsubishi got over a hundred rave reviews, and that Volkswagen dealership got more than a hundred bad reviews from a hundred people in its own neighbourhood.

By not going the extra inch, that VW dealership saved money, but spent loyalty.

A few years ago, my wife ordered a brand-new orange BMW Mini convertible. She was so excited to pick it up but had only seen it in the brochure. On the big day, she went to the dealership, met with the smiling salesman and was taken into a special room. The only object in the room was the new Mini. The salesman turned on the lights, and said, "Ta-da!"

It was a great way to reveal the car. Except it was red. Not orange.

My wife didn't know how to tell him, and when she did, the salesman was so apologetic. He fell over himself reordering the right colour pronto. But full marks for making the moment special. The worst thing a company can do is to be cavalier about a customer's business. Treat your customers with casual indifference for long enough and karma will whip its tail with surprising force. Success covers up many faults. When business is going well, companies become resistant to change. In other words, they become blind to their flaws. As Pixar president Ed Catmull wisely notes, success makes companies retreat and repeat. So if business is good, and the company is generating revenue while performing a minimal level of customer service, it will continue down that road. Until the economy hits a speed bump, that is, and the road turns into a cul-de-sac. Customers want to know they are valued. They need to feel their business is appreciated.

Just before the national Do Not Call List legislation went into effect, I received a telemarketing call from a bank asking if I would consider becoming a customer. Besides the interruption of my dinner, I had another problem with the call. I was already a customer of that bank. It's very revealing when that happens. It tells me the company doesn't do its homework. It tells me they don't really know me. It also tells me that in the great scheme of things, I don't really matter as a customer. The bank is so big it doesn't know who is a customer and who isn't.

Recently, I received a letter from a satellite TV company offering me a great offer to become a customer. That's great, except I'm already a customer. Besides that insult, they were offering a monthly rate that is better than the one I am currently paying. Cue the *Seinfeld* episode.

Companies complain they don't have enough revenue, they wince when their stock price dips, they complain the customer churn rate is too high, yet they don't make current clientele feel appreciated. They call us to pitch their services even though we are already customers. They mispronounce our names when they call. They offer better rates to non-customers. And they don't ever seem embarrassed by it.

The most listened-to episode of my radio show in 2012 was called "It's the Little Things," about how smart companies go the extra inch to make their customers feel appreciated. It's no wonder it was so popular and downloaded so often—people are starved for great service. They're even starved for *stories* of great service.

There's a dark joke inside the ad world that contains more than the usual kernel of truth. It's a fictitious slogan that gets quietly thrown around when an advertiser makes your eyes roll: *We're not happy until you're not happy.*

Who needs that kind of tension?

Chapter Thirteen

REID'S LAW
The Need for Tension

I n the mid-eighties, I worked with a famous photographer in Los Angeles named Reid Miles. Decades before, he gained fame as the designer of the iconic album covers for renowned jazz label Blue Note Records. Those covers are widely regarded as some of the best ever created. Reid shot many other famous album covers. He had a unique ability to add action to still photos, as the *Chicago IX: Greatest Hits* cover from 1975 demonstrates (See Figs. 26 and 27). He also did photography for advertising, including a shoot I did with him for DuPont carpets.

The late, great Reid Miles (he died in 1993) was a big personality with a matching voice. He reminded me a bit of comedian Rip Taylor; flamboyant and loud with a big, bushy moustache. He would pace around his studio swishing white wine in an oversized goblet, barking out instructions to his team. He completely art directed a photograph without touching a single prop on the set. As a matter of fact, he would take remarkable pictures without once touching the camera. He would tell his staff where he wanted the camera, would look through the lens and shout out his critique or praise of the framing, but he would never touch the equipment. When it came time to snap a photo, Reid would yell out "Hit me!" and his trusty assistant would push the button. In the course of watching Reid direct his staff to prepare for a shoot, he would constantly be in full "yell" mode. The air would be filled with a litany of "I hate that prop!" or "I said Egyptian blue, people. That's Persian blue!" or he would tell models "Do *not* smile. Hit me!"

On our way out to lunch one day, Reid's receptionist asked when we'd be returning. He looked back over his shoulder and said, "In an hour and a half. So you can start getting the shakies around two." I found that hilarious, and clearly Reid was very self-aware. He knew his presence created tension, hence his staff could start getting nervous about his return in about ninety minutes. Over lunch, I asked Reid why he constantly yelled at his (very impressive) staff. He said, "The absence of tension leads to contented oysters, but no pearls." When I got back to Toronto, I had that line boldly typeset and framed, with "Reid's Law" written under it in smaller type, and sent it to him. He loved it. (See Fig. 28.)

Reid's Law doesn't just apply to workplaces, it applies to brands. Brands need creative tension. Unbeaten Muhammad Ali became ten times more interesting when he suffered his first career loss to Joe Frazier. When invincible became vincible, fans leaned in. All the great brands in this world understand this principle.

A brand is not just a product. It's not just a logo. And it's not just a slogan. A brand is the sum total of a belief system. What a company believes, the guidelines it lives by, the goals it pursues, how it treats its customers, its philosophy behind pursuing business, the problem it was born to solve—those are the articles of faith that dictate how a company will behave. In other words, your brand is the collective intent of the people behind it, and the tension created between being profitable and being liked by your customers. The rest is art direction.

Competitors can copy your product, they can copy your prices, they can even copy your look, but they can *never* copy your culture. Culture cannot be mandated. In many ways, a brand is like a person. Think about the people you know and like. You make an evaluation based on how they treat you, how they treat other people, your history with them, their sense of humour, their warmth, their integrity, what you share in common and their capacity to give and take. There are even people in our lives who are difficult, but still worth the effort.

Same with a brand. Those same questions are posed, those same tensions exist and, to a large degree, the answers are clearly felt. If you're marketing an existing company, you have to take your company's temperature and make sure the brand on the inside is consistent with the brand on the outside. If there is a disconnect, it must be resolved. Always fix the internal workings first, then worry about the public face later. There is nothing more corrosive than a company doing rosy marketing while battling internal strife. That hemorrhaging will begin to seep through the fabric. If that's the case, it's time for cultural therapy. Heal the patient, then put on your marketing clothes.

On the other hand, if you're starting a new company, it's the perfect time to form and embed your cultural standards internally before expressing them externally. While getting a new business off the ground seems like a Herculean task, it is the time to begin as you mean to go on. Because no matter how big or small your company, every business has a culture. Your success will depend on the culture you create. Or in the case of an existing company, the kind of culture you nurture.

Nothing—repeat, nothing—is more important than your company culture. Is it a culture of money? Or is it a culture of creativity? Is it a culture of process, or a culture of ideas? Is it a customer-centric culture, or is it a share-price culture? Is it a culture of relationships, or is it a zone of transactions?

In other words, what do you stand for? The answer to that question should be something your customers care about. Ideally, it should be a battle you're fighting on their behalf. As we discussed earlier, Apple fights for your right to access computing power. Nike fights to get you off the couch. Airbnb fights the high cost of hotels.

So, what do you stand for?

If you have trouble answering that question quickly, you have a branding problem. If the answer to that question is self-serving, you have a big branding problem. If you have to pull the answer out of a drawer to remember, you have a massive branding problem.

In most shopping decisions, people choose to buy from people who are in the business for the love of it, as well as for the money. The order of that sentence is important. Steve Jobs often said that if you focus on profit, you will skimp on product. But if you focus on great products, profits will follow. Put another way, Deepak Chopra says, "If you chase the Goddess of Wisdom, the Goddess of Wealth will become jealous and pursue you." That is certainly true in my experience. The more Pirate focused on amassing knowledge that enhanced our product offering, the more revenue rolled in.

But again—Pirate's success was a sum of its parts. It wasn't just the directing capability, or the writing chops, or the eye for acting talent, or the passion for radio, or the five-star catering, or the beautiful studios or the creative radio seminars it hosted. That was the yeast that gave rise to the Pirate brand. As David Ogilvy once said, "It is almost always the total personality of the brand, rather than any trivial product difference, which decides the ultimate position in the market." Pirate didn't stand for any one of those things, but for the experience created by all of those things.

To put an even finer point on it, a recent survey by ad agency Young & Rubicam showed that brands are 200 percent more like other brands in their category than they were twenty years ago. So if the engineering and the nuts and the bolts are all pretty similar, the distinction rests in the intangibles. What your company stands for is vitally important, but it contains one dangerous tripwire—that stance often leads to parity positioning. In other words, dozens of companies claim to stand for "automotive excellence." Standing for "creative radio" is a tired declaration. Standing for "smart banking" is laughable.

To me, articulating what you stand for is but one side of the coin. The truly interesting question is on the other side: What do you stand against? The answer to that question is undoubtedly more intriguing, more revealing and ultimately more compelling, because it contains an interesting tension.

Think back to the famous Apple *1984* television commercial. It created such an impact because it positioned Apple for all time by clearly articulating what the company stood for: giving computing power to regular people. But what Apple stood *against* is what recruited such fierce loyalty. It railed against corporate overlords that hoarded power. That fight added dimension and colour and spunk. When Apple's warrior heaves that hammer at the giant screen and brings it crashing down in that *1984* ad, it wasn't just good filmmaking. It was a cherished hero story that resonates deeply in our subconscious—David and Goliath writ digitally. What Apple stands against has made it one of the most valuable companies in the world, more so than what it stands for. (And now, some thirty years later, Apple finds itself a Goliath. A strange upside of successfully battling giants.)

So when you are trying to build a new brand or recalibrating an existing one, ask yourself not only what your brand believes in, but what it doesn't. Listen for the echo of the founder's fist on the table. What you stand for will undoubtedly be admirable and laudable and in keeping with your product or service, but it will be largely unsurprising. It's hard to distinguish your company by just pinning your marketing on a category-wide virtue. I know that sounds like heresy, but it's true.

There's a reason most of the Ten Commandments are built around the word "not." "Thou shalt not covet thy neighbour's wife" is a lot more memorable than "Stay faithful." *Not* generates interesting tension.

By including what your brand stands against in the mix, your marketing suddenly takes on a more vivid texture. The heroes of fiction, from superheroes to gunfighters to detectives, all have one thing in common. They stand tall against a foe or an impossible situation. They rage against an injustice, an archenemy or world domination. Often they are the cavalry coming over the hill to the rescue of people they don't even know, inserting themselves into situations that require integrity and courage.

Now, all that may seem highfalutin for a brand, but it's not. The point here is that standing against something gives you more emotional resonance than standing for, say, safe city streets. That would have made Batman a pretty boring guy with pointy ears. Instead, he is a crime-fighting vigilante who dared to make a one-man stand against criminal masterminds. Standing against something brings the fight out in a brand, it adds grit to its personality, it rallies people. A fully dimensional brand with a clearly articulated for-and-against mission plants itself not only in customers' minds, but also in their hearts.

Back in the 1960s, Hall of Fame copywriter Ed McCabe wrote one of my favourite print ads, for a chain of cafeteria-style restaurants called Horn & Hardart. It showed a plate filled with interior decorating tchotchkes, arranged to look like food. The headline said it all: "You can't eat atmosphere." (See Fig. 29.)

It was clear what the chain stood against—overly fancy restaurants with bad food. Horn & Hardart could have gone the other way and waxed on about their good food. But we wouldn't be talking about that ad forty years later. It was the tension in that headline that still attracts attention. Its boldness made it impossible to ignore.

Like any interesting person, a brand can't feel like a one-note song. Politicians have always understood the power of tension. While they campaign on the issues they stand for, they also make hay from what they stand against, especially in rousing speeches and heated debates. "I will not stand idle while thousands of families live below the poverty line!" is a typical example of a cavalry statement. You may be skeptical of the authenticity in a particular politician, but the dual pro/con strategy is powerful. The strongest metals are forged in the hottest fires.

Stories need conflict. Actors need something to play against in order to express the truth of their characters. In *To Kill a Mockingbird*, Gregory Peck's character needed the bigotry of his small town to test his integrity. In *Zero Dark Thirty*, Jessica Chastain's character needs the dual tension of escalating terrorism on the ground and sexism in the ranks to reveal her guts and intelligence. Brands are no exception. Resistance reveals strengths of a company that smooth sailing cannot. The choices a company makes along its journey, especially the difficult ones, express its soul. The world watches and takes note.

It goes without saying that standing for nothing means it's easy to be negatively defined. Think Linens-N-Things—What did it stand for? Or dare I say General Motors—What does it stand for? And once the bailouts started, the public defined the auto giant as bloated and arrogant. If you won't define your brand, the world will happily do it for you. And you don't want that.

Your competitors will also define you. If their brand is fuzzy and vague and untended, your well-defined brand will shine twice as brightly. Conversely, if you have a worthy adversary with a sharply defined identity, the shade it throws will compel you to be stronger. For example, Nike's brilliant marketing drives Adidas to create powerful messaging, as it did with its "Impossible Is Nothing" campaign. Or think of the way Mercedes and BMW face off. A healthy category becomes like duelling banjos. If customers find the brands in a given category almost interchangeable, one of those brands is missing out on a huge opportunity to stand out. Most people think the top brands are all alike, so they don't do a lot of homework when choosing. They use intuition; they go on *feel*. When that happens, your efforts to convey what you stand for and against will kick in—or they won't.

As you can see, creating and nurturing a powerful brand requires an interesting alchemy. At the 2015 Cannes advertising festival, I went to hear shock-rocker Marilyn Manson speak. He was there to talk about his brand and how he navigates his dark ship through the shoals of pop culture. Beneath all the gothic imagery is an Ohio boy named Brian Warner, but he created his stage name based on tension—the beauty of Marilyn Monroe juxtaposed with the dread of Charles Manson. Two sides of a coin.

He was an articulate speaker, very intelligent and appealingly forthright. While analyzing his success, he offered up a fascinating insight. He said it was critical "not to empty the mystery bucket." Manson believed that holding something back was powerful marketing. If some questions were left unanswered, it would keep fans intrigued. It was an astute observation in an era where social media focuses on celebrity 25/8, where celebrities post their every move and tweet breathless thoughts to fans, and reality shows set up cameras in their homes. Manson was alluding to the Kim Kardashians of the world (Kardashian spoke the day before at the same event).

That rule also applies to brands. There should be a little magic held back. We marvel at Apple's products, but we really don't know how they build them. Look at your iPhone—Where are the screws? We're fascinated by Elon Musk's Tesla electric cars that are, for the first time, sexy *and* fast, but we don't really understand how he inspires his company to achieve what others have failed to do. We watch in awe as aging tennis star Roger Federer stays on top of a sport that demands youth, yet we don't fully grasp how he summons his finesse. I once read a comment from a sex therapist who maintains it is essential for every marriage to contain some mystery. If there's nothing left to hide, there is nothing left to seek.

I understand that concept fully in storytelling. I've always believed it is imperative to leave the circle broken. Let readers fill in strategic blanks, because people love to figure things out. In *The Godfather: Part II*, when Michael Corleone suddenly realizes his brother Fredo has lied to him in Cuba, it's just a fleeting moment that runs across Michael's face. But because it's left to the audience to figure out what just happened, the need to add two plus two gives the moment incredible tension.

Telling a compelling story that is rooted in your product is the most persuasive way of converting potential customers into paying customers. I learned that lesson early in my career from one of the most respected creative directors in the business—Hal Riney. He never strayed from the product in his storytelling. Every ad, every campaign came right out of the product. He never did a funny unrelated bit and then circled back to the product in the announcer section. He never told a joke and then tried to link it to the product. Riney didn't have to, because he found the actual product endlessly interesting. Bartles & Jaymes wine coolers, Henry Weinhard's Beer, Saturn cars, President Ronald Reagan's election advertising ("There's a bear in the woods . . ."). Every message came right out of the product. No exceptions. Riney's unwavering belief that every product had a story worth telling had a profound impact on me. He taught me to never use borrowed interest, to never use a weak bridge moment that begins with "On the other hand . . . ," to never veer away on a creative tangent then circle back to the product. Tell a story *about* the product.

At the core of every great story, the element that makes the story great is the aha moment. That's the moment a listener or a reader scratches their head and says, "What? I don't get it. I really don't . . . wait . . . *aha* . . . I got it!" In order to have an aha moment in your messages, the story can't be fully told. There has to be a small gap in the storytelling, a small bit of tension rooted in uncertainty. A break in the circle that listeners have to fill in themselves. It can't be so big as to create a gaping hole, and it can't be so small as to be insignificant. A great ad tells the viewer a story, takes them on a journey, then just near the end, the writer stops writing. A tiny, important piece of information is held back. But when readers get to that gap, they find themselves saying "What? . . . *aha!*"

When an audience is given a series of clues and sequential pieces of information that don't seem to fully add up, then suddenly it all clicks, that moment creates enormous impact. Stories with a perfectly situated tension/release moment resonate long after the ad has played out. That's why good writers leave breadcrumbs for their audience, letting them participate in the storytelling.

The same holds true for brands. While championing what your brand stands for, and digging your heels in for what you oppose, don't throw all the doors and windows wide open. Thankfully, a great deal of your appeal will be those intangibles we spoke of earlier. Much of your brand's value will be found in the soft assets, the assets your accountant can't understand. This is the magic. Steve Jobs was famous for protecting that magic. When a website leaked details about a top-secret Apple project, Jobs slammed the site with a lawsuit. He wasn't that interested in punishing the website, he was sending a message to his troops. He wanted them to know he demanded discretion. That's why there are no bloggers at Apple.

That means while you're creating or nurturing your brand by stating explicitly what you stand for and against, you still want to hold back the magic and the unique cultural aspects of your company. Your customers know the magic is there, they reap the benefit of that magic, but it is not fully revealed. So your customers remain intrigued and want to continue seeking.

At Pirate, the magic was in our taste, and our slavish dedication to the minutiae of radio. We were obsessed with analyzing it, breaking it down. At our seminars, we would give away seven hours of tips and insights. But the real magic—the writing and directing buckets—were never emptied. Maybe part of the reason was that they couldn't be emptied. How does one fully articulate the creative process? How do you tell someone how to get the best performance out of an actor when every actor requires a slightly different type of direction? But Pirate definitely had a magic, and people wanted to rub up against it.

In some ways, it's easier to protect the magic in a service business. The magic is contained in the people, in the hiring standards, in the shared culture. You're selling a unique ability, not a widget. When your business is selling widgets, the magic is found in the widget. When Sony co-founder Akio Morita first gave a Walkman to Steve Jobs, Jobs immediately took it apart to see how it worked. And we all know how that story ended. As Richard Branson says, all airlines start with the same equipment. What differs is the thinking, the zigging, the distinct cultures and standards.

All production companies own recording studios. As a matter of fact, I was always amazed when I travelled to studios in other cities or countries and discovered not only the same type of equipment in every studio but that we all used the identical brands. What separated Pirate from the herd was our culture. That culture was built on high standards, dictated by what we stood for and against. We stood for highly surprising radio, but what we stood against was the low esteem radio was traditionally given within the advertising industry. Radio was seen as TV's ugly sister. Neither clients nor copywriters got excited about radio. Radio was almost always recorded in small, bunker-like studios in basements. Radio was always given to the juniors or the unlucky, because it wasn't sexy enough for the senior creative teams. When I announced to my ad agency friends that I was going out on my own to start a radio production company, a very senior vice president pulled me aside and said, "You can't make money doing radio."

I completely disagreed with that. I knew in my heart that radio was the most freeing of all media for creative people. I knew that radio could be exciting, that you could hire even Hollywood actors for voiceover work at surprisingly reasonable rates, and that studios could be amazing creative spaces, not bunkers. Because of the degree of difficulty required to create award-winning radio commercials, I knew good radio could make a writer's career. Pirate stood for that standard of radio, while rebelling against the prevailing idea that radio was the boring rung on the bottom of the advertising ladder. That was the tension we used to our advantage.

When we started winning dozens of awards, the award shows would list us as "producers." We railed against that, too. We were "directors," just like film directors, except our medium was sound. We pushed hard on that, upsetting a lot of entrenched apple carts, but we wanted to elevate radio. Eventually we succeeded. To this day, radio award show credits list "directors" instead of producers.

Ten years after Pirate opened its doors, I read an interview with the founder of a new, competing audio production company. He was asked why he had chosen to start a commercial radio firm. He replied, "Because Pirate does 80 percent of the radio in this country, and that's just not right."

But it was understandable. Our brand was irresistible. We offered a high level of creativity, and did it while leveraging the tension between what we stood for and what we stood against. It was our *why*; it mattered to the people at Pirate.

There is one more place where tension is critical: deadlines. Creativity loves constraint, and the constraint of a deadline fuels creativity. Whenever I had two weeks to develop a campaign, I wouldn't really roll my sleeves up until about three or four days from the deadline. I noticed the same thing with our Pirate writers. I'd ask them how the campaign was going, say, ten days out, and they'd give me a casual "fine." I knew by the tone of their voices they hadn't started yet. Then about three days from the deadline, I would see them in their offices with the doors closed crunching it out. It was almost a self-imposed tension. Experience taught me that the tension of a deadline seems to unlock neural pathways, and the heat it forces on you sparks interesting connections. It's like suddenly going from regular gasoline to premium. Your brain burns more efficiently. Knowing this, I would impose tight deadlines when the job required a high degree of creativity. If the team presented work I wasn't happy with yet, nothing got results better than saying, "I want to see new ideas by noon tomorrow."

The lesson here is to use tight deadlines to your advantage. If you task a team in your office to generate creative ideas, give them a tight deadline. Not an impossible one, but a strict one. It's like the heightened playmaking in overtime hockey or a sudden contract agreement in a union dispute as the strike deadline approaches. In the world of creative problem solving, tension is your friend.

So keep those oysters on a short leash. Even when you're the oyster.

Chapter Fourteen

KEEPING YOUR SHISH ON YOUR KEBAB
Maintaining Your Personal Brand

Georges St-Pierre is a UFC fighter in a class by himself. He has an effortlessness in a world where most men grunt and strive and scream. But when St-Pierre wanted to attract lucrative endorsement contracts from advertisers, he grunted, strived and screamed.

To most marketers, the UFC was a blood sport. Too violent to associate with their products. Too male-centric. So St-Pierre hired advertising agency Sid Lee to help him cultivate his brand. Sid Lee's team had never branded a "person" before. Like most agencies, they worked with products and corporations. But they accepted the challenge and started with research. Results showed St-Pierre rated high in trust and toughness. Men admired his grit. Women found him sexy. With that, Sid Lee got to work.

The first task was to increase St-Pierre's fan base with quantifiable numbers that would attract bigger advertisers. When he suffered a knee injury, St-Pierre took the forced downtime as an opportunity to engage his fans. Sid Lee helped him refine his social media accounts so that the image he projected was consistent.

St-Pierre brought fans into his recovery process. He posted a series of videos on his Facebook page that showed him working through physical therapy. He had ongoing conversations with fans on Twitter. He gave updates on his progress. As a result, his Facebook fan base doubled to three million and his Twitter followers tripled to over 450,000.

But the biggest thing St-Pierre's ad agency did was to position him to advertisers—not as a violent cage fighter, but as an elite athlete. With that specific brand positioning, with a consistent message moving across all his social media accounts, and with a deep understanding of his audience, St-Pierre's endorsement deals doubled in fourteen months. And importantly, he was getting paid more for them. Georges St-Pierre had, in effect, borrowed the marketing techniques of big brands and changed his fortunes.

These days, everyone is a brand. Don't be offended by that— here's what I mean: You are unique, you have a skill set to offer the world, friends and employers have an opinion about you. You have a reputation.

That is the general definition of a brand. But smart brands know exactly who they are. One of the first things I tell clients is to review every single touch-point they have with customers. Make sure there is a consistency at every intersection. That every aspect of a company is professional, and that it accurately reflects the identity of the organization. Make sure there are no gaping holes.

Back to my shish kebab theory. A company has a multitude of communication points: a website, a Facebook page, a Twitter account, mainstream advertising, business cards, a storefront, signage, customer service, even on-hold messages. Each different, each with a unique function. All held together by the skewer of a consistent tone of voice.

The same rule applies to your personal brand. In our day, there are a lot of ways to project yourself to the world. You have a resumé, a website, you're on Facebook, Twitter and Instagram, you write blogs, you post items online, and so on. Those are the tasty items on your personal shish kebab. So let's borrow the lessons from big brands and apply them to you. First, let's see if your skewer is firmly in place.

If you're looking to market your personal services, a resumé is a good starting place to explore your personal brand. An estimated 90 percent of companies will only accept resumés online. Therefore, your e-mail address is usually the first thing prospective employers see from you. Your e-mail address is a form of marketing. It is a first impression. And it has an outsized impact on your chances of landing an interview or a meeting. So partybunny@hotmail.com is not a good idea. Neither is zombieslayer@gmail.com. If you are trying to market yourself, your e-mail should look and sound professional. Most hiring managers won't even look at a resumé if it comes attached to a novelty e-mail address.

In a study done in Amsterdam, seventy-three recruiters were shown six resumés, with similar credentials and experience levels. With everything else being equal, the ones with cutesy e-mail addresses were consistently rated lower—even though the resumé content was nearly identical. When recruiters are going through hundreds of resumés, the appropriateness of an e-mail address is a first-stage screening tool. Quirky e-mail addresses make people appear unprofessional, chipping away at their credibility.

One more tip: HR managers and recruiters don't like to see a resumé from a work-related address. It suggests you're looking for a job on another company's time. It's in bad taste. It makes hiring managers wonder if you might do the same thing to them. Use a personal e-mail address when job seeking. Learn from the big brands. Always be consistently professional.

A smart resumé is like a smart advertising campaign. It should be created with four questions in mind:

1. Who is your target audience?
2. What is your unique selling proposition?
3. How do you want your audience to feel?
4. What's the call to action?

Question one is critical: *Who is your target audience?* In order to impress your target audience, you have to know who your resumé is aimed at. Do your research. What specifically do hiring managers in your industry want to see? What characteristics do they share in common? What moves them? Your resumé will never be relevant if you don't know your target audience intimately.

When copywriters are being briefed on a new advertising campaign, more than half of that briefing consists of analyzing and understanding the target market. When Trevor Goodgoll did his brown paper exercise, exploring a marketing strategy on the agency walls, this is what he was drilling down to. Who are they? What is the demographic in terms of age, sex and income? What are the psychographic traits, their values, opinions, attitudes and lifestyles? What TV shows do they watch? What problem are they looking to solve? What are the obstacles between you and them?

This I know: Understanding your target audience is paramount. You want to tailor your resumé to this particular group, and you can't be relevant if you don't know them. Furthermore, you should be tailoring your resumé to each company. Never send out generic resumés. If you're talking to everyone, you're talking to no one.

Question two: *What is your unique selling proposition?* Put another way, what unique skills or life experiences do you bring to a company? This question is the heart of all advertising campaigns. Every effective advertisement pivots on the unique selling proposition— or USP—of a product. Every smart commercial is built around the main feature of the product. Why is this important? Because the

USP tells customers why they should care. It tells them why they should buy the product over all others.

It's the same with your resumé. Why should a company buy you over all the other applicants? Spend time on this. An American Express survey showed that 65 percent of managers are looking to hire people with specific experience, yet most people position themselves as generalists. Be specific. This should be the heart of your resumé. What makes you stand out over all your peers? If you were to write, "I do my best work between 6–8 a.m. before anyone gets into the office," your resumé is sitting pretty at the top of the pile. If you list your online gaming experience leading warrior clans as "leadership experience"—as one applicant to a technology company did on his resumé —it's headed into the big round file under the desk.

Question three: *How do you want your target audience to feel after they've read your resumé?* This is sophisticated marketing at its best. It's what separates smart brands from everyone else. It's not enough to merely list credentials and experience, just like it's not enough to list product benefits in an ad. As we discussed in chapter four, persuasive communication needs emotion. You don't want a hiring manager (or a client) to just comprehend your credentials, you want them to feel completely intrigued by your resumé. Enough to put you at the top of the list—and call for an interview. That means the language you choose is important. The tone you strike is critical. The readability of your resumé and the way it's organized should make people feel there is an interesting mind at work.

As a copywriter, I can tell you that smart writers sweat over the words they choose. Most resumés contain overused buzzwords: Creative. Effective. Motivated. Analytical. Innovative. Team player.

Those skills are important. But don't just say them, *demonstrate* them in your resumé and cover letter. Show, don't tell. That's the first rule of advertising. Your cover letter is the place where you have the biggest opportunity to showcase your personality. Clearly, there is a fine line between a compelling cover letter and an inappropriate one. The goal is to capture a snapshot of your personality while remaining professional. Ideally, it's a single page, so brevity is part of the charm. It's also the challenge. In a few paragraphs, you want to introduce yourself and intrigue the reader enough to drive them to your resumé. The letter should demonstrate that you are interesting, creative and highly motivated, without ever using those words. It shouldn't feel like a form letter or an overly stiff business memorandum. It should be a conversational letter from one person to another.

That means, if possible, it should ideally be addressed to a specific person. Maybe you saw them speak at a conference, or you read their blog, or maybe you have something else in common that you can reference. If the resumé has to be addressed to the HR department, you should still be real, be smart and be interesting. Ask yourself how you want the reader to *feel* after they've finished reading your letter. Then reverse-engineer the content.

Finally, question four: *What's the call to action?* Every effective advertisement asks for the sale. Call us for details, log on to our website, visit our store, reach for us in the dairy section. It is a critical element of marketing, so take that lesson to heart. It's surprising how many applicants never formally ask for the job. Even in business, asking for the sale is important. When I would meet with prospective clients, I would always make a point to say, "How can we do business together?" That sentence has led to a remarkable amount of revenue. Therefore, in your resumé, tell the company you want the job and suggest a next step. It could be as simple as, "I really want this job. What else can I do to convince you?" Or "Contact me if you want to talk Beatles, hockey or improving your marketing program."

Nice, personal and to the point.

Speaking of asking a prospective employer to contact you for an interview, make sure your voicemail is professional. It shouldn't be a silly, trying-to-be-funny message. It shouldn't be one of those overly long, impersonal prerecorded messages that phone companies provide. It goes without saying there should be an outgoing voicemail message if you are unavailable. A call from a prospective employer should never be picked up by a third party, like a roommate. Your voicemail should be *your* voice. With a short, professional and pleasant outgoing message saying you will call them back promptly. Think of the kind of message you would expect to hear if you called a smart company.

Let's talk profile pictures. In advertising, this would be the equivalent of a product shot. Visually, a photograph of the product is the most important part of a print ad or a commercial. More time and care is put into a product shot than any into other aspect of an advertisement, which is why it's referred to as the "beauty shot." Often, it's the only part of a commercial shoot the client shows up for. It's not unusual to look at the shooting schedule for a TV commercial, and see that it specifies one day to film the storyline with the actors and another day just for the product shot. Many photographers specialize in static product shots. There are car shooters, and food specialists and fashion pros. Marketers know nothing fuels purchase desire more than a beautiful photograph of the product.

The same applies to your profile picture, whether it's on a resumé or your company website. Face perception is one of the most highly developed skills in humans. Nature has taught us to make snap decisions in order to survive. In a mere hundred milliseconds, faces influence how we judge trustworthiness, enthusiasm, competence and danger. To begin with, it's paramount to *have* a profile photo. You are seven times more likely to be considered for a job if you have one. It's like selling a house. If there's no photo in the listing, you wonder what's wrong.

Many people choose scenery, pet pics, kooky photos or Twitter's default "egg" profile shots. All fine, as long as you're not hoping to look professional.

First rule: Choose a photo of your face. Second rule: Choose a photo of your face that actually looks like your face.

Don't laugh. Many people choose doctored photos, or favourite photos from when they were younger. One of the truisms in marketing is that you don't want to promise one thing, then deliver another. That bait and switch has led to the nagging cynicism that has infected marketing for years. If people see a smiling twenty-nine-year-old in a profile pic, and a smiling thirty-nine-year-old walks in for an interview, it ain't good. Everything about your resumé should be current, including photos. Some studies suggest that over 90 percent of recruiters use social media to screen candidates. And they spend a fifth of their time looking at profile photos and making snap judgments.

By the way, if you're unsure of the best photo to use, there is a website that will rate your profile shot. It's called PhotoFeeler. com. In partnership with Princeton University, the site helps you test profile photos. Once you're signed in, you simply upload your profile shot. Next, the site asks you to rate ten other profile photos. Then people, in return, rate your picture. Your photo is judged in three categories: Competence. Likeability. And influence.

I submitted my photo—the one on our cbc.ca/undertheinfluence website. The results were as follows: Competent, 77 percent; likable, 19 percent; influential, 95 percent.

I had to laugh. Then cry uncontrollably. Guess I'll be changing that photo. PhotoFeeler is a good disaster check. If one of the results is underperforming in a big way, like say, 19 percent, you may want to reconsider the photo. PhotoFeeler is collecting a lot of interesting feedback when it comes to photographs. For example, it surveyed sixty thousand ratings of eight hundred profile photos and suggests the following rules:

No sunglasses.

No selfies. (Get a professional photo.)

Smile. If your teeth are visible when you smile, even better.

Slightly squinch your eyes in a smiling way. Wide-open eyes suggest fear or sociopathy.

Head and shoulders are better than face only.

Dress for the job you want.

No vacation pics.

No photos with celebrities, it diminishes you.

And keep your head upright and straight. Apparently women, in particular, tend to tilt their heads in photos, which can make you look less self-assured. Remember, it only takes milliseconds of looking at a photo for someone to draw conclusions about who you are.

Now let's talk social media behaviour.

First of all, being *absent* from all social media sends up a red flag to potential employers. Nowadays, not being present on any kind of social media could be interpreted in the following ways:

1. You lack tech savvy.
   You're so out of touch that you're a liability.
2. You have nothing to offer.
   You are two-dimensional and uninteresting.
3. Or you've just done a panic delete.
   What exactly are you hiding?

Thirty-four percent of employers admit to checking their own employee's social media profiles, and that's just the percentage who admit it. Let's be realistic, if a recruiter is interested in your resumé, they've also googled you. And if you don't exist online anywhere, it raises more questions than it answers.

Yellow flags include use of profanity and too many questionable party pics. So google your image and see what pops up. When I did that a few years ago, I was a tad alarmed at what appeared. Then I realized there is another Terry O'Reilly who is an erotic novel writer.

Employers and clients judge self-monitoring. They want to see what *you* deem as acceptable public behaviour. You can do whatever you want on your social media. But know there are implications. Especially if you are advertising your services to potential clients or employers. As David Ogilvy once said, "Always give your product a first class ticket through life."

In the world of marketing, brands maintain a consistent image across many different media. That means messages have become all-terrain vehicles. While the formats and media may change, the tone, the content and the imagery remain professional, and— remember the shish kebab—should feel like it is all coming from the same place. Look at all your social media. Look at your website. Does it feel professional? Are you projecting a consistent identity across all your accounts? Are you tweeting interesting information? Are your blog posts smart and compelling? Do they spring from your experience? your skill set? your curiosity? Are they related to your industry?

Remember, social media is the first interview. As a matter of fact, employers consider social media to be an unfiltered look at you. Meaning it's more revealing than a job interview where you know you're being observed. As Jay Leno says, even Charles Manson can be on his best behaviour for a ten-minute job interview. Be smart and use your privacy settings, separating your personal life from your business life. But remember that anything said privately can become public in a heartbeat. All it takes is a quick screen capture shared with the world.

Big brands are exceptionally careful with their content. So be mindful of yours. With that, here are a few chilling stats to ponder:

Fifty-four percent of resumés are loaded with grammatical errors.

Thirty-three percent of people badmouth a former employer, a current boss or a fellow worker on social media.

Twenty percent post derogatory statements about certain groups, genders, races or religions.

Twenty-four percent lie about their qualifications. In a digitally connected world, it doesn't take prospective employers long to connect the dots. Or find the missing ones. A survey by Microsoft found that 70 percent of companies looking to hire someone say they found content online that caused them *not* to hire that candidate. Read that number again: 70 percent.

What you say online matters.

The messages you post are loaded with clues that prospective employers or clients can interpret in a number of ways. So be smart: tend to your brand every day. As marketer Seth Godin says: "Overload Google with a long tail of good stuff and always act like you're on *Candid Camera*." Because you are.

Selling yourself may be the most important campaign you ever undertake. In the good old days, it was a mailed resumé and a job interview. These days, while you're researching companies, companies are researching you. The digital world gives us many doors to knock on, but it also gives the world access to our many windows. So projecting a professional image is critical. Even if you're not actively looking for a job, making sure your personal brand reflects well on you and your company is always important.

Borrow a page from smart marketers; differentiate yourself first and foremost. Be interesting, be real and let your unique personality shine through. Your photo shouldn't matter, but it does. Don't send up any red or yellow flags. While too much filtering can feel inauthentic, you can still be fun; just be willing to stand behind what you post online. When in doubt, use restraint.

And this I know: Take care of your shish kebab.

Chapter Fifteen

THIS I KNOW

In my career, I've been privileged to work with the smartest marketers. The most creative writers and art directors. The wisest creative directors. The most gifted actors. And quite a few legendary communicators. In over thirty-five years of being an adman, I've created thousands of ads for the biggest brands in the country, and have been in countless high-level presentations. As a result of watching and listening intently, I've learned a lot. I've also made more than my fair share of mistakes along the way and learned the hard way that mistakes are the greatest teachers. Their sting ensures lessons are never forgotten.

THIS I KNOW:
Marketing is theatre.
In an era when people are exposed to over three thousand advertising messages a day, only the bold break through. I have seen, time and again, how ideas need to be fresh and why they need to be wrapped in the most surprising packages possible. We live in an attention economy. Marketing has to compete with entertainment, time-starved attention spans, ad-blocking software, remote

control skip buttons and general indifference. A car commercial isn't just competing with other car commercials, it's competing with all other commercials.

Look at the best marketers like WestJet, Coke, Apple and Nike; they never just market information. They create advertising theatre. Like WestJet's Christmas videos, or Coke's happiness vending machines, or Apple's Mac versus PC series, or anything Nike has ever done. Not a boring, eye-rolling commercial in the batch. And while a few of them are epic productions, most are incredibly simple ideas.

THIS I KNOW:
Don't whisper a dozen things, say one thing loudly.
The only effective marketing messages are single-minded. This circles back to the elevator pitch. A brand should have an elevator pitch, and so, too, should a commercial or an ad. If a commercial idea can't be summed up in one line, it's not ready to be a commercial yet. Sell one thing well per advertisement. In all my years in advertising, I have to say this is the biggest obstacle to great advertising. As I mentioned earlier, I lay most of the blame at the feet of advertisers, not their agencies. I've sat in endless meetings and recording sessions where clients overrule their agencies on this issue. Instead of selling one thing well, too many clients want to stuff ten pounds of potatoes into a five-pound bag. But in this cluttered marketing world, only an archer with a single-minded arrow pierces the apple. It's a funny thing. Advertisers create cluttered commercials, send them out into the clutter of the marketing world, then wonder why they don't really work. But as the top creative boss at Ogilvy & Mather recently said, "There's no shortage of brains in the industry. It's the vertebral column that tends to be missing."

Advertising agencies have to display more backbone when it comes to standing firm on single-minded messaging. They are being paid to be advertising experts, yet they often fold quickly when the five-pound potato bag starts straining at the seams. The best thing a creative director can do for a client is to fight for single-minded messages. It is the sign of a professional. I know the push-back from clients is brutal on this issue. But it's the only way the advertising is going to work.

Even at the highest levels of the advertising industry, this issue rages. Therefore, if you have no ad agency, you have to do your own policing. So promise me every advertisement you create will sell one benefit only. If you have five important benefits to talk about, that's five different ads. Anything less renders your marketing invisible.

THIS I KNOW:
Small brands need a big personality.
A small company can't compete directly with a larger company's budget, so take the fight to a different battlefield. I once wrote a radio commercial for the Art Gallery of Ontario. It was having a Matisse exhibit. It had a small budget but needed immediate attention for a time-limited exhibit. So I asked the AGO to send over slides of the Matisse paintings that would be on display. I was searching for inspiration. While perusing the slides, something occurred to me. Matisse was a master of colour and light, but you would never know it from his titles. So I wrote this radio commercial, which was read by a deep-voiced, eloquent British actor:

```
Large Cliff—Fish.
Woman in Striped Pullover, Violin on the Table.
Head of a Woman with Veil.
```

```
Head with Necklace.
Small Head with Comb.
Henri Matisse created some of the most cheerful
    and colourful art of the century.
He just sucked at titles.
The incredible Matisse Exhibit on now at the
    Art Gallery of Ontario. Don't miss it.
```

That commercial got a lot of attention, because it was surprising language coming from the AGO. The marketing folks at the gallery knew they needed to break through the clutter, and waxing poetic about the exhibit would appeal only to art aficionados. In order to be a success, they had to attract the general public, too. The Matisse exhibit was a success. Even though the Art Gallery had a tiny budget, it had a big, bold personality.

THIS I KNOW:
Radio is still powerful.

People always ask me if radio is on life-support. Radio is the ultimate survivor. It has endured movies, television, VCRs, DVRs, the Internet and social media. By the way, in the last five years, CBC Radio has had the best ratings in its eighty-year history. Radio is intimate. It is a human voice whispering in your ear. Most people listen to radio alone. It's not like TV, where the family settles in for an evening of entertainment. It's a solo activity. It's personal. That lesson was brought home to me while I was on a book tour a few years ago. When I met listeners of my radio show, they would immediately touch me when we met. They would grab my arm, hold my elbow, or not let go after we finished shaking hands. It was unnerving at first, but then I realized something. They were doing that because they felt a connection with me. We had a "relationship." We had spent a lot of time together. Think about the last time the host of your favourite morning radio show left the program. It's a jolt to the system. You feel off-balance. Your daily ritual is rocked. And it takes a lot of time to get used to the new host.

In other words, it's important.

Every year, CBC stages a fan event where people can come and meet their favourite radio and television hosts. I find the dynamics very interesting. In the presence of TV personalities, people stand back. There is some awe at work. There is an implied "distance" with television. A divide. But not so with radio. People would touch me for three hours straight. And I learned to welcome it. People feel they know you on radio. You're a friend. Without a doubt, that is radio's great power. It is the most personal medium of all.

That said, I had an uncomfortable moment with Bob Newhart once that involved both radio and television. It's the exception that proves the rule. I had directed Bob in about thirty radio commercials for Bell Mobility. The campaign idea was based on one-way telephone conversations, which was perfect for Bob, as he has a hilarious history of performing one-way phone conversations in his comedy routines. But when we recorded those commercials, Bob was in Los Angeles, and I was in Toronto. We recorded the sessions via a fibre-optic link between the two studios. We were never in the same room together, but we could hear each other with studio quality.

Bob and I had a routine where we would get on the phone a few days before the sessions to discuss the scripts. In one of those calls, he mentioned he was performing in Toronto soon, and offered a pair of tickets for my wife and me to attend his show. We happily accepted, and after that performance, his assistant invited us back to the green room to say hello. When we walked in, there was the famous Bob Newhart. There was the comedian I had watched on television for so many years. Plus, we had worked together on thirty radio commercials, so when we met, I gave Bob a hug.

He reacted in a low-key, stiff, eye-darting way. Easy to picture, if you know Bob's work.

See, Bob had spent hundreds of hours in my living room over the years. But I had spent zero in his. Those years made me feel like we had a relationship. While we had worked together over the course of a year, he had never laid eyes on me before. It was a funny moment in hindsight. Television personalities are not comfortable with huggers. They are used to respectable distances.

Here's the lesson: That distance disappears in radio. The gap closes. That is the magical, wonderful key to radio advertising. Remember that it's intimate, remember you're talking to one person, remember there's no need to shout. That's what makes it such a powerful medium.

THIS I KNOW:

Humour is the WD-40 of advertising.

All advertising is an interruption. But humour can open a lot of sticky doors. Using humour is a welcome way to make that intrusion polite and entertaining, and take the harsh creak out of the moment. Humour gives viewers a smile in return for spending the time, and hopefully the warmth of the moment will rub off on the brand. Humour also shows that an advertiser doesn't take itself too seriously. As the great commercial director Joe Sedelmaier once said, most ad people think they're creating *Birth of a Nation*, when in reality they're selling Jell-O.

THIS I KNOW:

Silence is powerful.

Bob Newhart was a master at making the smallest moment in a script the funniest moment. I always loved using short pauses for dramatic or humorous effect, but Bob taught me not to be afraid of *big* silence, that the courage of using a looooong pause pays off. I took that lesson to the limit in a commercial I wrote for organ donation. As I mentioned earlier, organ donation is an interesting challenge. As you may know, even if you've signed your organ donor card and registered as a donor online, your family can still override your wishes at the last moment. The problem is, most families don't know what your organ donor wishes are. In the small window available to harvest organs, you can't speak for yourself. And your family is in trauma. The doctor will ask your family for permission, and because they don't know your wishes, they usually offer up a grief-stricken no. So the important thing to impart in this commercial was that you have to tell your family you want to be an organ donor. Once they know, the chances are much greater that your wish will be honoured.

Unlike most public service announcements, I wasn't asking people to volunteer, I wasn't asking for money, and I wasn't even asking people to register as donors. I was asking them to make their wishes known to their family. The script I eventually wrote began by thanking people for signing their organ donor card. Then the voiceover said:

"But did you know it's still your family that makes the ultimate decision? That's why you have to discuss it with them. So, if you're listening to this right now—with someone in your family—look at them and say, 'I want to be an organ donor.' We'll wait a moment while you do that."

What followed was six seconds of silence.

Then the voiceover concluded by saying, "There, it's done. Thank you." I wanted listeners to act *during* the commercial. I couldn't count on listeners to talk to their families later that night, or the next day or the next week. Life gets in the way of good intentions. I needed them to act then and there. I wanted to make it awkward for someone to sit beside a loved one in a car and not say *anything* during that silence.

Every radio station in the country refused to air the spot. Why? What do radio stations hate most of all? Silence.

To try and save the commercial, I personally called the presidents of the half-dozen national radio networks in this country and took them through the idea. I explained why the issue was so pressing—Canada has one of the worst organ donation rates in the world—and that the silence was the trigger. In the end, they all agreed to run the commercial. That was seventeen years ago. The commercial still runs every April during Organ Donation Month, and many people have come up to me to say they had the conversation with their family because of that message.

But it would never have worked were it not for the roaring silence.

THIS I KNOW:

Creativity is an amplifier.

Advertising can't just be hard information. It doesn't have to be humorous, but it must provoke an emotion. Straight information rarely does that. Effective advertising should be interesting, provocative and surprising. Not blunt, boring and rude. An advertisement without a creative idea is like giving a speech to a hundred thousand people without a microphone. Creativity gets attention. Creativity amplifies the message. If we advertisers are going to take up real estate on radio, TV, posters, print pages and online, we must be a good host to people's attention spans. Hard-sell information is just clutter that begs to be skipped.

This is why the advertising industry has to take the blame for the growing issue of ad-blocking. Browsers now contain technology that will filter pop-up ads when accessing a website, or will disable Flash technology so autoplay video ads are blocked. Watch an evening of television between 8 and 11 p.m., and you will see roughly seventy commercials. Maybe two of them are any good. That's a lousy batting average. Plus, advertising is a frequency game. We need the public to see or hear our messages many times before they make a dent in people's awareness. People will only sit through a commercial a dozen times if it is really good. And smart. And entertaining. That's why advertisers need to up their creative game.

THIS I KNOW:
Good advertising should not look like a line of identical
bread loafs coming out of an oven.

Branding is an exercise in consistency. Creativity is not. I say this because many in marketing worship at the altar of consistency. As you know by now, I'm a fan of consistency when it comes to a brand image, but with one big caveat: Every ad in an advertising campaign should be surprising and different. Every piece of communication should feel new and fresh, while the entire campaign is held together by a consistent tone of voice and a consistent communication strategy.

Shish. Kebab.

Nike is a great example of this. No two commercials look alike, but they are all anchored by Nike's "Just Do It" attitude, which never changes. You know it's a Nike ad within seconds, yet no Nike ad looks the same. Every ad is a compelling story, and those stories are both big and small. Dan Wieden, the creative director of

Nike's ad agency, says, "Nike wants us to constantly surprise and amaze them." In my three decades in the biz, I think I had, maybe, three clients say that to me. That's why Nike's work is so effective. It breaks through. And that's why Nike has a 60 percent market share in athletic footwear.

THIS I KNOW:
Do not assign a creative task to a committee.

I'm with adman George Lois on this one. Large groups are okay if you're Amish and building a barn. Creativity is a small-team pursuit. Charge a small group of two or three smart people to solve a problem. Creativity should never be clouded by the politics of groups, drowned out by a cacophony of voices or smothered by agendas. Big groups are excellent at implementing a creative idea. Big groups will carry an idea far. They're just not good at coming up with one. As writer G.K. Chesterton once said, "I searched the parks in all your cities, and found no statues of committees."

THIS I KNOW:
Reward those who pay particular attention.

Every marketing campaign is an ongoing conversation with customers, as Mr. Springsteen reminded us. When advertisers lose track of the conversation, they lose customers forever. Great marketing is like a story with chapters. The goal is to be hyperaware of the ongoing conversation you're having with customers. Chapter to chapter.

Conversations create relationships. That was Springsteen's insight. When creating our radio show, I always try to acknowledge points we've made in the past when referenced a second time, so listeners know I'm aware they've been mentioned before. And I also put in small details to reward listeners who pay *close* attention. Those listeners are the show's biggest fans. No piece of music is randomly chosen. Every piece is picked to underscore—or juxtapose—what I'm talking about. For example, in the episode about "Ambush Marketing," where brands pretend to be one thing but are really something else, I underscored a story with Aerosmith's "Dude (Looks Like a Lady)." Only one listener e-mailed to say he got the joke, but that one e-mail made it worth it. Often, we'll have fun with running gags that only dedicated weekly listeners will understand. Sometimes I'll make a wry reference to a show that is a couple of years old. Only those paying *close* attention will connect the dots. It's a wink to our loyal listeners. That kind of shorthand creates a community.

THIS I KNOW:
The advertising industry needs way more female creative directors.
Men may occasionally do the grocery shopping, but women make the lists. Women control over 80 percent of all consumer spending, yet only 3 percent of the creative directors in North America are women. If the golden marketing rule is *know thy audience*, why aren't women in the driver's seat at agencies? It makes no sense to me. This has got to change.

THIS I KNOW:
People over fifty-five have the most money and buy the most products.
Yet, the advertising industry is infatuated with the eighteen- to thirty-four-year-old target market. There is a long-standing yet misguided belief that young people are more malleable in their

brand loyalties. And because they are thought to be in their big consuming years, brands breathlessly chase after them. Yet boomers have all the money, and buy the most products in almost every category—including soft drinks, cars and computers. And boomers are more than willing to switch brands. Not only that, they are about to inherit trillions of dollars. It's one of those odd disconnects in the marketing business that I shake my head at. But if you're a marketer looking for a robust market to chase, think boomers.

THIS I KNOW:
When a man goes into a fitting room with clothes, he's buying something.

A woman may not be. Men, generally speaking, shop with a mission. They are target-based shoppers. Most men don't window shop, and rarely go shopping without coming home with something. Women, generally speaking, like to graze. They can shop for a full afternoon, and buy nothing. Knowing that, retailers should design stores to help men complete their shopping tasks quickly and efficiently. On the other hand, retailers catering to women should give women lots of choices in a casual, relaxing atmosphere. The longer a woman shops, the greater the opportunity for a purchase. The shorter a man shops, the more likely the cash register will ring.

THIS I KNOW:
Phone numbers don't work in radio ads.

The only exception would be a company blessed with an extremely rare, easy-to-remember number. Few have one. Numbers are notoriously hard to remember. Especially ten-digit ones. Pizza Pizza may have had the best marketing phone number of all time, which was sung in a sticky jingle as "nine six seven, eleven-eleven." If offered a good rhyme and embedded the number in people's minds, which is all an ad for a pizza delivery service needs to do. Web URLs—which, because they are words, are easier to remember—have become the new phone numbers.

THIS I KNOW:
Great companies reward instinct.

Intuition is what catapults a company ahead of the competition. Most companies in this day and age don't value intuition. The business world is mostly run by MBAs, who value intellectual reason over emotion. Yet emotion drives human beings. Universities should be teaching courses on instinct. Students should be encouraged to love, honour and obey their gut feelings. They should be taught to listen to their hunches, because a hunch is creativity trying to tell you something. The day I started listening to my gut feelings is the day my career trajectory changed. I remember the moment.

It was during a meeting at Campbell Ewald. I was the junior writer in the room, and the senior creative people were struggling to come up with a new TV commercial for the agency's biggest client, Fiberglas Canada. I had an idea, but hesitated to put up my hand. When I finally mustered the courage, I nervously cleared my throat and suggested an idea in which a homeowner saves enough money by insulating with Fiberglas to put a down payment on a cottage—an absurdly small cottage. That idea became the flagship—and award-winning—commercial of the year for that client. The creative director was none other than Trevor Goodgoll, and he steered many big assignments my way after that. (See Fig. 30.)

Intuition jets across the ocean of a problem. Cold logic takes a rowboat.

THIS I KNOW:

There is a solution hiding inside absolutely everything.

So many of the marketing problems I've had to solve over the years seemed insurmountable at the outset. But by persistently drilling deeper, you always find a solution. If you're faced with a thorny marketing problem, don't give up. The solution is there, you just have to roll up your sleeves and start peeling the onion. Many times, the solution is hiding inside the obstacle. That's why I would often tell Pirate's creative department not to tunnel under an obstacle or detour around it, but rather, embrace it. Relieving the tension of an obstacle with a creative solution is one of the most powerful tools in marketing. Interesting to note that the use of the word "impossible" has dropped by 50 percent in the English language over the last hundred years. It doesn't surprise me.

THIS I KNOW:

Advertising is an art.

Many people scoff at that notion. But there are two types of creativity. One is pure expression, employed by artists and musicians, and the other is problem-solving creativity. This is the realm of business and industry. As adman John Hegarty says, marketing directors want advertising to be a science. They go down on their knees at night and plead with God to make it a science. But it never will be, because persuasion is an art. Remember the first time you persuaded your father to give you the keys to the car. Did you use science or artful persuasion? Exactly. Yes, there is a place for data and research and algorithms, but it still all comes down to a blank page and an idea. Pixar's Ed Catmull notes that art classes aren't about learning to draw. They're about learning to see. That is the art in advertising—observing human nature, understanding the heart of a brand and seeing the possibilities of creating a connection.

THIS I KNOW:

Unless you have big ambitions, you'll only have small outcomes.

This is the secret to creating a brand that is impossible to ignore. If you want to grow big, you need to think big. If you are a small company with a limited marketing budget, you must be audacious. If your marketing is safe or ordinary, your gains will be incremental at best. Think about it: according to a recent poll, 4 percent of ads are remembered positively, 7 percent are remembered negatively, 89 percent are not noticed or remembered at all. That should strike terror in the hearts of marketers everywhere. It means nearly 90 percent of all advertising dollars are wasted. Only big ideas break through. The biggest risk is complacency.

THIS I KNOW:

Marketing rules are meant to be broken.

There is a telling scene in the documentary *Hearts of Darkness: A Filmmaker's Apocalypse*. Directed in part by Eleanor Coppola, it documents the making of her husband's film, *Apocalypse Now*. In the scene, actor Dennis Hopper arrives on the set for his role as a photojournalist. He is wired, and bounces around Francis Ford Coppola saying he wants to ad lib his lines. That's when Coppola tells him, "You can't change your lines until you know your lines." It's an astute insight. Hopper has to know the intent of the scenes before he can suggest a different route. The same holds true in marketing. There are many rules and well-trodden routes of conventional thinking. A radio commercial has to be thirty seconds long. A billboard has to be seven words or less. A TV commercial has to be driven visually, not verbally. But in my experience, once you know the rules, breaking them can lead to memorable marketing.

For example, Mercedes wanted to advertise its small Smart cars on radio. So it created a series of quick, five-second ads. In a typical commercial break, you might hear six commercials. So Smart car tucked its five-second ads in between each regular commercial in the break. The last Smart car ad in that break simply said, "Look how easy it is to park a Smart car." It was a brilliant use of radio, and it cut through the clutter—and actually leveraged the clutter—because it broke the rules. I mentioned the Organ Donation Month radio ad earlier; the six-second gap of silence broke the cardinal rule of radio.

Often, when you go to view a video on YouTube, you have to sit through a commercial first. These are called "pre-rolls." Sometimes you have the option to skip the ad after six seconds. Knowing that, GEICO Insurance ran six-second commercials. So when you went to view a video, the GEICO ad fully played out in six seconds, with the announcer saying, "You can't skip this GEICO ad, because it's already over." A six-second video broke the rules. Most advertisers run twenty- to thirty-second ads on YouTube, and lose most of their viewers after the six-second mark. This is called a "bounce rate"—it measures how many viewers bounce away from the ad. The typical bounce rate is probably in the 60 to 70 percent zone. Fifty percent is considered excellent, and you've still lost half your audience. But GEICO got a zero percent bounce rate, because its ads were fully viewed in the short, six-second mandatory window. When Thomas Edison was asked about the rules at his lab, he said it best: "There are no rules here. We're trying to accomplish something."

THIS I KNOW:

If the strategy is right, the idea is good, the copy is strong and the visuals are powerful, but the ad is still wrong, your problem is tone.

It took me a long time to learn this lesson. Often we would work hard on an ad, come up with a bold idea, craft the visuals, wordsmith the copy, present it to the client—and the client would turn it down. The frustrating part was that the client couldn't articulate the problem. They just didn't like it. There's nothing more exasperating than getting vague feedback. Especially the words, "I just don't like it." Then at some point in my career, the problem came into focus.

Most often, when everything about the ad looked right and was still turned down, it was the *tone* of the ad that wasn't sitting right with the client. Tone is a crucial part of an advertisement, but you can't point to it. That makes it elusive. It's a feeling. Not an absolute. Every brand, every product, emits an appropriate tonality. *Friends* had a different tone than *Seinfeld*, even though both were sitcoms based on a group of close buddies. Mercedes has a different tone from BMW, even though they are both expensive luxury cars. Sears has a different tone from the Hudson's Bay Company, even though both are department stores. Even a Ford Explorer has a different tone from a Ford F-150. Both are made by the same company, both are trucks, but each with a completely different tonality. Explorers are comfortable SUVs for the city, F-150s are tough pickup trucks for the country. If you are a copywriter or an art director, you have to live the brand for a while to understand the tone. That's why I have a rule that a copywriter should never write about a product they have never held in their hand.

An ad can be off on tone by 10 percent, and that's all it takes for a client to say it's a no-go. They might not be able to put their finger on it, but it just doesn't *feel* right to them. It doesn't feel like their company. Or it's not what their company would say. Or it's not how they would say it. Creemore Springs, for instance, needs to feel like a small-town brewery in its marketing. That is its tone. If it started to sound like a mainstream brewery, it would dislocate its fans. Tim Hortons has to feel like Canada's coffee. Which is why Timmys had to abandon its established branding in the United States.

If you can't hire an ad agency and you are creating your own marketing, chances are you probably have a firm grasp on your company's tone. You live it every day. That is the great advantage of being inside. But if a marketing idea just doesn't *feel* right, even though it checks off all the other boxes, the culprit is probably tone. So tune your antennae appropriately.

THIS I KNOW:

Amateurs think marketing is all about selling.
Pros know it's about differentiation.

Yes, marketing is about selling. But before any serious selling can take place, a brand needs to differentiate itself in the market.

The marketplace is a crowded street. Customers have endless choices. They neither understand nor care about how hard it is to deliver consistent quality and personalized experiences. That is the privilege of having market power. As I've said many times in this book, people shop on feel most of the time. If you stand for something, you're going to have people for you and against you. If you stand for nothing, you will have no one for you and no one against you. Your branding must differentiate your company first and foremost. It must have its own unique voice, its own unique look. It must stake out a clear piece of real estate; it must have a distinct personality.

Then the selling starts.

THIS I KNOW:

Adjectives are the kryptonite of advertising.

I always try to avoid adjectives in my advertising work. Advertising has planted big, wet kisses on adjectives since the first heyday of this business in the 1920s. Early advertising agency founders like Albert Lasker figured out that when copy used adjectives, products became more seductive. More distinctive. More desirable. Lasker understood desire. And he was right. Products flew off the shelves. But along the way, adjectives got tossed around too casually, like Sinatra throwing twenties around in a nightclub. Bigger, brighter, faster, cheaper, tastier, smoother and all the other flashy descriptors began to lose their power. Every product claimed them, whether they were true or not. Soon, those words no longer moved the public. And that happened a long, long time ago.

To me, the best copywriters find ways to describe products without using adjectives. Great writing makes you feel a product benefit without going to the cliché. If you challenge yourself to limit the use of adjectives in your marketing, it makes for harder writing but more persuasion. Great copywriting should be surprising, interesting and even more engaging than good magazine writing. If you've peppered your copy with adjectives, you weaken the persuasion one more click with each one. As the book *The Cluetrain Manifesto* put it so beautifully: "Adjectives are like the blank tiles in Scrabble. You can use them anywhere, but they have no value."

THIS I KNOW:

Marketing is a glorious puzzle.

It has a lot of pieces, but putting the big picture together has kept me happy and engaged for over thirty years.

THIS, TOO, I KNOW:

Marketing should be a joy.

If you tackle marketing with enthusiasm and endless curiosity, it will not only return your investment ten-fold, but it will also be fun and a joy to do. Yes, there are stressful moments—I had hair when I started in this business—but on the whole, I wouldn't have wanted to do anything else. I agree with Oprah on this one. You know you're in a sweet spot when what you're doing energizes you instead of depleting you.

Afterword

The true measure of this book is whether you feel energized by the time you hit this page.

I hope you do.

Marketing is difficult to do when you don't have an advertising agency on speed dial. Hopefully, it doesn't feel as daunting as it did before you read these words. Marketing, when done right, is remarkably effective. Success just depends on getting the fundamentals right. You want all your coordinates locked in early. It's like a plane leaving Toronto for London, England, and being one inch off-course at takeoff. But the time it lands, it's in Russia.

But get the foundation right, have a clear understanding of the business you're in, distill your selling message down to a concise sentence, figure out a smart strategy and you're miles ahead of most marketers. Add to that the secret sauce of storytelling, counterintuitive thinking and perfectly timed messages.

Then, your competitors just might find you "really, completely irritating."

Wishing you the best of luck.

See you next week.

Notes

6   "Coke clobbered Coke."
From the terrific and thought-provoking book *Buying In:
The Secret Dialogue between What We Buy and Who We Are*
by Rob Walker (New York: Random House, 2008). Rob
is an uncompromising observer of the marketing world.
Sometimes I wince, but usually because he's right.

7   "That commercial was inspired by an interesting moment."
The Care and Feeding of Ideas by Bill Backer (New York:
Crown, 1993). Backer passed away as I was writing this
book, and he was one of the greats of the ad biz. His
famous Coke hilltop commercial was the cherry on top of
the last episode of *Mad Men*. Enough said.

17   "I have used that line for over thirty years . . ."
The Marketing Imagination by Theodore Levitt (New York:
Free Press, 1983). I read this book when I was in my
second year of copywriting. It was a little over my head at
the time, but upon rereading it I can't believe how much
stayed with me.

22   "I read an article about Comedy Central . . ."
"The Laugh Factory" by Jonah Weiner, *New York Times Magazine*, June 21, 2015.

41   "Lenox also made fine china . . ."
Positioning: The Battle for Your Mind by Al Ries and Jack Trout (New York: McGraw-Hill, 1986). This is one of the bibles of the advertising business. Ries and Trout put forward the concept of "positioning" in such a clear and powerful way that it has influenced Madison Avenue to this day.

43   "Then there are times when a company is facing a strategic hurdle . . ."
Leap: A Revolution in Creative Business Strategy, by Bob Schmetterer (Hoboken, NJ: John Wiley & Sons, 2003). A great read from an adman with a sharp eye for the insights of marketing. The kind of insights most people miss.

53   "One of my favourite television campaigns . . ."
Written, by the way, by Julian Koenig, the famous Doyle Dane Bernbach copywriter who revolutionized advertising by writing all those wonderful Volkswagen ads in the 1960s, with headlines like "Lemon" and "Think Small." His daughter Sarah Koenig is the co-creator/host of the popular podcast *Serial*.

55   "Laser eye surgeons often have difficulty . . ."
Tell to Win: Connect, Persuade, and Triumph with the Hidden Power of Story by Peter Guber (New York: Crown Business,

2011), one of the most successful movie producers in Hollywood. As he's listened to hundreds of movie pitches, it's interesting to hear his take on purposeful storytelling.

57 "So here's what Rob Walker did."
Walker even noted on each eBay listing that the description was a work of fiction!

60 "Now, humour isn't the only answer to effective marketing . . ."
Marketing the Moon: The Selling of the Apollo Lunar Program, by David Meerman Scott and Richard Jurek (Cambridge, MA: MIT Press, 2014). This is an absolutely gorgeous book in a large format, so well written and researched.

61 "When companies like Duncan Hines . . ."
Ad Women: How They Impact What We Need, Want, and Buy, by Juliann Sivulka (Amherst, NY: Prometheus Books, 2009). Every woman (and man) in the advertising business should read this book about the history of women on Madison Avenue and their enormous (but rarely documented) influence.

68 "Of the many marketing philosophies I hold dear . . ."
Apples, Insights and Mad Inventors: An Entertaining Analysis of Modern Marketing by Jeremy Bullmore (Chichester, UK: John Wiley & Sons, 2006). He began his career as a copywriter in 1954, so he truly is a Mad Man. A very witty and wise book about brands.

⁶⁹ "Each ad featured a different classical composer . . ."
From the wonderful book *Me, and Other Advertising Geniuses*, by Charlie Brower (New York: Doubleday, 1974). An absolutely hilarious and insightful book from the man who rose from copywriter to CEO of the mighty BBDO ad firm. He was famous for saying there is no such thing as hard sell and soft sell—only smart sell and stupid sell. Don't you love him already?

⁷⁴ "With that answer, the fog lifted."
A story told to me by the creative director on the account, the wonderful raconteur Doug Linton. One of the best storytellers in Canadian advertising.

⁷⁵ "Storytelling can also help sell intangible benefits . . ."
From the *Little Teal Book of Trust: How to Earn It, Grow It, and Keep It to Become a Trusted Advisor in Sales, Business and Life* by Jeffrey Gitomer (New Jersey: FT Press, 2008). A little gem of a book on the slippery subject of trust.

⁷⁵ ". . . I'm going to poison you and marry your sister."
A hilarious line about trust that I overheard somewhere along the line. A lack of trust is the underpinning of every soap opera ever done.

⁷⁵ "So instead of saying 'trust me' . . ."
Read Henry Beckwith's excellent book *Selling the Invisible: A Field Guide to Modern Marketing* (New York: Warner Books, 1997). It's one of my favourite marketing books. Chock full of quick, short chapters—each one containing an insight into the difficult process of selling services you can't see or hold in your hand.

77 'Think of the incredibly challenging context . . ."
A listener told me an amusing story about her father.
He was a car dealer in the 1950s, selling Triumphs in
Montreal. He was flown to Germany by VW and offered
a Beetle distributorship. Having just come from England
after the war, his response was, "No one is going to buy
that ugly, German car." Whenever he got tipsy at parties
many years later, he would tell that story, then turn
around and say, "Kick me."

77 'When Disney considered cars for the lead role . . ."
*The New Advertising: The Great Campaigns from Avis to
Volkswagen* by Robert Glatzer (New York: Citadel, 1970).
A great book from 1970, written just as the first decade of
the advertising creative revolution was coming to a close.
Glatzer had a front-row seat.

81 "The P&G team called the new spray Febreze . . ."
As told by Charles Duhigg in his book *The Power of Habit:
Why We Do What We Do in Life and Business* (New York:
Random House, 2012), a fascinating look at how we create
the habits in our lives and why.

99 "Before a new business pitch . . ."
From the must-read book *Predatory Thinking: A Masterclass
in Out-Thinking the Competition* by Dave Trott (London,
UK: Pan Macmillan, 2013). He was the creative director
anchoring the famous British ad firm Gold Greenlees
Trott. One of the most astute essayists in the ad biz.

105 "When producer Brian Grazer was trying to sell . . ."
From Grazer's book, *A Curious Mind: The Secret to a Bigger Life* (New York: Simon & Schuster, 2015). I saw Grazer speak at the Cannes advertising festival. He is one of the most successful producers in Hollywood and understands the concept of differentiation—ever seen his hair? He is endlessly curious and that trait is his secret sauce.

113 'The colour purple is not appetizing . . ."
As told in the fascinating book, *A Beautiful Constraint: How to Transform Your Limitations into Advantages, and Why It's Everyone's Business* by Adam Morgan and Mike Barden (Hoboken, NJ: John Wiley & Sons, 2015). I have always believed creativity loves constraint and the authors articulate this philosophy beautifully in these pages.

123 "It's called Banana Republic."
"Banana Republic: Turning Khaki into Gold" by Dinah Eng, *Fortune*, March 18, 2013.

128 'The biggest gains in business . . ."
Songwriters Look at Songwriting by Paul Zollo (Cincinnati, OH: Writer's Digest Books, 1991). I highly recommend this book. It's a collection of interviews with songwriters, and their insights are riveting. For example, Paul Simon says he much prefers an interesting mistake to a safe move. Smart and intriguing stuff.

144 "How did Oreo put that response . . ."
Advertising Age, 84, no 8 (February 25, 2013).
A must-read publication for the marketing mind.

153 "Psychologist and writer Dan Ariely . . ."
Dan Ariely, "3 Main Lessons of Psychology," May 5, 2008,
http://danariely.com/2008. Dan is a thought leader and
looks at life from the most unexpected angles.

157 "Successful marketers are endlessly curious . . ."
Again, from *A Curious Mind*, by Brian Grazer.

166 "Ever walk into an Apple retail store . . ."
As noted by ex-P&G Global Marketing Officer Jim Stengel
in his book *Grow: How Ideals Power Growth and Profit at the
World's Greatest Companies* (New York: Crown Business,
2011). An interesting read from someone who sat on one of
the loftiest perches in the marketing world.

171 "A supermarket chain in California . . ."
"A Retail Gig That Employees Don't Hate," by
Claire Zillman, *Fortune*, August 1, 2015.

172 "The Four Seasons Hotels chain, for example . . ."
Four Seasons: The Story of a Business Philosophy
by Isadore Sharp (New York: Portfolio, 2009). Hard to
imagine the Four Seasons began as a motor hotel in
Toronto, but it's true. And the story of how a motor hotel
became one of the world's most admired luxury hotel
companies is well worth a read. Sharp was an innovator.

174 "According to a survey IBM recently did . . ."
"Redefining Boundaries: Insights from the Global C-suite
Study," IBM–Global C-suite Study, November 2015,
http://goo.gl/dJE4bP.

174. "It's also interesting to note that when
companies lose customers . . ."
Jill Griffin, *Customer Loyalty: How to Earn It, How to Keep It*
(San Francisco: Jossey-Bass, 1997).

175. "There were a hundred business reasons . . ."
"Humans Are Underrated" by Geoff Colvin,
Fortune, July 23, 2015, 110.

178. "I read an interesting article on Disney World . . ."
From *Business Insider*: www.businessinsider.com
/sc/disney-institute-customer-experience-2016-2.

193. "Another little touch we incorporated . . ."
The Pirate stopwatch was created by the wonderful folks
at Taxi. The highly talented creative director there named
Zak left to start his own agency called Zulu Alpha Kilo.
See what he did there?

194. "Typical word-of-mouth referral rates . . ."
Stat noted by Bob Mirman during a homebuilding
conference in Dallas, Texas, in 2014. Mirman is the CEO
of Eliant, a company that provides customer experience
solutions to the building trade.

208. "The same holds true for brands."
As noted by Leander Kahney in his book *Inside Steve's
Brain* (New York: Portfolio, 2008). Many books have
been written about Apple and Jobs. This is one of the
better ones.

213 "Georges St-Pierre is a UFC fighter . . ."
Sam Sheridan's beautiful phrase describing the core
element of champions, from his insightful book
The Fighter's Mind: Inside the Mental Game (New York:
Atlantic Monthly Press, 2010). A wonderful writer getting
inside the minds of men who inflict violence for a living.

215 "In a study done in Amsterdam . . ."
Study conducted by Department of Social and
Organizational Psychology at VU University, Amsterdam,
as quoted in *Mail Online*: www.dailymail.co.uk
/sciencetech/article-3002421/Is-EMAIL-address
-affecting-career-Employers-likely-recruit-people
-use-underscores-cute-words.html.

219 "The same applies to your profile picture . . ."
Libby Kane, "8 Mistakes You Should Never Make on
LinkedIn." *Forbes*, www.forbes.com, March 4, 2013.

223 "Twenty-four percent lie about their qualifications."
Microsoft survey: *Online Reputation in a Connected World*
(January 2010).

226 "Don't whisper a dozen things . . ."
Them fightin' words were spoken by Tham Khai Meng,
Worldwide Chief Creative Officer of Ogilvy & Mather at
the Cannes advertising festival.

238 "Advertising is an art."
*Creativity, Inc.: Overcoming the Unseen Forces That Stand
in the Way of True Inspiration* by Ed Catmull (New York:
Random House, 2009). One of the best books ever written

on the subject of managing creativity—from the leader
of Pixar.

239 "Unless you have big ambitions . . ."
One more thing about Trott's *Predatory Thinking*.
He takes no prisoners in his view of what really works
in marketing. So refreshing.

242 "Amateurs think marketing is all about selling."
Victor Milligan, "The New CMO Agenda: Shifting to a
Customer-Obsessed Model," *Advertising Age*,
http://adage.com, September 21, 2015.

243 "Adjectives are the kryptonite of advertising."
One day in 1943, Albert Lasker abruptly announced
that he was leaving the ad business and handed his
advertising agency over to his three vice presidents. Their
names were Foote, Cone & Belding—which still exists as
one of the biggest firms in the ad world.

243 "To me, the best copywriters find ways . . ."
The Cluetrain Manifesto by Rick Levie, Christopher
Locke, Doc Searls, and David Weinberger (New York:
Basic Books) is a remarkable book written back in 2000.
Its premise was that the Internet was then rendering
conventional marketing obsolete and corporations needed
to sit up and take notice. The title comes from a comment
made by an employee about his company: "The clue train
stopped there four times a day for ten years and they
never took delivery."

Acknowledgements

Craig Pyette kept putting notes in the margin like "What do you mean here?" and "What?" and "I don't follow you." Then occasionally he would scribble "Ha!" I would strive for the Ha's. He's a great editor who also happens to be a great guy.

The marketing team at Knopf Canada. Think Navy SEAL Team, only smarter, more resourceful and way more fun.

My agent, Bev Slopen. Ten pounds of dynamite in a five-pound bag.

My wife and business partner, Debbie. She is the first set of eyes on everything I write. She is my gyroscope. It's always better when we're together.

Our three daughters, Shea, Callie and Sid. They are all smart, funny and savvy. My wife and I have no idea how this happened.

My parents, Mel and Betty. When I told them I wanted to write commercials for a living, they just said, "Go get 'em."

Finally, thanks to that director who pulled me out of *Romper Room* in 1963 to be in a TV commercial for a local bakery. Look what happened.

Image Credits

"Trevor Goodgoll . . ." Photo by Jamie Morren.

"The commercial that established . . ." Photo by the author, of Apple's original "1984" TV ad.

"A brilliant creative expression . . ." Photo courtesy of DDB Worldwide.

"This ingenious solution . . ." Photo courtesy of ITAR-TASS.

"Actors John Hodgman and Justin Long . . ." Photo by the author, of original TV ad.

"The classic print campaign . . ." Photo by the author, of original ad in *Collier's*.

"Note the horizontal . . ." City of Chicago website.

"Volvo puts your junk . . ." Courtesy of Volvo.

"Proudly the worst . . ." Photo courtesy of KesselsKramer, Hans Brinker Budget Hotel.

"Hans Brinker Budget Hotel . . ." Photo courtesy of KesselsKramer, Hans Brinker Budget Hotel.

"The story fishermen . . ." Photo by the author, of original ad in *Life*.

"Marilyn Monroe's passing . . ." Photo by the author, of original *Life* cover.

"Not just a receipt . . ." Photo courtesy of Bossa Nova Films, Brazil.

"This is what listeners . . ." Photo by the author, of original Hudson's Bay ad viewed through Shazam app.

"I'll let you figure . . ." Photo by the author, of original ad on DailyTelegraph.com.au.

"The right message . . ." Photo courtesy of Virgin Atlantic.

"A beautifully timed . . ." Photo courtesy of Virgin Atlantic.
"This tweet proved . . ." Tweeted by @Oreo.

"We aim to please . . ." Photo by the author.

"Nudge, nudge . . ." Best efforts were made to source this photo.

"Just look at the tweeter's . . ." Photo courtesy of Peter Shankman.

"Before you can choose . . ." Photo by the author.

"Viva Las Vegas" Photo by the author.

"The kind of surprise . . ." Photo courtesy of Diamond Resorts International.

"One of over two . . ." Photo courtesy of Taxi Toronto.

"Reid Miles set a new . . ." Photo by Sidney O'Reilly of album cover.

"Reid Miles took the still . . ." Photo by Sidney O'Reilly of album cover.

"An art director and . . ." Photo courtesy of Reid Miles.

"Ed McCabe knew . . ." Photo by the author of original ad.

"I nervously presented . . ." Photo courtesy of Joe Sedelmaier.

Index

bounce rates, 240

Bourne Identity (Ludlum), 26

branding

    Coke and, 6, 8

    consistency of, 68, 233

    as differentiation, 242

    difficulty of, 67

    inconsistency and, 67–68

    as knowing what company stands for, 202

    of person, 213–14

    telephone calls and, 181

brand(s)

    clarity of storyline and, 76

    consistency of images across media, 222

    creative tension and, 200

    defined, 67, 200, 214

    differentiation among, 62, 67

    and elevator pitch, 226

    and e-mail address, 215

    emotion and true value of, 66

    general public retention of impression of, 12

    and imposition of a view, 77

    as interchangeable vs. standing out, 206

    internal vs. external, 201

    likeness among, 202–3

    magic/intangibles in, 206–7, 208

    and marketing strategy, 45

    negative definition of, 205

    personal, 214–15, 223

    resumé and, 215–19

    shape-shifting and, 69

    small, and big personality, 227–28

    social media personal vs. business accounts and, 148

    stories and, 68

    total personality of, 202

    what stands for/against, 203–5

Branson, Richard, 142, 176–78, 209

Bretton's, 42–43

brinksmanship, in presentations, 102–4

Britain

    attic insulation/cleaning in, 150–51

    nudging in, 150–51

British Rail, 51–52, 67

Broadway, New York City, 86–87

Brooks, Bonnie, 140–41

Buckley's Cough Mixture, marketing strategy, 35, 36

budgets

    creativity vs., 15

    and going narrow and deep vs. wide and shallow, 94

    and identification of greatest areas of opportunity, 82

Buenos Aires, Madero Este real estate development, 124–26

building trade, small touches and word-of-mouth referrals in, 194

Bullmore, Jeremy, 62

Burlingham, Bo, *Small Giants: Companies That Choose to Be Great Instead of Big*, 169–70

Bush, George W., 148

Cameron, David, 151

Campbell Ewald advertising agency, xiii–xv, 237

Cannes advertising festival, 59–60

Caples, John, 159

car dealerships

    and small gestures, 195–96

    See also names of individual car companies

car rental companies, 39–40

Carter, Jimmy, 29

Dr. Scholl's Fast Flats, 138–39
Drucker, Peter, 169
Duhigg, Charles, *The Power of Habit*, 134–37
Duncan Hines, 61
DuPont industrial plastic, 131

Eastwood, Clint, 74
   in *Dirty Harry*, 26
Eaton's, 35
eBay
   stories used to sell items on, 57–58, 73
   trust and, 75
   See also online stores
Edison, Thomas, 240
El Al, 28
elevator pitch(es)
   airline industry and, 28
   brands and, 226
   and competition, 23
   core message and, 28–29
   definition, 21–22
   as detonators, 31
   difficulty of articulating, 23
   driving purpose and, 17
   examples of, 24–31
   and feeling, 17
   fist-slams and, 22–23
   as forced clarity, 22
   gap in market and, 23–24
   knowing what business company is in and, 18
   and marketing strategy, 32
   movie studios and, 25–28
   new companies and founding spark, 23
   and *People* magazine, 19
   and persuasion, 29
   as plot idea of book, 76
   refining of, 31
   sentences vs. paragraphs and, 24

single-minded marketing messages and, 21, 226
   and storyline, 69
   and storytelling, 72
   as tests of ideas, 31
   time and, 23
   uniqueness of business and, 22, 23–24
e-mail addresses
   as form of marketing, 215
   personal vs. work-related, 215
   and resumés, 215
emoticons, as nudges, 161
emotion
   and acting on messages, 62–63
   in advertising, 232
   animation and, 61–62
   and book simile for marketing, 76
   and brand differentiation, 62
   and brand's true value, 66
   communications and, 62
   and customer pull, 17, 58–59
   and customer purchases, 56
   and decision-making, 64
   examples, 56–58
   and feeling in marketing, 53, 58
   hiring for skills, 170, 176
   information vs., 56
   injection into information, 62
   and knowing what business company is in, 16–17
   logic vs., 66
   and moon landing, 60–61
   and movie choices, 64
   in resumés, 217
   skills in customer service, 169–70
   and social media, 63
   stories and, 56–58

Sears vs., 241

human nature, understanding of

    and counterintuitive thinking, 114–15

    and nudging, 162–63

humour

    and advertising as interruption/intrusion, 59, 230

    comedy vs., 59

    in global cinema ad, 59–60

    marketing strategy vs., 14–15

    remembering and, 60

Hurricane Sandy, and lapses in marketing taste, 147

"I love New York" campaign, 86–87

IBM, Apple vs., 3, 13, 17

"I'd like to buy the world a Coke," 7, 8

"I'd like to teach the world to sing," 8

ideas

    counterintuitive, 121, 123

    fragility of, 101

    generation vs. selling of, 95–96

    mirroring past ideas vs. being counterintuitive, 123–24

    systematic serendipity and no bad ideas, 128

Instagram, 148

Internet, trust and, 75–76

intuition

    and competition, 237

    value of, 128

Issenberg, Sasha, *The Victory Lab*, 157–58

"It's the Little Things" (O'Reilly; radio show episode), 197

Ivory soap, 42

J. Walter Thompson (advertising agency), 65

Jackson, Samuel L., in *Snakes on a Plane*, 26

Jamieson Vitamins, 188–89

JCPenney

    and mittens, 145–46

    and Super Bowl blackout, 145–46

Jobs, Steve

    "2007 D5 Convention" conversation, 69

    and customer service, 166

    elevator pitch to Sculley, 29

    and magic in brand, 208

    message of, 3

    presenting new Apple products, 107

    on profit vs. product, 202

    Walkman given by Morita to, 209

    and *why* of going into business, 13

Jordan, Michael, 30

joy, marketing as, 244

"Just Do It" (Nike), 3–4, 18, 72, 233

Kardashian, Kim, 206

Kawasaki motorcycles, 74

Kelley, Kevin, 79

Kelly, Cathal, 49

Kennedy, John F., 60

Kenneth Cole, and Arab Spring revolutions, 147

KFC, 13

Kilmer, Val, 138

knowing what business company is in

    advantages of, 18

    advertising agencies uncovering, 5

    Coke as, 6, 8

    customer belief of, 12

elevator pitches and, 32
examples of, 34–35, 36–37
formulation of, 34
gap in market and, 36, 37
great vs. good, 46
humour vs., 14–15
internal rethinking and, 43–44
market analysis and, 36, 37
master plan for, 35–36
opportunity identification
  and, 36, 37
smaller companies and, 44–45
tactics vs., 45–47
uniqueness of company and,
  37–38
What-if games and plan formulation, 85
Matthiessen, Peter, 174
McCabe, Ed, 204–5
McLaren, Malcolm, xi, 37
medication bottles, small labels
  on, 188–89
Mercedes
  Audi vs., and Super Bowl
    blackout, 144
  BMW vs., 41–42, 206, 241
  Smart Cars, 240
Mercedes-Benz Superdome,
  Super Bowl blackout,
  143–46
Metro subway system, Paris,
  43–44
Meyer, Danny, 169–70, 171, 176, 181
Miami Heat, 30–31
Miami International Airport,
  customer service at, 179
Michaels arts and crafts stores,
  Weather Channel and, 90–91
Michelin
  change of tagline, 17, 63–64
  feeling and, 63–64
  in safety vs. tire business, 2
Mickey Mouse toys, 62

Microsoft
  Apple vs., 69
  and creation of world, 77
  as in *Forbes* list of World's
    Most Valuable Brands, 18
Miles, Reid, 199–200
MindTrap (board game), 121–23
mixed martial arts, 47–48
M&Ms, 35
Molson
  as in party vs. beer business,
    1–2, 9, 17
  in party vs. beer business, 4
Monroe, Marilyn, 133–34, 206
Morita, Akio, 209
Morton's steakhouse, 167–68, 183
mouthwashes, 41
Musk, Elon, 207

NASA, 60–61
National Hockey League (NHL),
  49
Neptune Theatre, Halifax, free
  tickets to, 194–95
Neville, John, 194–95
New Seekers, 8
New York City, 85–87
New York Times Magazine,
  Consumed column, 56–58
Newhart, Bob, 229–30, 231
Nike
  Adidas vs., 206
  and battle on customer's
    behalf, 202
  creation of world, 76
  feeling and, 63, 64
  and "Just Do It," 3–4, 18, 72,
    233
  as maturing company, 25
  in motivation vs. shoe busi-
    ness, 3–4, 9, 17
  and storytelling, 71
  Taxi pitching business of,

into, 174–75
for customer relations/
service, 181–83
in marketing strategy and
competition, 36, 37
nudges and, 151–52
real-time, 148
in small gestures, 190
social misfortunes and, 147
for storytelling, 80
in timing, 137–38, 142
and turning complaints into
customer service, 172–73
See also greatest area of
opportunity
O'Reilly on Advertising (radio
show), xvii
O'Reilly Radio Inc., xv–xvi
Oreo cookies
AMC Theatres and, 146
and Super Bowl blackout,
144, 145
organ donations, 153–54, 231–32,
240
original spark
and elevator pitches, 23
veering from, 15
and *why* of going into
business, 13–14, 16
Orlando Magic basketball
organization, 180
Orr, Bobby, 49
Orwell, George, *1984*, 2–3, 4
Oz, Frank, 26

pain-points
and checking in with cus-
tomers for feedback, 187–88
elimination of, and loyalty,
187–88
patterns/recurring, 188
as small, rectifiable nuisances, 188–89

Tim Hortons, and avail-
ability/unavailability of
orders, 190
Panasonic, 102
Pantene hair products, Weather
Channel and, 90
Parikhal, John, 132
parity positioning, 203
parking spaces
in malls, with bulbs showing
availability, 189
Pirate providing maps for,
187
reserved, 187
passion
KFC and, 14
objectivity vs., 5
and presentations, 95–96
PBS, and Super Bowl blackout,
144–45
PC, Macintosh vs., 68–69
Peck, Gregory, 205
People magazine, 19, 88–89
Pepsi
Challenge, 5–6
Coca-Cola vs., 42, 103, 143
Sculley leaving for Apple, 29
performance art, presentations
as, 107–8
Perna, Bill, 118–21
persuasion
advertising as news vs., 16
as art, 238
and buying of ideas, 95
confidence and, 105–7
elevator pitches and, 29
Lasker and, 16
passion and, 95–96
timing and, 139–40
Phelps, Michael, 25
PhotoFeeler.com, 220–21
Pickett, Plunkett and Puckett
(Postaer), 98–99

selling new ideas/campaigns
to existing clients, 100–101
silence in, 110
standing out from competition, 104
structure needed for, 109
and telling clients what to
think, 110
tips list for, 108–11
two kinds of, 99–101
and types of presenters, 95–96
price
and brand consistency, 67–68
perception vs., 74
small gestures vs., 187
and value, 72
Procter & Gamble, 81–82
products
quantity vs. quality, 54, 62
wanting benefit from, vs.
product itself, 17–18
profile pictures, 219–21
profit
being liked by customers vs.,
200
product vs., 202
"The Profit of One Degree"
(Weather Trends
International), 91–92
Psychedelic Psunday (radio show),
93–94
purchase cycles, beats in, 139
puzzle, marketing as, 243

Quallofil, 118

radio
advantages of, 210
and Colombian kidnappings,
89–90
"drive times" and, 93
greatest area of opportunity
and, 92–93

as personal medium, 228–30
Psychedelic Psunday, 93–94
seminars on commercials, xvi
as still powerful/important,
228–30
television vs., 228, 229, 230
radio advertising
affordability, vs. TV, 119
airings as narrow and deep
vs. wide and shallow,
92–93, 94
campaign for MindTrap, 122
five-second ads in, 240
low esteem given to, vs. TV,
210
phone numbers in, 236–37
print vs., 119
and purchasing, 141
Shazam and, seeing mer-
chandise, 141
silence in, 231–32, 240
Sparhawk Golden Ale, 119–21
without mentioning product
name, 119–21
Radio City Music Hall, and NFL
Draft, 168
Ragù, 42
Rapala, Lauri, 133–34
Rapala lures, 133–34
Reagan, Ronald, 29
The Real Madmen (Cracknell),
97–98
real-time advertising, social
media and, 143–48
recording studio business
about, 209–11
food provision, 192–93
script timing/tips, 193–94
Reid's Law, 200
repeat customers. *See* loyalty
reputation, 75–76
restaurants
and customer service, 169–70,

Slow Down GPS app, 140
small details/gestures
    airports and, 190
    in building trade, 194
    care dealerships and, 195–96
    and competitive advantage,
        186
    and customer appreciation,
        197
    as customer service, 186
    examples, 190
    hotels and, 190, 191–92
    and loyalty, 185–86
    opportunities, 190
    in Pirate food provision,
        192–93
    thank-you calls/cards, 194
    theatres, and free tickets,
        194–95
    as word-of-mouth advertis-
        ing, 189
*Small Giants: Companies That
    Choose to Be Great Instead of
    Big* (Burlingham), 169–70
Snakes on a Plane (movie), 26
Snickers, and JCPenney in Super
    Bowl blackout, 145
Snyder, Blake, *Save the Cat*, 28
social media
    ability to react instantly,
        143–48
    absence from, 221–22
    badmouthing on, 223
    consistency in messaging on,
        147, 222
    derogatory statements on, 223
    emotion and, 63
    employers checking employ-
        ees', 221–22
    employment recruiters and,
        220, 222
    as first interview, 222–23
    hotels accessing, 173–74

and lack of mystery, 206
lying about qualifications
    on, 223
personal vs. business
    accounts on, 148
profile pictures, 220
qualities of information
    shared on, 147
and real-time advertising,
    143–48
self-monitoring of, 222
separation of personal from
    business life on, 222–23
and Super Bowl blackout, 144
Under the Influence on, 147–48
Virgin America and, 177
social misfortunes, as selling
    opportunities, 147
solutions
    counterintuitive thinking
        and difficulties of finding,
        115–16
    hiding inside obstacles, 238
    obstacles and new, 163
    to persistent problems, 116
Sony, 209
Southwest Airlines, 175, 183
Sparhawk Golden Ale, 118–21
"Speed Bumps" (O'Reilly; radio
    series episode), 149–50
Spin Neapolitan Pizza chain, 91
Splash (movie), 105
Springsteen, Bruce, 79, 234
Star Trek, 64
Starbucks
    in coffee theatre business, 2
    and weather forecast, 142
Start with Why (Sinek), 12–13
Steinway Pianos, 69–70, 71, 73
Stolley, Richard, 19
stories
    and brands, 68
    and emotion, 56–58

radio vs., 228, 229, 230
Tell to Win (Guber), 30–31
Tennant, Mike, xvi–xvii
tension
    deadlines and, 211
    as profitability vs. being
        liked by customers, 200
    in storytelling, 208
    what company stands
        against, and, 204, 205
Tesla electric cars, 207
TGI Friday's, and JCPenney in
    Super Bowl blackout, 145
Thaler, Richard, *Nudge,* 150,
    161–62
thank-you calls/cards, 194
theatre, marketing as, 225–26
theatres, free tickets from, 194–95
thoughtful touches. *See* small
    details/gestures
Three Mile Island nuclear reac-
    tor meltdown, 134
Tide, and Super Bowl blackout,
    144
Tim Hortons
    and availability/unavailabil-
        ity of orders, 190
    marketing strategy, 35
    tone of, 242
Time magazine, 19
Timex Torture Tests, 53–54, 55
timing
    and advertising annoyance/
        anger, 132
    big data algorithms and,
        132–33
    counterintuitive thinking
        and, 129
    importance of, 131, 132–33
    luck and, 133–34
    and nudging, 138–39, 151–52
    opportunism and, 137–38, 142
    and persuasion, 139–40

and pregnancy shopping, 136
and pushback against over-
    timeliness, 137
real-time opportunities and,
    148
receptiveness and, 138–39
and tipping point, 138–39
Virgin legroom advertising
    and, 143
To Kill a Mockingbird (movie),
    205
tone, 241–42
Top Gun (movie), 137–38
touch-points
    and brand definition, 214
    consistency in, 214
    as marketing acts, 189–90
    Pirate and, 192–94
Touchstone, and *Splash,* 105
Toys "R" Us, 122
True Religion jeans, 55
trust, storytelling and, 75–76
24 (Grazer; series), 134
Twins (movie), 27–28
Twitter
    AMC Theatres vs. Oreo
        cookies on, 146
    during Clinton/Bush
        speeches, 148
    event hashtags, 148
    immediate feedback, 148
    Oreo cookies and, 144
    and Super Bowl blackout,
        143–44
    Taco Bell vs. Old Spice on, 146
"2007 D5 Convention" conversa-
    tion (Jobs; Gates), 69
Tylenol, 40, 46

Uber, 75
Ultimate Fighting
    Championship (UFC)
    and competition, 38–39

and mixed martial arts,
47–48
St-Pierre and, 213–14
Under the Influence (O'Reilly;
radio show), xvii, 71, 147–48
unique selling propositions
(USPs), 216–17
uniqueness of business
and competition, 23–24
and elevator pitches, 22, 23–24
and marketing strategy,
37–38
United States
Navy, and *Top Gun,* 138
nudge squad, 151
and welfare payments vs.
assistance to poor, 160
The Unpublished David Ogilvy
(Ogilvy), 16

value
price and, 72
secondary meaning and,
72–73
storytelling and, 72–73
Veet, 141–42
The Victory Lab (Issenberg),
157–58
Virgin airlines
collection of change for charity, 191
customer service, 176–78
legroom advertising, 142–43
luggage care advertising,
143
vitamin bottles. *See* medication
bottles, small labels on
voicemail, 219
Volkswagen, creation of world,
77–79
Volvo automobiles
and delivery of merchandise
to cars, 117–18, 128

marketing strategy, 34, 36
misspelling of name in pitch,
98
and strategy vs. tactics, 45
and What-If games, 118
voter turnout, 157–59
VQA (Vintners Quality
Alliance), 82–85
"Vuja Dé," 125–26, 129

Walker, Rob
eBay experiment, 56–58, 73
Significant Objects, 57–58
Walmart
Amazon online competition
with, 116–17
competition and Walton's
meetings with managers,
157
and customers delivering
packages, 116–17, 128
and same-day delivery,
116–17, 128
Walton, Sam, 157
Warner, Brian, 206
Watts, Pete, xii
weather
as greatest area of opportunity, 90–92
Starbucks and, 142
Weather Channel
and Michaels arts and crafts
stores, 90–91
and Pantene hair products, 90
Weather Trends International,
"The Profit of One
Degree," 91–92
websites
brand consistency in, 222
marketing consistency and,
68
profile pictures on, 219–20
shish kebab theory and, 68,

TERRY O'REILLY, who has won hundreds of international advertising awards, was the co-founder of Pirate Radio and Television in Toronto and New York. He is in demand as a speaker and sought as a juror for international awards panels. Since 2005, he has appeared on CBC Radio as host of *O'Reilly on Advertising*, *The Age of Persuasion* and most recently *Under the Influence*, which is carried also in the United States on SiriusXM and WBEZ Chicago.